Writing Spaces: Readings on Writing

Series Editors, Charles Lowe and Pavel Zemliansky

WRITING SPACES: READINGS ON WRITING

Series Editors, Charles Lowe and Pavel Zemliansky

Volumes in *Writing Spaces: Readings on Writing* offer multiple perspectives on a wide-range of topics about writing, much like the model made famous by Wendy Bishop's "The Subject Is . . ." series. In each chapter, authors present their unique views, insights, and strategies for writing by addressing the undergraduate reader directly. Drawing on their own experiences, these teachers-as-writers invite students to join in the larger conversation about developing nearly every aspect of the craft of writing. Consequently, each essay functions as a standalone text that can easily complement other selected readings in writing or writing-intensive courses across the disciplines at any level.

Writing Spaces

Readings on Writing
Volume 1

Edited by
Charles Lowe and Pavel Zemliansky

Parlor Press
West Lafayette, Indiana
www.parlorpress.com

Parlor Press LLC, West Lafayette, Indiana 47906

Printed in the United States of America
S A N: 2 5 4 - 8 8 7 9

Library of Congress Cataloging-in-Publication Data

Writing spaces : readings on writing. Volume 1 / edited by Charles Lowe and Pavel Zemliansky.
    p. cm.
Includes bibliographical references and index.
ISBN 978-1-60235-184-4 (pbk. : alk. paper) -- ISBN 978-1-60235-185-1 (adobe ebook)
1. College readers. 2. English language--Rhetoric. I. Lowe, Charles, 1965- II. Zemliansky, Pavel.
PE1417.W735 2010
808'.0427--dc22

                    2010019487

Cover design by Colin Charlton.
This book is printed on acid-free paper.

Parlor Press, LLC is an independent publisher of scholarly and trade titles in print and multimedia formats. This book is available in paperback, cloth, and Adobe eBook formats from Parlor Press on the World Wide Web at http://www.parlorpress.com. For submission information or to find out about Parlor Press publications, write to Parlor Press, 816 Robinson St., West Lafayette, Indiana, 47906, or e-mail editor@parlorpress.com.

For Wendy Bishop

Contents

Acknowledgments

When we began discussing the possibility of a project like *Writing Spaces*, almost two years ago, we immediately thought that we'd like it to resemble Wendy Bishop's unique series "The Subject Is . . ." in approach, style, and tone. As we publish the first volume of *Writing Spaces*, we pay tribute to Wendy's work and to the influence she has had on us. We were privileged to participate in "The Subject Is . . ." series, one as a co-editor, the other—as a contributor. We remember being intrigued by the possibility of essays, which spoke to students and teachers alike, illuminating complex topics in an accessible manner. We also remember reading "The Subject Is . . ." books, assigning them to our first-year writers, and hearing a somewhat-surprised "this is pretty good for a textbook" reaction from them.

Like Wendy's series, *Writing Spaces* could not exist without the collaborative efforts of so many in our field, all teachers of writing who were, at one time, writing students as well. We appreciate the hard work and patience of our editorial board members in reviewing the chapters of this collection, and they deserve an extra special thanks from us for the helpful revision strategies and encouragement they provided the authors of this volume: Linda Adler-Kassner, Chris Anson, Stephen Bernhardt, Glenn Blalock, Bradley Bleck, Robert Cummings, Peter Dorman, Douglas Eyman, Alexis Hart, Jim Kalmbach, Judith Kirkpatrick, Carrie Lamanna, Carrie Leverenz, Christina McDonald, Joan Mullin, Dan Melzer, Nancy Myers, Mike Palmquist, James Porter, Clancy Ratliff, Keith Rhodes, Kirk St. Amant, and Christopher Thaiss. To our Assistant Editors, Craig Hulst and Terra Williams, and our Graphics Editor, Colin Charlton: this collection is indebted to you for the ideas that you contributed in its genesis and production, and the many hours you spent working to prepare the manuscripts. Thanks to Richard Haswell for the help he gave in reading all of the drafts and tagging them with the keyword system implemented on CompPile. And finally to David Blakesley, thanks for your support in publishing the print edition through Parlor Press, and the many great ideas and feedback that you always contribute to a project.

Introduction: Open Source Composition Texts Arrive for College Writers

Robert E. Cummings

Let me ask you this: which of the following statements is most memorable?*

A) Hasta la vista, baby.

B) I need your clothes, your boots, and your motorcycle.

C) I'll be bahk.

D) From government to non-profit organizations, teachers to text-book publishers, we all have a role to play in leveraging twenty-first century technology to expand learning and better serve California's students, parents, teachers and schools.

If you answered "D," you might need to get out more often. But you will probably be proven correct.

Of course all of these statements are the pronouncements of California's current governor, Arnold Schwarzenegger. While in the first three instances he serves as a robotic killing machine (*Terminator 2* and *The Terminator*), in the last statement he serves as a harbinger of

---

a major change in the way textbooks are written, reviewed, published, and distributed in America ("Free Digital"). Long after the Terminator is terminated in our collective pop culture memories, the effects of open source textbooks will be felt.

The arrival of open source texts for the classroom is coming in fits and starts, but with the debut of the first volume of *Writing Spaces*, college writing students can now join the movement. *Writing Spaces* combines peer-reviewed texts, composed for student writers, by teachers in the field, and arranged by topics student writers will immediately understand.

What help are we offering for students learning to write in the college environment?

- Understanding the shift from high school to college writing
- Strategies for group writing
- Defining and employing stages of the writing process
- Finding real help in writing through an engagement with rhetorical concepts, such as the rhetorical triangle, or genre, or principles of the canon, such as invention
- Coming to terms with plagiarism, how the academy defines it, and how to avoid common traps
- Appreciating the role of argument in the classroom, and constructively addressing fatigue with argumentation
- Why you should use "I" in your writing
- Metacognition and the necessary role of reflection in a robust revision process
- Strategies for recognizing the natural role of procrastination, and how to defeat it
- Realistic conceptions of online writing environments such as Wikipedia, and information on how to use such sites to further the goals of composition
- Creative strategies for generating writing ideas, including journaling, conversation (face-to-face and electronic), role play, drumming, movement, and handwriting

If you are struggling with a writing project, we think you will also appreciate the organization of *Writing Spaces*. Through the use of the keyword index on the website, you can quickly scan the table of contents to find chapters which help with your specific problems. Once a writer clicks on a particular keyword, only the articles which address that specific problem appear; we will also have an expanded index in the print edition. This "just in time delivery" method for the help writers need not only provides clear help in the moment of composing confusion, but also places the concept in the context of several approaches from multiple articles so that when writers have the cognitive space to look at the writing concept in context, the keyword system gives them the ability to do just that.

But how else does this text differ from other composition texts geared for students? Let's start with free. Not only, as so many computer coders have said before, free like "beer" but free like "speech" (and maybe even free like a puppy, too) (cf. Wikipedia and Williams). Our text arrives to you free of charge, and freely available on the web. Thus, you can refer to it without limitation, through laptops and phones. And your teachers can assign it in your classroom without giving a second thought to whether or not it can be accessed, how much the bookstore will charge for it, and whether or not their prices will prevent or deter you from acquiring the text in a fall semester class until just before Thanksgiving. Nor will your teachers need to worry about sending the bookstore their readings for the fall semester before the prior February, as is a common practice on most campuses. Perhaps best of all, free means there is no need to for you to either rent the book or sell it back at the end of the semester for twenty-five cents on the dollar. And if you would prefer reading from the printed page, versions of this content will be for sale through Parlor Press.

Also, the content in this electronic volume evokes the "free as in speech" concept as well. This text is written largely by teachers of writing and donated free of charge to *Writing Spaces*. But because ours is a peer-reviewed publication, contributors can earn credit within the traditional tenure and promotion system. As students, you are ensured a quality of content which ranks as high as any in our field, and authors' content is evaluated for its veracity and utility in teaching writing— not whether it will sell.

This distinction between "gratis" and "libre" comes from the open source process in the computer coding world to describe a collaborative authoring process where the coding/writing product could be altered by the software user. But now we see how the open source process has expanded to fundamentally alter the textbook publishing model. As students, parents, and legislators have lately pointed out, the textbook marketplace has long been broken: students must purchase texts required for courses, and the faculty who require those texts have no control over pricing. With the arrival of systems such as *Writing Spaces*, faculty can select peer-reviewed materials that students can either access for free on a website, or pay to print, and contributing authors are given academic credit for their original work.

Like many open source projects, *Writing Spaces* is just beginning. While even the most dedicated fan of *The Terminator* series would be hard pressed to think of "The Governator" as a progressive fomenter of equitable access to texts in higher education, there will no doubt be more and more government officials who see "free" and become acquainted with the open source publishing model. But you no longer need to wait to be told about the usefulness of open source textbooks in your writing classroom; you are reading it now. The fundamental shift toward a collaborative and responsive textbook publishing model has clearly begun in the world of composition. Thanks for being a part of it.

WORKS CITED

"Free Digital Textbook Initiative Review Results." *California Learning Resource Network.* n.d. Web. 15 May 2010.

The Terminator. Dir. James Cameron. TriStar, 1984. DVD.

Terminator 2: Judgment Day. Dir. James Cameron. TriStar, 1991. DVD.

Wikipedia contributors. "Gratis versus Libre." *Wikipedia, The Free Encyclopedia.* Wikipedia, The Free Encyclopedia, 18 Apr. 2010. Web. 15 May 2010.

Williams, Sam. *Freedom: Richard Stallman's Crusade for Free Software.* Sevastapol, CA: O'Reilly, 2002. Print. Also available online at <http://oreilly.com/openbook/freedom/>. 15 May 2010.

WRITING SPACES

What Is "Academic" Writing?

L. Lennie Irvin

Introduction: The Academic Writing Task

As a new college student, you may have a lot of anxiety and questions about the writing you'll do in college.* That word "academic," especially, may turn your stomach or turn your nose. However, with this first year composition class, you begin one of the only classes in your entire college career where you will focus on learning to write. Given the importance of writing as a communication skill, I urge you to consider this class as a gift and make the most of it. But writing is hard, and writing in college may resemble playing a familiar game by completely new rules (that often are unstated). This chapter is designed to introduce you to what academic writing is like, and hopefully ease your transition as you face these daunting writing challenges.

So here's the secret. Your success with academic writing depends upon how well you understand what you are doing as you write and then how you approach the writing task. Early research done on college writers discovered that whether students produced a successful piece of writing depended largely upon their representation of the writing task. The writers' mental model for picturing their task made a huge difference. Most people as they start college have wildly strange ideas about what they are doing when they write an essay, or worse—they have no clear idea at all. I freely admit my own past as a clueless freshman writer, and it's out of this sympathy as well as twenty years of teaching college writing that I hope to provide you with something useful. So grab a cup of coffee or a diet coke, find a comfortable chair with good light, and let's explore together this activity of academic writing you'll be asked to do in college. We will start by clearing up some of those wild misconceptions people often arrive at college possessing. Then we will dig more deeply into the components of the academic writing situation and nature of the writing task.

MYTHS ABOUT WRITING

Though I don't imagine an episode of *MythBusters* will be based on the misconceptions about writing we are about to look at, you'd still be surprised at some of the things people will believe about writing. You may find lurking within you viral elements of these myths—all of these lead to problems in writing.

Myth #1: The "Paint by Numbers" myth

Some writers believe they must perform certain steps in a particular order to write "correctly." Rather than being a lock-step linear process, writing is "recursive." That means we cycle through and repeat the various activities of the writing process many times as we write.

Myth #2: Writers only start writing when they have everything figured out

Writing is not like sending a fax! Writers figure out much of what they want to write as they write it. Rather than waiting, get some writing on the page—even with gaps or problems. You can come back to patch up rough spots.

Myth #3: Perfect first drafts

We put unrealistic expectations on early drafts, either by focusing too much on the impossible task of making them perfect (which can put a cap on the development of our ideas), or by making too little effort because we don't care or know about their inevitable problems. Nobody writes perfect first drafts; polished writing takes lots of revision.

Myth #4: Some got it; I don't—the genius fallacy

When you see your writing ability as something fixed or out of your control (as if it were in your genetic code), then you won't believe you can improve as a writer and are likely not to make any efforts in that direction. With effort and study, though, you can improve as a writer. I promise.

Myth #5: Good grammar is good writing

When people say "I can't write," what they often mean is they have problems with grammatical correctness. Writing, however, is about more than just grammatical correctness. Good writing is a matter of achieving your desired effect upon an intended audience. Plus, as we saw in myth #3, no one writes perfect first drafts.

Myth #6: The Five Paragraph Essay

Some people say to avoid it at all costs, while others believe no other way to write exists. With an introduction, three supporting paragraphs, and a conclusion, the five paragraph essay is a format you should know, but one which you will outgrow. You'll have to gauge the particular writing assignment to see whether and how this format is useful for you.

Myth #7: Never use "I"

Adopting this formal stance of objectivity implies a distrust (almost fear) of informality and often leads to artificial, puffed-up prose. Although some writing situations will call on you to avoid using "I" (for example, a lab report), much college writing can be done in a middle, semi-formal style where it is ok to use "I."

The Academic Writing Situation

Now that we've dispelled some of the common myths that many writers have as they enter a college classroom, let's take a moment to think about the academic writing situation. The biggest problem I see in freshman writers is a poor sense of the writing situation in general. To illustrate this problem, let's look at the difference between speaking and writing.

When we speak, we inhabit the communication situation bodily in three dimensions, but in writing we are confined within the two-dimensional setting of the flat page (though writing for the web—or multimodal writing—is changing all that). Writing resembles having a blindfold over our eyes and our hands tied behind our backs: we can't see exactly whom we're talking to or where we are. Separated from our audience in place and time, we imaginatively have to create this context. Our words on the page are silent, so we must use punctuation and word choice to communicate our tone. We also can't see our audience to gauge how our communication is being received or if there will be some kind of response. It's the same space we share right now as you read this essay. Novice writers often write as if they were mumbling to themselves in the corner with no sense that their writing will be read by a reader or any sense of the context within which their communication will be received.

What's the moral here? Developing your "writer's sense" about communicating within the writing situation is the most important thing you should learn in freshman composition.

Figure 1, depicting the writing situation, presents the best image I know of describing all the complexities involved in the writing situation.

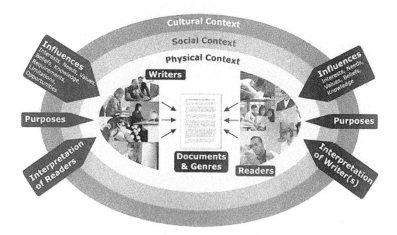

Figure 1. Source: "A Social Model of Writing." Writing@CSU. 2010. Web. 10 March 2010. Used by permission from Mike Palmquist.

Looking More Closely at the "Academic Writing" Situation

Writing in college is a fairly specialized writing situation, and it has developed its own codes and conventions that you need to have a keen awareness of if you are going to write successfully in college. Let's break down the writing situation in college:

Who's your audience?	Primarily the professor and possibly your classmates (though you may be asked to include a secondary outside audience).
What's the occasion or context?	An assignment given by the teacher within a learning context and designed to have you learn and demonstrate your learning.
What's your message?	It will be your learning or the interpretation gained from your study of the subject matter.
What's your purpose?	To show your learning and get a good grade (or to accomplish the goals of the writing assignment).
What documents/ genres are used?	The essay is the most frequent type of document used.

So far, this list looks like nothing new. You've been writing in school toward teachers for years. What's different in college? Lee Ann Carroll, a professor at Pepperdine University, performed a study of student writing in college and had this description of the kind of writing you will be doing in college:

> What are usually called 'writing assignments' in college might more accurately be called 'literacy tasks' because they require much more than the ability to construct correct sentences or compose neatly organized paragraphs with topic sentences. . . . Projects calling for high levels of critical literacy in college typically require knowledge of research skills, ability to read complex texts, understanding of key disciplinary concepts, and strategies for synthesizing, analyzing, and responding critically to new information, usually within a limited time frame. (3–4)

Academic writing is always a form of evaluation that asks you to demonstrate knowledge and show proficiency with certain disciplinary skills of thinking, interpreting, and presenting. Writing the paper is never "just" the writing part. To be successful in this kind of writing, you must be completely aware of what the professor expects you to do and accomplish with that particular writing task. For a moment, let's explore more deeply the elements of this college writing "literacy task."

Knowledge of Research Skills

Perhaps up to now research has meant going straight to Google and Wikipedia, but college will require you to search for and find more in-depth information. You'll need to know how to find information in the library, especially what is available from online databases which contain scholarly articles. Researching is also a process, so you'll need to learn how to focus and direct a research project and how to keep track of all your source information. Realize that researching represents a crucial component of most all college writing assignments, and you will need to devote lots of work to this researching.

The Ability to Read Complex Texts

Whereas your previous writing in school might have come generally from your experience, college writing typically asks you to write on unfamiliar topics. Whether you're reading your textbook, a short story, or scholarly articles from research, your ability to write well will be based upon the quality of your reading. In addition to the labor of close reading, you'll need to think critically as you read. That means separating fact from opinion, recognizing biases and assumptions, and making inferences. Inferences are how we as readers connect the dots: an inference is a belief (or statement) about something unknown made on the basis of something known. You smell smoke; you infer fire. They are conclusions or interpretations that we arrive at based upon the known factors we discover from our reading. When we, then, write to argue for these interpretations, our job becomes to get our readers to make the same inferences we have made.

The Understanding of Key Disciplinary Concepts

Each discipline whether it is English, Psychology, or History has its own key concepts and language for describing these important ways of understanding the world. Don't fool yourself that your professors' writing assignments are asking for your opinion on the topic from just your experience. They want to see you apply and use these concepts in your writing. Though different from a multiple-choice exam, writing similarly requires you to demonstrate your learning. So whatever writing assignment you receive, inspect it closely for what concepts it asks you to bring into your writing.

Strategies for Synthesizing, Analyzing, and Responding Critically to New Information

You need to develop the skill of a seasoned traveler who can be dropped in any city around the world and get by. Each writing assignment asks you to navigate through a new terrain of information, so you must develop ways for grasping new subject matter in order, then, to use it in your writing. We have already seen the importance of reading and research for these literacy tasks, but beyond laying the information out before you, you will need to learn ways of sorting and finding meaningful patterns in this information.

In College, Everything's an Argument: A Guide for Decoding College Writing Assignments

Let's restate this complex "literacy task" you'll be asked repeatedly to do in your writing assignments. Typically, you'll be required to write an "essay" based upon your analysis of some reading(s). In this essay you'll need to present an argument where you make a claim (i.e. present a "thesis") and support that claim with good reasons that have adequate and appropriate evidence to back them up. The dynamic of this argumentative task often confuses first year writers, so let's examine it more closely.

Academic Writing Is an Argument

To start, let's focus on argument. What does it mean to present an "argument" in college writing? Rather than a shouting match between two disagreeing sides, argument instead means a carefully arranged and supported presentation of a viewpoint. Its purpose is not so much to win the argument as to earn your audience's consideration (and even approval) of your perspective. It resembles a conversation between two people who may not hold the same opinions, but they both desire a better understanding of the subject matter under discussion. My favorite analogy, however, to describe the nature of this argumentative stance in college writing is the courtroom. In this scenario, you are like a lawyer making a case at trial that the defendant is not guilty, and your readers are like the jury who will decide if the defendant is guilty or not guilty. This jury (your readers) won't just take your word that he's innocent; instead, you must convince them by presenting evidence that proves he is not guilty. Stating your opinion is not enough—you have to back it up too. I like this courtroom analogy for capturing two importance things about academic argument: 1) the value of an organized presentation of your "case," and 2) the crucial element of strong evidence.

Academic Writing Is an Analysis

We now turn our attention to the actual writing assignment and that confusing word "analyze." Your first job when you get a writing assignment is to figure out what the professor expects. This assignment may be explicit in its expectations, but often built into the wording of the most defined writing assignments are implicit expectations that you might not recognize. First, we can say that unless your professor specifically asks you to summarize, you won't write a summary. Let me say that again: don't write a summary unless directly asked to. But what, then, does the professor want? We have already picked out a few of these expectations: You can count on the instructor expecting you to read closely, research adequately, and write an argument where you will demonstrate your ability to apply and use important concepts you have been studying. But the writing task also implies that your essay will be the result of an analysis. At times, the writing assignment may even explicitly say to write an analysis, but often this element of the task remains unstated.

So what does it mean to analyze? One way to think of an analysis is that it asks you to seek How and Why questions much more than What questions. An analysis involves doing three things:

1. Engage in an open inquiry where the answer is not known at first (and where you leave yourself open to multiple suggestions)

2. Identify meaningful parts of the subject

3. Examine these separate parts and determine how they relate to each other

An analysis breaks a subject apart to study it closely, and from this inspection, ideas for writing emerge. When writing assignments call on you to analyze, they require you to identify the parts of the subject (parts of an ad, parts of a short story, parts of Hamlet's character), and then show how these parts fit or don't fit together to create some larger effect or meaning. Your interpretation of how these parts fit together constitutes your claim or thesis, and the task of your essay is then to present an argument defending your interpretation as a valid or plausible one to make. My biggest bit of advice about analysis is not to do it all in your head. Analysis works best when you put all the cards on the table, so to speak. Identify and isolate the parts of your analysis, and record important features and characteristics of each one. As patterns emerge, you sort and connect these parts in meaningful ways. For me, I have always had to do this recording and thinking on scratch pieces of paper. Just as critical reading forms a crucial element of the literacy task of a college writing assignment, so too does this analysis process. It's built in.

Three Common Types of College Writing Assignments

We have been decoding the expectations of the academic writing task so far, and I want to turn now to examine the types of assignments you might receive. From my experience, you are likely to get three kinds of writing assignments based upon the instructor's degree of direction for the assignment. We'll take a brief look at each kind of academic writing task.

The Closed Writing Assignment

- Is Creon a character to admire or condemn?
- Does your advertisement employ techniques of propaganda, and if so what kind?
- Was the South justified in seceding from the Union?
- In your opinion, do you believe Hamlet was truly mad?

These kinds of writing assignments present you with two counter claims and ask you to determine from your own analysis the more valid claim. They resemble yes-no questions. These topics define the claim for you, so the major task of the writing assignment then is working out the support for the claim. They resemble a math problem in which the teacher has given you the answer and now wants you to "show your work" in arriving at that answer.

Be careful with these writing assignments, however, because often these topics don't have a simple yes/no, either/or answer (despite the nature of the essay question). A close analysis of the subject matter often reveals nuances and ambiguities within the question that your eventual claim should reflect. Perhaps a claim such as, "In my opinion, Hamlet was mad" might work, but I urge you to avoid such a simplistic thesis. This thesis would be better: "I believe Hamlet's unhinged mind borders on insanity but doesn't quite reach it."

The Semi-Open Writing Assignment

- Discuss the role of law in Antigone.
- Explain the relationship between character and fate in Hamlet.
- Compare and contrast the use of setting in two short stories.
- Show how the Fugitive Slave Act influenced the Abolitionist Movement.

Although these topics chart out a subject matter for you to write upon, they don't offer up claims you can easily use in your paper. It would be a misstep to offer up claims such as, "Law plays a role in Antigone" or "In Hamlet we can see a relationship between character and fate." Such statements express the obvious and what the topic takes for granted. The question, for example, is not whether law plays a role in Antigone, but rather what sort of role law plays. What is the nature of this role? What influences does it have on the characters or actions or theme? This kind of writing assignment resembles a kind of archeological dig. The teacher cordons off an area, hands you a shovel, and says dig here and see what you find.

Be sure to avoid summary and mere explanation in this kind of assignment. Despite using key words in the assignment such as "explain," "illustrate," analyze," "discuss," or "show how," these topics still ask you to make an argument. Implicit in the topic is the expectation that you will analyze the reading and arrive at some insights into patterns and relationships about the subject. Your eventual paper, then, needs to present what you found from this analysis—the treasure you found from your digging. Determining your own claim represents the biggest challenge for this type of writing assignment.

The Open Writing Assignment

- Analyze the role of a character in Dante's The Inferno.
- What does it mean to be an "American" in the 21st Century?
- Analyze the influence of slavery upon one cause of the Civil War.
- Compare and contrast two themes within *Pride and Prejudice.*

These kinds of writing assignments require you to decide both your writing topic and you claim (or thesis). Which character in the Inferno will I pick to analyze? What two themes in Pride and Prejudice will I choose to write about? Many students struggle with these types of assignments because they have to understand their subject matter well before they can intelligently choose a topic. For instance, you need a good familiarity with the characters in The Inferno before you can pick one. You have to have a solid understanding defining elements of American identity as well as 21st century culture before you can begin to connect them. This kind of writing assignment resembles riding a bike without the training wheels on. It says, "You decide what to write about." The biggest decision, then, becomes selecting your topic and limiting it to a manageable size.

Picking and Limiting a Writing Topic

Let's talk about both of these challenges: picking a topic and limiting it. Remember how I said these kinds of essay topics expect you to choose what to write about from a solid understanding of your subject? As you read and review your subject matter, look for things that interest you. Look for gaps, puzzling items, things that confuse you, or connections you see. Something in this pile of rocks should stand out as a jewel: as being "do-able" and interesting. (You'll write best when you write from both your head and your heart.) Whatever topic you choose, state it as a clear and interesting question. You may or may not state this essay question explicitly in the introduction of your paper (I actually recommend that you do), but it will provide direction for your paper and a focus for your claim since that claim will be your answer to this essay question. For example, if with the Dante topic you decided to write on Virgil, your essay question might be: "What is the role of Virgil toward the character of Dante in The Inferno?" The thesis statement, then, might be this: "Virgil's predominant role as Dante's guide through hell is as the voice of reason." Crafting a solid essay question is well worth your time because it charts the territory of your essay and helps you declare a focused thesis statement.

Many students struggle with defining the right size for their writing project. They chart out an essay question that it would take a book to deal with adequately. You'll know you have that kind of topic if you have already written over the required page length but only touched one quarter of the topics you planned to discuss. In this case, carve out one of those topics and make your whole paper about it. For instance, with our Dante example, perhaps you planned to discuss four places where Virgil's role as the voice of reason is evident. Instead of discussing all four, focus your essay on just one place. So your revised thesis statement might be: "Close inspection of Cantos I and II reveal that Virgil serves predominantly as the voice of reason for Dante on his journey through hell." A writing teacher I had in college said it this way: A well tended garden is better than a large one full of weeds. That means to limit your topic to a size you can handle and support well.

Three Characteristics of Academic Writing

I want to wrap up this section by sharing in broad terms what the expectations are behind an academic writing assignment. Chris Thaiss and Terry Zawacki conducted research at George Mason University where they asked professors from their university what they thought academic writing was and its standards. They came up with three characteristics:

1. Clear evidence in writing that the writer(s) have been persistent, open-minded, and disciplined in study. (5)

2. The dominance of reason over emotions or sensual perception. (5)

3. An imagined reader who is coolly rational, reading for information, and intending to formulate a reasoned response. (7)

Your professor wants to see these three things in your writing when they give you a writing assignment. They want to see in your writing the results of your efforts at the various literacy tasks we have been discussing: critical reading, research, and analysis. Beyond merely stating opinions, they also want to see an argument toward an intelligent audience where you provide good reasons to support your interpretations.

The Format of the Academic Essay

Your instructors will also expect you to deliver a paper that contains particular textual features. The following list contains the characteristics of what I have for years called the "critical essay." Although I can't claim they will be useful for all essays in college, I hope that these features will help you shape and accomplish successful college essays. Be aware that these characteristics are flexible and not a formula, and any particular assignment might ask for something different.

Characteristics of the Critical Essay

"Critical" here is not used in the sense of "to criticize" as in find fault with. Instead, "critical" is used in the same way "critical thinking" is used. A synonym might be "interpretive" or "analytical."

1. It is an argument, persuasion essay that in its broadest sense MAKES A POINT and SUPPORTS IT. (We have already discussed this argumentative nature of academic writing at length.)

2. The point ("claim" or "thesis") of a critical essay is interpretive in nature. That means the point is debatable and open to interpretation, not a statement of the obvious. The thesis statement is a clear, declarative sentence that often works best when it comes at the end of the introduction.

3. Organization: Like any essay, the critical essay should have a clear introduction, body, and conclusion. As you support your point in the body of the essay, you should "divide up the proof," which means structuring the body around clear primary supports (developed in single paragraphs for short papers or multiple paragraphs for longer papers).

4. Support: (a) The primary source for support in the critical essay is from the text (or sources). The text is the authority, so using quotations is required. (b) The continuous movement

of logic in a critical essay is "assert then support; assert then support." No assertion (general statement that needs proving) should be left without specific support (often from the text(s)). (c) You need enough support to be convincing. In general, that means for each assertion you need at least three supports. This threshold can vary, but invariably one support is not enough.

5. A critical essay will always "document" its sources, distinguishing the use of outside information used inside your text and clarifying where that information came from (following the rules of MLA documentation style or whatever documentation style is required).

6. Whenever the author moves from one main point (primary support) to the next, the author needs to clearly signal to the reader that this movement is happening. This transition sentence works best when it links back to the thesis as it states the topic of that paragraph or section.

7. A critical essay is put into an academic essay format such as the MLA or APA document format.

8. Grammatical correctness: Your essay should have few if any grammatical problems. You'll want to edit your final draft carefully before turning it in.

Conclusion

As we leave this discussion, I want to return to what I said was the secret for your success in writing college essays: Your success with academic writing depends upon how well you understand what you are doing as you write and then how you approach the writing task. Hopefully, you now have a better idea about the nature of the academic writing task and the expectations behind it. Knowing what you need to do won't guarantee you an "A" on your paper—that will take a lot of thinking, hard work, and practice—but having the right orientation toward your college writing assignments is a first and important step in your eventual success.

DISCUSSION

1. How did what you wrote in high school compare to what you have/will do in your academic writing in college?

2. Think of two different writing situations you have found yourself in. What did you need to do the same in those two situations to place your writing appropriately? What did you need to do differently?

3. Think of a writing assignment that you will need to complete this semester. Who's your audience? What's the occasion or context? What's your message? What's your purpose? What documents/genres are used? How does all that compare to the writing you are doing in this class?

WORKS CITED

Carroll, Lee Ann. *Rehearsing New Roles: How College Students Develop as Writers*. Carbondale: Southern Illinois UP, 2002. Print.

Thaiss, Chris and Terry Zawacki. *Engaged Writers & Dynamic Disciplines: Research on the Academic Writing Life*. Portsmouth: Boynton/Cook, 2006. Print.

So You've Got a Writing Assignment. Now What?

Corrine E. Hinton

It's the first day of the semester and you've just stepped foot into your Intro to American Politics class.[*] You grab a seat toward the back as the instructor enters, distributes the syllabus, and starts to discuss the course schedule. Just before class ends, she grabs a thin stack of papers from her desk and, distributing them, announces, "This is your first writing assignment for the term. It's due two weeks from Thursday, so I suggest you begin early." Your stomach clenches. For some people, a writing assignment causes a little nervous energy, but for you, it's a deep, vomit-inducing fireball that shoots down your body and out your toes. As soon as the assignment sheet hits your hands, your eyes dart wildly about, frantically trying to decipher what you're supposed to do. How many pages is this thing supposed to be? What am I supposed to write about? What's Chicago style? When is it due? You know your instructor is talking about the assignment right now, but her voice fades into a murmur as you busy yourself with the assignment sheet. The sound of shuffling feet interrupts your thoughts; you look up and realize she's dismissed the class. You shove the assignment into your bag, convinced you're doomed before you've even started.

---

[*] This work is licensed under the Creative Commons Attribution-Noncommercial-Share Alike 3.0 United States License and is subject to the Writing Spaces Terms of Use. To view a copy of this license, visit http://creativecommons.org/licenses/by-nc-sa/3.0/us/ or send a letter to Creative Commons, 171 Second Street, Suite 300, San Francisco, California, 94105, USA. To view the Writing Spaces Terms of Use, visit http://writingspaces.org/terms-of-use.

So you've got a writing assignment. Now what? First, don't panic. Writing assignments make many of us nervous, but this anxiety is especially prevalent in first year students. When that first writing assignment comes along, fear, anxiety, avoidance, and even anger are typical responses. However, negative emotional reactions like these can cloud your ability to be rational, and interpreting a writing assignment is a rational activity and a skill. You can learn and cultivate this skill with practice. Why is learning how to do it so important?

First, you can learn how to manage negative emotional responses to writing. Research indicates emotional responses can affect academic performance "over and above the influence of cognitive ability or motivation" (Pekrun 129). So, even when you have the knowledge or desire to accomplish a particular goal, your fear, anxiety, or boredom can have greater control over how you perform. Anything you can do to minimize these reactions (and potentially boost performance) benefits your personal and intellectual wellness.

Learning to interpret writing assignment expectations also helps encourage productive dialogue between you and your fellow classmates and between you and your instructor. You'll be able to discuss the assignment critically with your peers, ask them specific questions about information you don't know, or compare approaches to essays. You'll also be able to answer your classmates' questions confidently. Many students are too afraid or intimidated to ask their instructors for help, but when you understand an instructor's expectations for an assignment, you also understand the skills being assessed. With this method, when you do not understand a requirement or expectation, you'll have more confidence to approach your instructor directly, using him as valuable resource that can encourage you, clarify confusion, or strengthen your understanding of course concepts.

What follows is a series of practical guidelines useful for interpreting most college writing assignments. In my experience, many students already know and employ many of these strategies regularly; however, few students know or use all of them every time. Along the way, I'll apply some of these guidelines to actual assignments used in university classrooms. You'll also be able to get into the heads of other students as they formulate their own approaches to some of these assignments.[1]

Guidelines for Interpreting Writing Assignments

1. Don't Panic and Don't Procrastinate

Writing assignments should not incite panic, but it happens. We've already discussed how panicking and other negative reactions work against you by clouding your ability to analyze a situation rationally. So when your instructor gives you that writing assignment, don't try to read the whole assignment sheet at breakneck speed. Instead, take a deep breath and focus. If your instructor talks about the assignment, stop what you're doing and listen. Often, teachers will read through the assignment aloud and may even elaborate on some of the requirements. Write down any extra information or advice your instructor provides about the requirements, his or her expectations, changes, possible approaches, or topic ideas. This information will be useful to you as you begin thinking about the topic and formulating your approach. Also, pay attention to your classmates' questions. You might not need those answers now, but you may find them helpful later.

If you're an undergraduate student taking more than one class, it's not uncommon to have several writing assignments due within days of each other. Hence, you should avoid procrastinating. People procrastinate for different reasons. Maybe you wait because you've always been able to put together a decent paper the night before it's due. Perhaps you wait because avoiding the assignment until the last minute is your response to academic stress. Waiting until the last minute to complete a writing assignment in college is a gamble. You put yourself at risk for the unexpected: your printer runs out of ink, your laptop crashes and you didn't backup your work, the Internet in the library is down, the books you need are checked out, you can't locate any recent research on your topic, you have a last-minute emergency, or you have a question about the assignment you can't find the answer to. The common result of situations like these is that if the student is able to complete the assignment, it is often a poor representatatoin of her actual knowledge or abilities. Start your assignment as soon as possible and leave yourself plenty of time to plan for the unexpected.

2. Read the Assignment. Read It Again. Refer to It Often

The ability to read critically is a useful skill. When you read a textbook chapter for your history course, for example, you might skim it for major ideas first, re-read and then highlight or underline important items, make notes in the margins, look up unfamiliar terms, or compile a list of questions. These same strategies can be applied when reading writing assignments.

The assignment sheet is full of material to be deciphered, so attack it the same way you would attack your history book. When Bailey[2], an undergraduate at a university in Los Angeles, was asked to respond to a biology writing assignment, here's what she had to say about where she would start:

> When getting a writing assignment, you should read it more than once just to get a knowledge of what they're [the instructors] really asking for and underline important information, which is what I'm doing now. Before starting the assignment, always write some notes down to help you get started.

Here are some other strategies to help you become an active, critical reader of writing assignments:

1.   Start by skimming, noting anything in particular that jumps out at you.
2.   As soon as you have the time and the ability to focus, re-read the assignment carefully. Underline or highlight important features of the assignment or criteria you think you might forget about after you've started writing.
3.   Don't be afraid to write on the assignment sheet. Use the available white space to list questions, define key terms or concepts, or jot down any initial ideas you have. Don't let the margins confine your writing (or your thoughts). If you're running out of space, grab a fresh sheet of paper and keep writing. The sooner you starting thinking and writing about the assignment, the easier it may be to complete.

As you begin drafting, you should occasionally refer back to the official assignment sheet. Maintaining constant contact with your teacher's instructions will help keep you on the right track, may remind you of criteria you've forgotten, and it might even spark new ideas if you're stuck.

3. Know Your Purpose and Your Audience

Instructors give writing assignments so students can demonstrate their knowledge and/or their ability to apply knowledge. On the surface, it may seem like the instructor is simply asking you to answer some questions to demonstrate that you understand the material or to compare and contrast concepts, theorists, or approaches. However, assessing knowledge is usually just one reason for the assignment. More often than not, your instructor is also evaluating your ability to demonstrate other critical skills. For example, she might be trying to determine if you can apply a concept to a particular situation, if you know how to summarize complex material, or if you can think critically about an idea and then creatively apply that thinking to new situations. Maybe she's looking at how you manage large quantities of research or how you position expert opinions against one another. Or perhaps she wants to know if you can form and support a sound, credible argument rather than describing your opinion about a certain issue.

Instructors have different ways of conveying what they expect from their students in a writing assignment. Some detail explicitly what they intend to evaluate and may even provide a score sheet. Others may provide general (even vague) instructions and leave the rest up to you. So, what can you do to ensure you're on the right track? Keep reading through these guidelines, and you'll learn some ways to read between the lines. Once you identify all the intentions at work (that is, what your instructor is trying to measure), you'll be able to consider and address them.

Audience is a critical component to any writing assignment, and realistically, one or several different audiences may be involved when you're writing a paper in college. The person evaluating your essay is typically the audience most college students consider first. However, your instructor may identify a separate audience to whom you should tailor your response. Do not ignore this audience! If your business instructor tells you to write a research proposal that will be delivered to members of the local chamber of commerce, then adapt your response to them. If you're in an engineering course, and your instructor asks you to write a product design report about a piece of medical equipment geared toward medical practitioners (and not engineers), you should think differently about your terminology, use of background information, and what motivates this particular audience when they read your report. Analyzing the background (personal, educational, professional), existing knowledge, needs, and concerns of your audience will help you make more informed decisions about word choice, structure, tone, or other components of your paper.

4. Locate and Understand the Directive Verbs

One thing you should do when interpreting a writing assignment is to locate the directive verbs and know what the instructor means by them. Directive verbs tell you what you should do in order to formulate a written response. The following table lists common directive verbs used in writing assignments:

Table 1. Frequently used directive verbs.

analyze	defend	illustrate
apply	describe	investigate
argue	design	narrate
compare	discuss	show
consider	explain	summarize
contrast	explore	synthesize
create	evaluate	trace

You might notice that many of the directive verbs have similar general meanings. For example, although explore and investigate are not necessarily synonyms for one another, when used in writing assignments, they may be asking for a similar structural response. Understanding what those verbs mean to you and to your instructor may be the most difficult part of understanding a writing assignment. Take a look at this sample writing assignment from a philosophy course:

Philosophy Writing Assignment *

"History is what the historian says it is." Discuss.

All papers are to be typed, spell-checked and grammar-checked. Responses should be 2000 words. They should be well written, with a logical flow of thought, and double-spaced with 1" margins on all sides. Papers should be typed in 12-pitch font, using Courier or Times Roman typeface. Indent the first line of each new paragraph five spaces. Also include a title page so that the instructor can identify the student, assignment and course number.

Proper standard English is required. Do not use slang or a conversational style of writing. Always avoid contractions (e.g. "can't" for "cannot") in formal essays. Always write in complete sentences and paragraphs! Staple all papers in the upper left-hand corner and do not put them in a folder, binder or plastic cover.

All written work, citations and bibliographies should conform to the rules of composition laid down in The Chicago Manual of Style (15th edition), or Charles Lipson's Doing Honest Work in College (chapter 5). A paper that lacks correct citations and/or a bibliography will receive an automatic 10% reduction in grade.

* Sample undergraduate philosophy writing assignment, courtesy of Dr. Kenneth Locke, Religious Studies Department, University of the West.

You may interpret the word discuss in one way, while your instructor may have a different understanding. The key is to make certain that these two interpretations are as similar as possible. You can develop a mutual understanding of the assignment's directive verbs and calculate an effective response using the following steps:

1. Look up the verb in a dictionary and write down all of the definitions.
2. List all possible synonyms or related terms and look those up as well; then, see if any of these terms suggest a clearer interpretation of what the assignment is asking you to do.
3. Write down several methods you could use to approach the assignment. (Check out guideline eight in this essay for some common approaches.)

4. Consult with your instructor, but do not be discouraged if he/
she is unwilling to clarify or provide additional information;
your interpretation of the directions and subsequent approach
to fulfilling the assignment criteria may be one of its purposes.

5. Consult a trusted peer or writing center tutor for assistance.

6. Figure out what you know.

When deciphering an assignment's purpose is particularly challenging, make a list. Think about what you know, what you think you
know, and what you do not know about what the assignment is asking
you to do. Putting this list into a table makes the information easier to
handle. For example, if you were given an assignment that asked you
to analyze presentations in your business ethics class, like the assignment in Figure 2, your table might look like Table 2 below:

Business Writing Assignment Presentation Analysis

During three weeks of class, you'll observe several small group presentations on business ethics given by your fellow classmates. Choose
two of the presentations and write a short paper analyzing them. For
each presentation, be sure to do the following:

1. In one paragraph, concisely summarize the group's main conclusions

2. Analyze the presentation by answering any two of the following three:

   a. With which of the group's conclusions do you agree? Why?
   With which of the conclusions do you disagree? Why? (include specific examples of both)

   b. What particular issue of ethics did the group not address or
   only address slightly? Analyze this aspect from your perspective.

   c. In what way could you apply one or more of the group's
   conclusions to a particular situation? (The situation could
   be hypothetical, one from your personal or professional experience, or a real-world example).

The paper should be no more than 3 pages in length with 12-pt
font, 1 ½ line spacing. It is due one week after the conclusion of presentations.

Your grade will depend upon

1. the critical thought and analytical skills displayed in the paper;
2. your use of ethical principles from chapter 7 of our textbook;
3. the professionalism, correctness, and logic of your writing.

Table 2. Sample knowledge table for undergraduate business writing assignment.

What I Know	What I Think I Know	What I Don't Know
Need to observe and take notes on 2 presentations	Concisely means "short," so my summaries should be shorter than the other parts of the paper.	What does the professor mean by "critical thought"?
Need to summarize each groups' conclusions	I think I need to apply my own understanding of ethics to figure out which issue the group didn't address	How does the professor evaluate "professionalism"? How do I demonstrate this?
2–3 pages long; 12 pt font and 1 ½ spacing	I think I understand everything from chapter 7	Do I need to apply both groups' conclusions to the same situation or to two different ones?
Need to include personal opinion	I think it's okay to say "I" in the paper.	How much personal opinion should I include and do I need specific examples to support my opinion?
Need to answer 2 of the 3 questions under part 2	I don't think I need an introduction.	Should I separate my essay into two parts, one for each group I observed?

After reviewing the table, you can see that this student has a lot of thoughts about this assignment. He understands some of the general features. However, there are some critical elements that need clarification before he submits the assignment. For instance, he's unsure about the best structure for the paper and the way it should sound. Dividing your understanding of an assignment into a table or list can help you identify the confusing parts. Then, you can formulate specific questions that your instructor or a writing center consultant can help you answer.

6. Ask Yourself: Do I Need an Argument?

Perhaps one of the most important things to know is whether or not your instructor is asking you to formulate and support an argument. Sometimes this is easy to determine. For example, an assignment many instructors include in their courses is a persuasive paper where you're typically asked to choose an issue, take a position, and then support it using evidence. For many students, a persuasive paper is a well known assignment, but when less familiar assignment genres come up, some students may be confused about argument expectations. This confusion may arise because the instructor uses a directive verb that is easily misinterpreted. What about the verb explain? Does it make you think of words like summarize, review, or describe (which would suggest more facts and less opinion)? Or, do you associate it with words like debate, investigate, or defend (which imply the need for a well-supported argument)? You can also look for other clues in the assignment indicating a need for evidence. If your instructor mentions scholarly citations, you'll probably need it. If you need evidence, you'll probably need an argument. Still confused? Talk to your instructor.

7. Consider the Evidence

If your assignment mentions a minimum number of required sources, references a particular citation style, or suggests scholarly journals to review during your research, then these are telltale signs that you'll need to find and use evidence. What qualifies as evidence? Let's review some of the major types:

- Personal experience
- Narrative examples (historical or hypothetical)
- Statistics (or numerical forms of data) and facts
- Graphs, charts, or other visual representatives of data
- Expert opinion
- Research results (experimental or descriptive)

Each of these offers benefits and drawbacks when used to support an argument. Consider this writing assignment from a 200-level biology class on genetics:

Biology Writing Assignment

Genes & Gene Research

Purpose:

This writing assignment will ask you to familiarize yourself with genes, the techniques gene researchers use when working with genes, and the current research programs investigating genes. The report is worth 10% of your final grade in the course.

In a research report of at least 1500 words, you should address the following:

1. Generally, what is a gene and what does it do? Create a universally applicable definition for a gene.

2. Choose a specific gene and apply your definition to it (i.e., what does this particular gene do and how does it work?)

3. Recreate the history of the gene you've chosen including the gene's discovery (and discoverer), the motivation behind the research into this gene, outcomes of the research, and any medical, social, historical, or biological implications to its discovery.

4. Explore the current research available on your gene. Who is conducting the research, what are the goals (big/small; long-term/short-term) of the research, and how is the research being funded?

Research should be properly documented using CSE (Council of Science Editors) style.

The report should be typewritten, double spaced, in a font of reasonable size.

This instructor asks students to demonstrate several skills, including definition, summary, research, and application. Nearly all of these components should include some evidence, specifically scientific research studies on the particular gene the student has chosen. After reading it, here's what Bailey said about how she would start the assignment: "This assignment basically has to do with who you are, so it should be something simple to answer, not too difficult since you should know yourself." Ernest, another student, explains how he would approach the same assignment: "So, first of all, to do this assignment, I would go on the computer, like on the Internet, and I would . . . do research about genes first. And . . . everything about them, and then I would . . . start with the first question, second question, third and fourth, and that's it." For Bailey, using her own life as an example to illustrate genetic inheritance would be the best way to start responding to the assignment. Ernest, on the other hand, thinks a bit differently; he knows he needs "research about genes" to get started, and, like many students, figures the internet will tell him everything he needs to know. So, how do you know what evidence works best? Know the field you're writing in: what type(s) of evidence it values, why it's valuable, and what sources provide that evidence. Some other important questions you should ask yourself include

- Where, in the paper, is the most effective place for this evidence?
- What type of evidence would support my argument effectively?
- What kind of evidence would most convince my audience?
- What's the best way to integrate this evidence into my ideas?
- What reference/citation style does this discipline use?

If your writing assignment calls for evidence, it is important that you answer these questions. Failure to do so could cost you major points—in your assignment and with your instructor.

8. Calculate the Best Approach

When you decide how to approach your paper, you're also outlining its basic structure. Structure is the way you construct your ideas and move from one idea to the next. Typical structural approaches include question/answer, comparison/contrast, problem/solution, methodology, cause/effect, narration/reflection, description/illustration, classification/division, thesis/support, analysis/synthesis, and theory/application. These patterns can be used individually or in combination with each other to illustrate more complex relationships among ideas. Learning what structures are useful in particular writing situations starts with reviewing the assignment. Sometimes, the instructor clearly details how you should structure your essay. On the other hand, the assignment may suggest a particular structural pattern but may not actually reflect what the instructor expects to see. For example, if the prompt asks four questions, does that mean you're supposed to write a paragraph for each answer and then slap on an introduction and a conclusion? Not necessarily. Consider what structure would deliver your message accurately and effectively.

Knowing what structures are acceptable within the discipline is also important. Many students are uncomfortable with rigidity; they wonder why their chemistry lab reports must be presented "just so." Think about the last time you looked at a restaurant menu. If you're looking for appetizers, those items are usually listed at the front of the menu whereas desserts are closer to the back. If a restaurant menu listed the desserts up front, you might find the design unfamiliar and the menu difficult to navigate. The same can be said for formalized writing structures including lab reports or literature reviews, for example. Examining scholarly publications (journal articles or books) within that field will help you identify commonly used structural patterns and understand why those structures are acceptable within the discipline.

9. Understand and Adhere to Formatting and Style Guidelines

Writing assignments usually provide guidelines regarding format and/or style. Requirements like word count or page length, font type or size, margins, line spacing, and citation styles fall into this category. Most instructors have clear expectations for how an assignment should look based on official academic styles, such as the Modern Language Association (MLA), the American Psychological Association (APA), the Chicago Manual of Style (CMS), or the Council of Science Editors (CSE). If your instructor specifically references a style then locate a copy of the manual, so you'll know how to cite source material and how to develop your document's format (font, spacing, margin size, etc.) and style (use of headings, abbreviations, capitalization).

Occasionally, an instructor may modify a standard style to meet her personal preferences. Follow any additional formatting or style guidelines your instructor provides. If you don't, you could lose points unnecessarily. They may also refer you to scholarly journals to use as models. Don't ignore these! Not only will you be able to review professional examples of the kinds of work you're doing (like lab reports, lit reviews, research reports, executive summaries, etc.), you'll also learn more about what style of writing a discipline values.

10. Identify Your Available Resources and Ask Questions

Even after following these steps, you may still have questions. When that happens, you should know who your resources are and what they do (and don't do). After Nicole read the business ethics assignment (provided earlier in this chapter), she said, "I would send a draft to [the instructor] and ask him if he could see if I'm on the right track." Nicole's instincts are right on target; your primary resource is your instructor. Professors may appear intimidating, but they are there to help. They can answer questions and may even offer research recommendations. If you ask ahead of time, many are also willing to review a draft of your project and provide feedback. However, don't expect your teacher to proofread your paper or give you the "right" answer. Writing assignments are one method by which instructors examine your decision making, problem solving, or critical thinking skills.

The library is another key resource. Reference librarians can help you develop an effective research process by teaching you how to use the catalog for books or general references, how to search the databases, and how to use library equipment (copy machines, microfiche, scanners, etc.). They will not choose your topic or conduct your research for you. Spending some time learning from a reference librarian is worthwhile; it will make you a more efficient and more effective student researcher, saving you time and frustration.

Many institutions have student support centers for writing and are especially useful for first year students. The staff is an excellent source of knowledge about academic expectations in college, about research and style, and about writing assignment interpretation. If you're having trouble understanding your assignment, go to the writing center for help. If you're working on a draft and you want to review it with someone, they can take a look. Your writing center tutor will not write your paper for you, nor will he serve as an editor to correct grammar mistakes. When you visit your university's writing center, you'll be able to discuss your project with an experienced tutor who can offer practical advice in a comfortable learning environment.

The above are excellent resources for student assistance. Your instructor, the librarians, and the writing center staff will not do the work for you. Instead, they'll teach you how to help yourself. The guidelines I've outlined here are meant to do exactly the same. So the next time you've got a writing assignment, what will you do?

DISCUSSION

1. Think about a previous writing assignment that was a challenge for you. What strategies did you use at the time? After reading the chapter, what other strategies do you think might have been useful?

2. Choose two verbs from the list of frequently used directive verbs (Table 1). Look up these verbs (and possible synonyms) in the dictionary and write down their definitions. If you saw these verbs in a writing assignment, what potential questions might you ask your professor in order to clarify what he/she means?

3. Choose two of the sample assignments from the chapter and create a chart similar to Table 2 for each assignment. What differences do you notice? If these were your assignments, what evidence do you think would best support your argument and why (review guideline seven for help)?

4. What advice would you give to first year college students about writing, writing assignments, or instructor expectations? Structure this advice in the form of a guideline similar to those included in the chapter.

NOTES

1. My thanks to Dr. Kenneth Locke from University of the West for contributing a sample assignment to this project and to the students who participated in this exercise; their interest, time, and enthusiasm helps bring a sense of realism to this essay, and I am indebted to them for their assistance.

2. The names of student participants in this document have been changed to retain confidentiality.

WORKS CITED

Bailey. Biology Writing Assignment. Rec. 20 July 2009. Digital Voice Recorder. University of the West, Rosemead, California.

Ernest. Biology Writing Assignment. Rec. 20 July 2009. Digital Voice Recorder. University of the West, Rosemead, California.

Nicole. Business Writing Assignment. Rec. 20 July 2009. Digital Voice Recorder. University of the West. Rosemead, California.

Pekrun, Reinhard, Andrew J. Elliot, and Markus A. Maier. "Achievement Goals and Achievement Emotions: Testing a Model of Their Joint Relations with Academic Performance." *Journal of Educational Psychology* 101.1 (February 2009): 115–135.

The Inspired Writer vs. the Real Writer

Sarah Allen

Several years ago, in a first year writing course, a student nervously approached me after class, asking if we could talk about her latest draft of a formal paper.[*] She was worried about the content of the draft, about the fact that in writing about her writing process (the assignment for the paper), she found her tone to be at best frustrated, at worst grumbling and whiney. "I don't really like writing. Is that okay?" she asked.

This is the first time that I remember a student confessing aloud (to me) that she did not like writing, and I remember struggling for an appropriate response—not because I couldn't fathom how she had the gall to admit this to me, a writing teacher, but because I couldn't understand why admitting to not liking writing worried her. In the next class, I asked my students if they liked writing. I heard a mixed response. I asked them if they assumed that someone like me, a writing teacher/scholar, always liked writing. The answer was a resounding "yes." I rephrased, "So you believe that every day I skip gleefully to my computer?" Again, though giggling a bit, my students answered "yes." And, at last, one student piped up to say, "Well, you're good at it, right? I mean, that's what makes you good at it."

My student, quoted above, seems to suggest that I am good at writing because I like doing it. But I'd have to disagree on at least two points: First, I wouldn't describe my feelings toward writing as being a "like" kind of thing. It's more of an agonistic kind of thing. Second, I am not "good" at writing, if being good at it means that the words, the paragraphs, the pages come easily.

On the contrary, I believe that I write because I am driven to do so—driven by a will to write. By "will," I mean a kind of purposeful-ness, propensity, diligence, and determination (which, I should men-tion, does not lead to perfection or ease . . . unfortunately). But, I should qualify this: the will to write is not innate for me, nor is it al-ways readily available. In fact, the common assumption that a will to write must be both innate and stem from an ever-replenishing source never ceases to surprise (and annoy) me. I've worked with a lot of envi-ably brilliant and wonderful writers—teachers, students, scholars, and freelancers. I've yet to meet one who believes that she/he is innately and/or always a brilliant writer, nor have I met one who says she/he always wants to write.

And yet, I confess that I find myself to be genuinely surprised when some well-respected scholar in my field admits to struggling with his writing. For example, David Bartholomae (a very successful scholar in the field of Rhetoric and Composition) confesses that he didn't learn to write until after he completed his undergraduate studies, and that he learned it through what must have been at least one particularly traumatic experience: his dissertation was rejected for being "poorly written" (22–23).

If at first glance the rejection of a dissertation means little to you, let me explain: imagine spending years (literally, years) on a piece of writing (a very long piece of writing), for which you've sacrificed more than you ever thought you'd sacrifice for anything (your time, your freedom, sleep, relationships, and even, at times, your sanity), only to have it rejected. And worse, it's rejected for being "poorly written," which is like being booted off of a pro-league baseball team for not being able to tie your shoes properly. We're talking basics here, or so we (writers) like to think. And yet, if writing were nothing more than "practicing the basics," why's it so hard—hard even for one of the best of the best in my field?

It's alarming how many great scholars have admitted to struggling with writing. Bartholomae is not the only one. In a rather famous ad-mission, one of the "fathers" of the field of Rhetoric and Composition, Peter Elbow—the guy who put freewriting on the map, wrote one of the first book-length studies of the writing process, and has been the virtual MLK, Jr. for voice-in-writing (yeah, that guy)—dropped out of graduate school because he suffered so badly from writer's block.[1]

My own story of my frustrated struggle with writing is not nearly so heroic as Elbow's or Bartholomae's. I did not fight the dragon beasts of poor writing skills or writer's block, return to the (writing) field as the victorious knight, and then settle in for a long, successful reign as one of the rulers of the land of Rhetoric and Composition. Rather, mine was (and, sometimes, still is) more Hamlet-like, more like a battle with a ghost—the ghost being the "Inspired Writer."

The Inspired Writer, as I understand her/him, is a figure for whom writing comes easily—the sort of Romantic hero who writes purely out of an awe-full state, generating perfect prose without the frustrated process of revision (or failure). This Inspired Writer is everywhere, in all the great stories of great writers who were so full of "writerliness" that they were tormented by their need to write; they were relentlessly pursued by their muses . . . as was evidenced by their inked hands, tangled hair, ringed eyes, and profoundly watchful stares. They did not have to go crawling about in the muck of what-everybody's-already-written, across the desert of what-could-I-possibly-say, and over the mountain of an-audience-who-probably-knows-a-lot-more-than-I-do.

Of course, the great irony of this figure's story is that the Inspired Writer is really the transcendent distortion of real-life writers. It's much more likely that most of those great, real-life writers got their inked hands from gripping too hard their quills or pens in frustration, as they hovered over pages with more slashes, margin-notes, and edits than clean, untouched sentences set in perfect lines. They probably got their tangled hair from wrenching it; their ringed eyes from spending too many hours staring at black squiggles over white pages; and their profoundly watchful stares from their consequent, bad eyesight.

The fact is that they, too, had to answer to the great works that had been written before them; they, too, had to struggle with their own fears about sounding stupid; and they, too, had to answer to an often discerning and demanding audience. Yet, despite reality, the awesome figure of the Inspired Writer still holds sway, hovering over us like bad lighting, blinding us to our own work.

The pervasiveness of this myth of the Inspired Writer and the continued celebration of her/him works against us, as writers, for we often assume that if writing does not come easily, then our writing is not good—and in turn, that we cannot be good writers. Consequently, we believe that the writing that comes easily is the only good writing, so we will turn in papers that have been drafted quickly and without revision, hoping for the best (grade).

Now, in the days when I was clawing my way through classes as an English major, literature teachers didn't spend much time on revision. I don't ever remember being told anything about strategies for revision. I remember doing peer reviews, where we read each other's drafts and marked punctuation problems, having no idea how to examine— much less comment on—structure and analysis. Other than the five-paragraph formula I'd learned in high school, I had no idea what a paper should or could look like. In other words, when I was learning to write college papers some fifteen years ago, I was totally on my own. The most useful strategy in my bag of tricks? Trial and error. And believe me, good grades or no, having had the opportunity recently (thanks to my mother moving and insisting, "take your STUFF!") to look at the papers I wrote back then, I see an awful lot of the latter.

You see, the awful, honest truth is that I'm no rabbit, no natural digger, no lover of thick, tangled messes, and I had no idea how to find my way through the knotted ideas at work in any first drafts, much less how to dig my way into more root (e.g. to go further with my claims, to push the analysis, to discover the "so what" of my work). I didn't find this place (the page) to be a comfy, hide-out-worthy home. In fact, I confess that I still don't. I have always loved to read, but writing has been much more work than I ever anticipated. And even after so many years of graduate school, and even more years of teaching writing and of writing scholarship, when one might think I should have fully embraced and embodied the status of "veteran" digger, I still, very often feel like I'm trudging through some thick of hard branches and harder roots to find my way down a page.

After years of reflecting on this trudging and of talking with students about how they, too, often feel as though they are trudging down a page—through ideas, among the cacophony of words (our own and others')—I've come to this (admittedly, unimpressive) realization: this is, for many of us, an alien discourse. I'm not like my two closest friends from graduate school, whose parents were academics. We didn't talk at breakfast about "the problematic representations of race in the media." Instead, my father told racist jokes that my sisters and I didn't recognize—until later—were racist. We didn't talk at dinner about "the mass oppression of 'other(ed)' cultures by corporate/

national tyrants." My sisters and I talked about how the cheerleaders were way cooler than we were because they had better clothes, cars, hair, bodies, and boyfriends, and that we would, consequently, be losers for the rest of our lives.

Again, this is an alien discourse, even now. Well, not this. This is more like a personal essay, but the papers I was supposed to write for my literature classes, those were strange. I didn't normally think in the order that a paper would suggest—first broadly, then moving to specifics, which are treated as isolated entities, brought together in transitions and at the end of the paper. I didn't understand, much less use, words like "Marxism," "feminism," or even "close reading." I didn't know that Shakespeare may not have been Shakespeare. I didn't know that Hemingway was a drunk. I didn't know that really smart people spent their entire careers duking it out about who Shakespeare really was and whether Hemingway's alcoholism influenced his work.

I didn't know the vocabulary; I didn't know the issues; I didn't think in the right order; I didn't quote properly; and I was far too interested in the sinking, spinning feeling that writing—and reading—sometimes gave me, instead of being interested in the rigorousness of scholarly work, in modeling that work, and in becoming a member of this strange discourse community. Consequently, when a teacher finally sat me down to explain that this was, in fact, a community—one that occurred on pages, at conferences, in coffee shops, and over listservs—and that if I wanted to stay on the court, I'd have to learn the rules of the game, I was both intrigued and terrified. And no surprise, writing then became not just a way to induce the sinking, spinning thing of which I spoke earlier, but a way to think, a way to act—e.g. a way to figure out little things, like who "Mr. W.H." is in Shakespeare's dedication to his Sonnets, as well as big things, like how we can better fight the "isms" of this world.

No doubt, the sinking, spinning feeling that I experience when I write or read comes and goes now, but it always did. I feel it alternately, as it shares time with the "trudging" feeling I described earlier. But, please don't think that this trudging comes from having to learn and practice the writing conventions of an alien community. Rather, the feeling of "trudging" is a consequence, again, of that haunting specter, the Inspired Writer. The feeling comes from the expectation that writing should come from "the gods" or natural talent, and it is a consequence, too, of the expectation that this inspiration or talent should be always available to us—always there, though sometimes hidden, in some reservoir of our beings.

Thus, even now, when I hit a blank spot and the sentence stumbles off into white space, I feel . . . inadequate . . . or worse, like a fraud, like I'm playing a game that I've got no business playing. The reader is gonna red-card me. And what makes it worse: I have to write. Writing teacher and scholar or not, I have to write memos and emails and resumes and reports and thank you notes and on and on.

But the upshot of all of this is that you'd be amazed what talking about this frustration (and all of the attendant fears) will do for a writer, once she/he opens up and shares this frustration with other writers, other students, teachers . . . with anyone who has to write. For example, once my students see that everyone sitting in this classroom has a gnawing fear about their work failing, about how they don't have "it," about how they don't feel justified calling themselves "writers," because most of them are "regular folks" required to take a writing class, well . . . then we can have ourselves a getting-down-to-it, honest and productive writing classroom. Then, we can talk about writer's block—what it is, what causes it, and what overcomes it. We can talk about how to develop "thick skins"—about how to listen to readers' commentaries and critiques without simultaneously wanting to rip our writings into tiny pieces, stomp them into a trashcan, and then set fire to them. And most importantly, then, we can talk about writing as a practice, not a reflection of some innate quality of the writer.

My work, for example, is more a reflection of the scholarship I spend the most time with than it is a reflection of me, per se. One strategy I learned in graduate school (and I swear, I picked it up by watching my first year composition students) is to imitate other, successful pieces of writing. By "imitate," of course I don't mean plagiarize. I mean that I imitate the form of those texts, e.g. the organization, and the ways that they engage with, explore, and extend ideas.

For example, a Rhetoric and Composition scholar named Patricia Bizzell has written scholarship that I use a lot in my own work. In fact, even when I don't use her work directly, I can see her influence on my thinking. A couple of years ago, after reading one of her books for about the hundredth time (seriously), I noticed that her articles and chapters are organized in predictable kinds of ways (not predictable as in boring, but predictable as in she's-a-pro). She seems to have a formula down, and it works. Her work is consistently solid—i.e. convincing, important—and using that formula, she's able to tackle really dense material and make it accessible to readers.

To be more specific, she tends to start with an introduction that demonstrates, right away, why the coming work is so important. For example, in "Foundationalism and Anti-Foundationalism in Composition Studies," she starts off the article by reminding us, basically (I'm paraphrasing here), that everybody's down with "the social," that we are all invested in examining how language—and writing—occurs in a context and how that context dictates meaning. So, for example, the word "we" in the previous sentence is a reference to Rhetoric and Composition teachers and scholars; however, in this sentence, it's not a reference to a group of people, but to the word "we," as it occurs in the previous sentence. See? Meaning changes according to context.

So, Bizzell starts with this premise: that everybody's down with the social, that we're invested in examining contexts, that we know that meaning happens in those contexts. Then, she introduces the problem: that we still want something pre-contextual (e.g. I know what "we" means because I can step outside of any contexts—including this one—and examine it objectively). Then, she gives two in-depth examples of where she sees the problem at work in the field. She then examines how we've tried to address that problem, then how we've failed at addressing it, and then she poses another/new perspective on the problem and, consequently, another/new way of addressing it.

This is her formula, and I imitate it, frequently, in my own work. It's rigorous, thorough, and like I said earlier, accessible. It works. But, sometimes I'm working on something totally different, something new (to me), and that formula starts to box me in too much; the formula becomes a tomb instead of a foundation. That's when I turn to outside readers.

Now, this one, actually, is a tougher strategy to use . . . because it requires that you share a piece of work that looks like a train wreck to you with another human being—ideally, another smart, patient, open-minded human being. I have four people I send my work out to consistently. One is my boss; one my mentor; one a (very successful) peer; and the other, a senior colleague I come dangerously close to worshipping. In other words, I don't send my stuff to my mom. I don't give it to my best friend, my boyfriend, my dance teacher, or my sisters. I only send my stuff to people who seem to be a lot better at writing scholarship than I feel like I am.

Again, it's hard to do, but I can't tell you how many students I'll see in my office over the course of a semester who will say, "But my mom read my paper, and she says it looks great"—while gripping a paper marked with a D or F. Mom may have been the final authority when you were negotiating curfews and driving and dating, but unless Mom's a (college-level) writing teacher, she'll be no more of an expert in college-level writing than your dentist will. Send it to her if you want an outside reader, but don't expect her final word to be similar to your teacher's final word. And while I'm on my soapbox . . . don't let anyone edit your papers . . . including your mom. It's called "collusion"—a kind of plagiarism—and it's really easy to spot, especially if you were the Comma Splice King in the first paper and use commas flawlessly in the second.

More importantly, keep in mind that if you only use your mom, or your coach, or some other person who's not in the same class, then you may be making the revision process (and the reading for that person) more difficult than necessary, since that reader will have no idea what you've read in class, what you've talked about in class, or what the assignment guidelines and grading criteria are. Writing occurs—and is assessed—in a context, remember?

The best strategy for finding and using readers is to start with the teacher (no, it's not cheating). Ask him/her to read a draft before you submit the final. Then, share the paper with a classmate, as well as someone who's not in the class. That way, you'll get an "insider's" perspective as well as an "outsider's."[2] I've heard students say that using anyone but the teacher for feedback seems to be a waste of time. However, I find that when a student brings me a draft, I (and most writing professors) read it in terms of how it should be revised, not how I'd grade it. So, after you revise based on the teacher's feedback, get other readers to take a look, again, at the newly revised version and have them read it as a finished product. This will help you get a better sense of how it's working as a text that will be graded.

The best piece of advice I can give you, though, is to tell the Inspired Writer to shut up and let you write. If you have to, find out about a few of your favorite writers. I guarantee that they struggle, too. If not them, try talking to your classmates and/or your teacher. Again, if they have written anything in their lives worth writing, then it took some effort to do so. And, once the insecurities are out there, so to speak, and not trapped in Pandora's little box to drive us mad with their "what if" whispers, you may discover that there's more to the writing process than just getting lost in branches and stumbling over roots.

There's nothing quite like finding that the black squiggles you typed onto that white page actually invoke a feeling in or change the mind of your reader(s). Of course, too, there's the emotion, revelation, clench of teeth, slackening of shoulders, or any other response, that a text elicits from even its own writer. The latter is, for my part, the biggest reason why I write—even now, and even and especially as I write scholarship. For me, the text is like a fire in the room. And I am often awed by the way it moves, sleeps, devours, and sustains, while I am simultaneously trying to master it (knowing full well that if I let it go, it will run riot, but knowing, too, that I can't push too hard or it will disappear altogether).

For what I've found in my own relationship to writing, and in talking to my students about theirs, is that it's about the connection, really—even if the connection is an antagonistic one. We like to think that thinking isn't for nothing; that communicating with another (even and especially with ourselves) is never entirely in vain; that what we have to say is perhaps/probably not brilliant but is, still, worth the attempt of saying, of writing, and of considering/being considered. No doubt, a whole lot of practice can give us the means to write in such a way that not only we, the writers, but others will want to listen, will want to read. And in that listening-talking, reading-writing relation, a collision, the inevitable momentary connection, happens.

Maybe we smack the dirt and roots; maybe we smack white space. Maybe a reader's jaw drops at the "gets it" insight of some obscure line in your paper that you don't even remember writing because you spent forty-five minutes working on the line right after it. Maybe you make someone stop and think for just a moment about something they've never considered before. Maybe you make friends with a bunch of classmates because of that story you wrote about the roadtrip you took last summer to a music festival. Maybe you inspired a heated class debate because of that paper you wrote about your personal project for saving the world.

But for all the misunderstandings, all the fears and so-called failings that happen among writer and paper and reader, there's always another white page, and there's always more to say. This is why we must write, why we must continue to practice: to keep talking, keep thinking, keep revising. Nobody's ever got the final word, not even on the page. We've all got the will to write: it's called "communication." Maybe you do so in music or in paint or in graphics or, even, in gossip. But here, in these black squiggles on this white page, you've listened to something I've had to say. Maybe you've not listened closely; maybe you're yawning or rolling your eyes. But if this is a decent piece of writing, you're giving some response right now—a smile? An exasperated sigh? A tensed shoulder? A clenched fist? Whatever the case, here, response is happening. And that's at least a (good) start.

Discussion

1. What are you most anxious about, when writing? For example, do you worry most about grammar and mechanics? About organization? About the deadline? About page length? Why?

2. No doubt most students are at least peripherally, if not entirely, concerned with what grade they get on a paper. Given that pressure and/or in addition to that pressure, what are you most anxious about, when sharing your writing with others—e.g. classmates and/or the teacher? For example, do you worry most about your audience thinking your ideas are stupid? About readers misunderstanding your argument? About your peers/teacher judging you according to how well you write?

3. How are your answers to numbers 1 and 2 related? For example, does your anxiety about the deadline have anything to do with your anxiety about readers misunderstanding your argument? If so, how and/or why?

4. What, if any, strategies do you use to address these anxieties? Do they work?

Notes

1. See his "Autobiographical Digression" in the second chapter of *Writing without Teachers*.

2.   Most universities have a Writing Center, too, and that can be a valuable resource, since the staff are trained to read papers and often allot as much as an hour to focus on your draft.

WORKS CITED

Bartholomae, David. "Against the Grain." *Writers on Writing*. Ed. by Tom Waldrep. New York, NY: Random House, 1985. 19–29.

Bizzell, Patricia. "Foundationalism and Anti-Foundationalism in Composition Studies." *Academic Discourse and Critical Consciousness*. Pittsburgh, PA: U of Pittsburgh P, 1992. 202–221.

Elbow, Peter. *Writing without Teachers*. New York, NY: Oxford UP, 1973.

Backpacks vs. Briefcases: Steps toward Rhetorical Analysis

Laura Bolin Carroll

First Impressions

Imagine the first day of class in first year composition at your university.* The moment your professor walked in the room, you likely began analyzing her and making assumptions about what kind of teacher she will be. You might have noticed what kind of bag she is carrying—a tattered leather satchel? a hot pink polka-dotted backpack? a burgundy brief case? You probably also noticed what she is wearing—trendy slacks and an untucked striped shirt? a skirted suit? jeans and a tee shirt?

It is likely that the above observations were only a few of the observations you made as your professor walked in the room. You might have also noticed her shoes, her jewelry, whether she wears a wedding ring, how her hair is styled, whether she stands tall or slumps, how quickly she walks, or maybe even if her nails are done. If you don't tend to notice any of these things about your professors, you certainly do about the people around you—your roommate, others in your residence hall, students you are assigned to work with in groups, or a prospective date. For most of us, many of the people we encounter in a given day are subject to this kind of quick analysis.

Now as you performed this kind of analysis, you likely didn't walk through each of these questions one by one, write out the answer, and add up the responses to see what kind of person you are interacting with. Instead, you quickly took in the information and made an informed, and likely somewhat accurate, decision about that person. Over the years, as you have interacted with others, you have built a mental database that you can draw on to make conclusions about what a person's looks tell you about their personality. You have become able to analyze quickly what people are saying about themselves through the way they choose to dress, accessorize, or wear their hair.

We have, of course, heard that you "can't judge a book by its cover," but, in fact, we do it all the time. Daily we find ourselves in situations where we are forced to make snap judgments. Each day we meet different people, encounter unfamiliar situations, and see media that asks us to do, think, buy, and act in all sorts of ways. In fact, our saturation in media and its images is one of the reasons why learning to do rhetorical analysis is so important. The more we know about how to analyze situations and draw informed conclusions, the better we can become about making savvy judgments about the people, situations and media we encounter.

IMPLICATIONS OF RHETORICAL ANALYSIS

Media is one of the most important places where this kind of analysis needs to happen. Rhetoric—the way we use language and images to persuade—is what makes media work. Think of all the media you see and hear every day: Twitter, television shows, web pages, billboards, text messages, podcasts. Even as you read this chapter, more ways to get those messages to you quickly and in a persuasive manner are being developed. Media is constantly asking you to buy something, act in some way, believe something to be true, or interact with others in a specific manner. Understanding rhetorical messages is essential to help us to become informed consumers, but it also helps evaluate the ethics of messages, how they affect us personally, and how they affect society.

Take, for example, a commercial for men's deodorant that tells you that you'll be irresistible to women if you use their product. This campaign doesn't just ask you to buy the product, though. It also asks you to trust the company's credibility, or ethos, and to believe the messages they send about how men and women interact, about sexuality, and about what constitutes a healthy body. You have to decide whether or not you will choose to buy the product and how you will choose to respond to the messages that the commercial sends.

Or, in another situation, a Facebook group asks you to support health care reform. The rhetoric in this group uses people's stories of their struggles to obtain affordable health care. These stories, which are often heart-wrenching, use emotion to persuade you—also called pathos. You are asked to believe that health care reform is necessary and urgent, and you are asked to act on these beliefs by calling your congresspersons and asking them to support the reforms as well.

Because media rhetoric surrounds us, it is important to understand how rhetoric works. If we refuse to stop and think about how and why it persuades us, we can become mindless consumers who buy into arguments about what makes us value ourselves and what makes us happy. For example, research has shown that only 2% of women consider themselves beautiful ("Campaign"), which has been linked to the way that the fashion industry defines beauty. We are also told by the media that buying more stuff can make us happy, but historical surveys show that US happiness peaked in the 1950s, when people saw as many advertisements in their lifetime as the average American sees in one year (Leonard).

Our worlds are full of these kinds of social influences. As we interact with other people and with media, we are continually creating and interpreting rhetoric. In the same way that you decide how to process, analyze or ignore these messages, you create them. You probably think about what your clothing will communicate as you go to a job interview or get ready for a date. You are also using rhetoric when you try to persuade your parents to send you money or your friends to see the movie that interests you. When you post to your blog or tweet you are using rhetoric. In fact, according to rhetorician Kenneth Burke, rhetoric is everywhere: "wherever there is persuasion, there is rhetoric. And wherever there is 'meaning,' there is 'persuasion.' Food eaten and digested is not rhetoric. But in the meaning of food there is much rhetoric, the meaning being persuasive enough for the idea of food to be used, like the ideas of religion, as a rhetorical device of statesmen" (71–72). In other words, most of our actions are persuasive in nature.

What we choose to wear (tennis shoes vs. flip flops), where we shop (Whole Foods Market vs. Wal-Mart), what we eat (organic vs. fast food), or even the way we send information (snail mail vs. text message) can work to persuade others.

Chances are you have grown up learning to interpret and analyze these types of rhetoric. They become so commonplace that we don't realize how often and how quickly we are able to perform this kind of rhetorical analysis. When your teacher walked in on the first day of class, you probably didn't think to yourself, "I think I'll do some rhetorical analysis on her clothing and draw some conclusions about what kind of personality she might have and whether I think I'll like her." And, yet, you probably were able to come up with some conclusions based on the evidence you had.

However, when this same teacher hands you an advertisement, photograph or article and asks you to write a rhetorical analysis of it, you might have been baffled or felt a little overwhelmed. The good news is that many of the analytical processes that you already use to interpret the rhetoric around you are the same ones that you'll use for these assignments.

The Rhetorical Situation, Or Discerning Context

One of the first places to start is context. Rhetorical messages always occur in a specific situation or context. The president's speech might respond to a specific global event, like an economic summit; that's part of the context. You choose your clothing depending on where you are going or what you are doing; that's context. A television commercial comes on during specific programs and at specific points of the day; that's context. A billboard is placed in a specific part of the community; that's context, too.

In an article called "The Rhetorical Situation," Lloyd Bitzer argues that there are three parts to understanding the context of a rhetorical moment: exigence, audience and constraints. Exigence is the circumstance or condition that invites a response; "imperfection marked by urgency; it is a defect, an obstacle, something waiting to be done, a thing which is other than it should be" (Bitzer 304). In other words, rhetorical discourse is usually responding to some kind of problem. You can begin to understand a piece's exigence by asking, "What is this rhetoric responding to?" "What might have happened to make the rhetor (the person who creates the rhetoric) respond in this way?"

The exigence can be extremely complex, like the need for a new Supreme Court justice, or it can be much simpler, like receiving an email that asks you where you and your friends should go for your road trip this weekend. Understanding the exigence is important because it helps you begin to discover the purpose of the rhetoric. It helps you understand what the discourse is trying to accomplish.

Another part of the rhetorical context is audience, those who are the (intended or unintended) recipients of the rhetorical message. The audience should be able to respond to the exigence. In other words, the audience should be able to help address the problem. You might be very frustrated with your campus's requirement that all first-year students purchase a meal plan for on-campus dining. You might even send an email to a good friend back home voicing that frustration. However, if you want to address the exigence of the meal plans, the most appropriate audience would be the person/office on campus that oversees meal plans. Your friend back home cannot solve the problem (though she may be able to offer sympathy or give you some good suggestions), but the person who can change the meal plan requirements is probably on campus. Rhetors make all sorts of choices based on their audience. Audience can determine the type of language used, the formality of the discourse, the medium or delivery of the rhetoric, and even the types of reasons used the make the rhetor's argument. Understanding the audience helps you begin to see and understand the rhetorical moves that the rhetor makes.

The last piece of the rhetorical situation is the constraints. The constraints of the rhetorical situation are those things that have the power to "constrain decision and action needed to modify the exigence" (Bitzer 306). Constraints have a lot to do with how the rhetoric is presented. Constraints can be "beliefs, attitudes, documents, facts, traditions, images, interests, motives" (Bitzer 306). Constraints limit the way the discourse is delivered or communicated. Constraints may be something as simple as your instructor limiting your proposal to one thousand words, or they may be far more complex like the kinds of language you need to use to persuade a certain community.

So how do you apply this to a piece of rhetoric? Let's say you are flipping through a magazine, and you come across an advertisement that has a large headline that reads "Why Some People Say 'D'OH'

When You Say 'Homer'" ("Why"). This ad is an Ad Council public service announcement (PSA) to promote arts education and is sponsored by Americans for the Arts and NAMM, the trade association of the international music products industry.

Since you want to understand more about what this ad means and what it wants you to believe or do, you begin to think about the rhetorical situation. You first might ask, "what is the ad responding to? What problem does it hope to address?" That's the exigence. In this case, the exigence is the cutting of arts funding and children's lack of exposure to the arts. According to the Ad Council's website, "the average kid is provided insufficient time to learn and experience the arts. This PSA campaign was created to increase involvement in championing arts education both in and out of school" ("Arts"). The PSA is responding directly to the fact that kids are not getting enough arts education.

Then you might begin to think about to whom the Ad Council targeted the ad. Unless you're a parent, you are probably not the primary audience. If you continued reading the text of the ad, you'd notice that there is information to persuade parents that the arts are helpful to their children and to let them know how to help their children become more involved with the arts. The ad tells parents that "the experience will for sure do more than entertain them. It'll build their capacity to learn more. In fact, the more art kids get, the smarter they become in subjects like math and science. And that's reason enough to make a parent say, 'D'oh!,' For Ten Simple Ways to instill art in your kids' lives visit AmericansForTheArts.org" ("Why"). Throughout the text of the ad, parents are told both what to believe about arts education and how to act in response to the belief.

There also might be a secondary audience for this ad—people who are not the main audience of the ad but might also be able to respond to the exigence. For example, philanthropists who could raise money for arts education or legislators who might pass laws for arts funding or to require arts education in public schools could also be intended audiences for this ad.

Finally, you might want to think about the constraints or the limitations on the ad. Sometimes these are harder to get at, but we can guess a few things. One constraint might be the cost of the ad. Different magazines charge differently for ad space as well as placement within the magazine, so the Ad Council could have been constrained by how much money they wanted to spend to circulate the ad. The ad is also only one page long, so there might have been a limitation on the amount of space for the ad. Finally, on the Ad Council's webpage, they list the requirements for organizations seeking the funding and support of the Ad Council. There are twelve criteria, but here are a few:

1. The sponsor organization must be a private non-profit 501(c)3 organization, private foundation, government agency or coalition of such groups.

2. The issue must address the Ad Council's focus on Health & Safety, Education, or Community. Applications which benefit children are viewed with favor—as part of the Ad Council's Commitment to Children.

3. The issue must offer a solution through an individual action.

4. The effort must be national in scope, so that the message has relevance to media audiences in communities throughout the nation. ("Become")

Each of these criteria helps to understand the limitations on both who can participate as rhetor and what can be said.

The exigence, audience and constraints are only one way to understand the context of a piece of rhetoric, and, of course, there are other ways to get at context. Some rhetoricians look at subject, purpose, audience and occasion. Others might look at the "rhetorical triangle" of writer, reader, and purpose.

An analysis using the rhetorical triangle would ask similar questions about audience as one using the rhetorical situation, but it would also ask questions about the writer and the purpose of the document. Asking questions about the writer helps the reader determine whether she or he is credible and knowledgeable. For example, the Ad Council has been creating public service announcements since 1942 ("Loose Lips Sink Ships," anyone?) and is a non-profit agency. They also document their credibility by showing the impact of their campaigns in several ways: "Destruction of our forests by wildfires has been reduced from 22 million acres to less than 8.4 million acres per year, since our Forest Fire Prevention campaign began" and "6,000 Children were paired with a mentor in just the first 18 months of our mentoring campaign" ("About"). Based on this information, we can assume that the Ad Council is a credible rhetor, and whether or not we agree with the rhetoric they produce, we can probably assume it contains reliable information. Asking questions about the next part of the rhetorical triangle, the purpose of a piece of rhetoric, helps you understand what the rhetor is trying to achieve through the discourse. We can discern the purpose by asking questions like "what does the rhetor want me to believe after seeing this message?" or "what does the rhetor want me to do?" In some ways, the purpose takes the exigence to the next step. If the exigence frames the problem, the purpose frames the response to that problem.

The rhetorical situation and rhetorical triangle are two ways to begin to understand how the rhetoric functions within the context you find it. The key idea is to understand that no rhetorical performance takes place in a vacuum. One of the first steps to understanding a piece of rhetoric is to look at the context in which it takes place. Whatever terminology you (or your instructor) choose, it is a good idea to start by locating your analysis within a rhetorical situation.

The Heart of the Matter—The Argument

The rhetorical situation is just the beginning of your analysis, though. What you really want to understand is the argument—what the rhetor wants you to believe or do and how he or she goes about that persuasion. Effective argumentation has been talked about for centuries. In the fourth century BCE, Aristotle was teaching the men of Athens how to persuade different kinds of audiences in different kinds of rhetorical situations. Aristotle articulated three "artistic appeals" that a rhetor could draw on to make a case—logos, pathos, and ethos.

Logos is commonly defined as argument from reason, and it usually appeals to an audience's intellectual side. As audiences we want to know the "facts of the matter," and logos helps present these—statistics, data, and logical statements. For example, on our Homer ad for the arts, the text tells parents that the arts will "build their capacity to learn more. In fact, the more art kids get, the smarter they become in subjects like math and science" ("Why"). You might notice that there aren't numbers or charts here, but giving this information appeals to the audience's intellectual side.

That audience can see a continuation of the argument on the Ad Council's webpage, and again much of the argument appeals to logos and draws on extensive research that shows that the arts do these things:

- Allow kids to express themselves creatively and bolster their self-confidence.
- Teach kids to be more tolerant and open.
- Improve kids' overall academic performance.
- Show that kids actively engaged in arts education are likely to have higher SAT scores than those with little to no arts involvement.
- Develop skills needed by the 21st century workforce: critical thinking, creative problem solving, effective communication, teamwork and more.
- Keep students engaged in school and less likely to drop out. ("Arts")

Each bullet above is meant to intellectually persuade parents that they need to be more intentional in providing arts education for their children.

Few of us are persuaded only with our mind, though. Even if we intellectually agree with something, it is difficult to get us to act unless we are also persuaded in our heart. This kind of appeal to emotion is called pathos. Pathetic appeals (as rhetoric that draws on pathos is called) used alone without logos and ethos can come across as emotionally manipulative or overly sentimental, but are very powerful when used in conjunction with the other two appeals.

Emotional appeals can come in many forms—an anecdote or narrative, an image such as a photograph, or even humor. For example, on their web campaign, People for the Ethical Treatment of Animals (PETA) uses an image of a baby chick and of Ronald McDonald wielding a knife to draw attention to their Chicken McCruely Un-Happy Meal. These images are meant to evoke an emotional response in the viewer and, along with a logos appeal with the statistics about how cruelly chickens are treated, persuade the viewer to boycott McDonalds.

Pathos can also be a very effective appeal if the rhetor has to persuade the audience in a very short amount of time, which is why it is used heavily in print advertisements, billboards, or television commercials. An investment company will fill a 30-second commercial with images of families and couples enjoying each other, seeming happy, and surrounded by wealth to persuade you to do business with them.

The 30-second time spot does not allow them to give the 15-year growth of each of their funds, and pathetic appeals will often hold our interest much longer than intellectual appeals.

The ad promoting the importance of art uses humor to appeal to the audience's emotional side. By comparing the epic poet Homer to Homer Simpson and his classic "d'oh!" the ad uses humor to draw people into their argument about the arts. The humor continues as they ask parents if their kids know the difference between the Homers, "The only Homer some kids know is the one who can't write his own last name" ("Why"). The ad also appeals to emotion through its language use (diction), describing Homer as "one very ancient dude," and describing The Odyssey as "the sequel" to The Iliad. In this case, the humor of the ad, which occurs in the first few lines, is meant to draw the reader in and help them become interested in the argument before the ad gets to the logos, which is in the last few lines of the ad.

The humor also makes the organization seem real and approachable, contributing to the ethos. The humor might lead you to think that Americans for the Arts is not a stuffy bunch of suits, but an organization you can relate to or one that has a realistic understanding of the world. Ethos refers to the credibility of the rhetor—which can be a person or an organization. A rhetor can develop credibility in many ways. The tone of the writing and whether that tone is appropriate for the context helps build a writer's ethos, as does the accuracy of the information or the visual presentation of the rhetoric.

In the Homer ad, the ethos is built in several ways. The simple, humorous and engaging language, such as "Greek Gods. Achilles Heel. Trojan Horse. All of these icons are brought to us by one very ancient dude—Homer. In The Iliad and its sequel, The Odyssey, he presented Greek mythology in everyday language" ("Why") draws the audience in and helps the tone of the ad seem very approachable. Also, the knowledge of Greek mythology and the information about how the arts help children—which also contribute to the logos appeal—make the ad seem credible and authoritative. However, the fact that the ad does not use too many statistics or overly technical language also contributes to the ethos of the ad because often sounding too intellectual can come across as pompous or stuffy.

Aristotle's artistic appeals are not the only way to understand the argument of rhetoric. You might choose to look at the claim or the unstated assumptions of a piece; someone else might consider the visual appeal of the rhetoric, like the font, page layout, types of paper, or images; another person might focus on the language use and the specific word choice and sentence structure of a piece. Logos, pathos, and ethos can provide a nice framework for analysis, but there are numerous ways to understand how a piece of rhetoric persuades (or fails to persuade).

Looking at the context and components of a piece of rhetoric often isn't enough, though, because it is important to draw conclusions about the rhetoric—does it successfully respond to the exigence? Is it an ethical approach? Is it persuasive? These kinds of questions let you begin to create your own claims, your own rhetoric, as you take a stand on what other people say, do, or write.

Beginning to Analyze

Once you have established the context for the rhetoric you are analyzing, you can begin to think about how well it fits into that context. You've probably been in a situation where you arrived way underdressed for an occasion. You thought that the dinner was just a casual get together with friends; it turned out to be a far more formal affair, and you felt very out of place. There are also times when discourse fails to respond to the situation well—it doesn't fit. On the other hand, successful discourses often respond very well to the context. They address the problem, consider the audience's needs, provide accurate information, and have a compelling claim. One of the reasons you work to determine the rhetorical situation for a piece of discourse is to consider whether it works within that context. You can begin this process by asking questions like:

- Does the rhetoric address the problem it claims to address?
- Is the rhetoric targeted at an audience who has the power to make change?
- Are the appeals appropriate to the audience?
- Does the rhetor give enough information to make an informed decision?
- Does the rhetoric attempt to manipulate in any way (by giving incomplete/inaccurate information or abusing the audience's emotions)?

- What other sub-claims do you have to accept to understand
  the rhetor's main claim? (For example, in order to accept the
  Ad Council's claim that the arts boost math and science scores,
  you first have to value the boosting of those scores.)
- What possible negative effects might come from this rhetoric?

Rhetorical analysis asks how discourse functions in the setting in which
it is found. In the same way that a commercial for denture cream seems
very out of place when aired during a reality television show aimed at
teenagers, rhetoric that does not respond well to its context often fails
to persuade. In order to perform analysis, you must understand the
context and then you must carefully study the ways that the discourse
does and does not respond appropriately to that context.

The bottom line is that the same basic principles apply when you
look at any piece of rhetoric (your instructor's clothing, an advertisement, the president's speech): you need to consider the context and the
argument. As you begin to analyze rhetoric, there are lots of different
types of rhetoric you might encounter in a college classroom, such as

- Political cartoon
- Wikipedia entry
- Scholarly article
- Bar Graph
- Op-Ed piece in the newspaper
- Speech
- YouTube video
- Book chapter
- Photograph
- PowerPoint Presentation

All of the above types of discourse try to persuade you. They may ask
you to accept a certain kind of knowledge as valid, they may ask you
to believe a certain way, or they may ask you to act. It is important to
understand what a piece of rhetoric is asking of you, how it tries to
persuade you, and whether that persuasion fits within the context you
encounter it in. Rhetorical analysis helps you answer those questions.

Implications of Rhetorical Analysis, Or Why Do This Stuff Anyway?

So you might be wondering if you know how to do this analysis already—you can tell what kind of person someone is by their clothing, or what a commercial wants you to buy without carefully listening to it—why do you need to know how to do more formal analysis? How does this matter outside a college classroom?

Well, first of all, much of the reading and learning in college requires some level of rhetorical analysis: as you read a textbook chapter to prepare for a quiz, it is helpful to be able to distill the main points quickly; when you read a journal article for a research paper, it is necessary to understand the scholar's thesis; when you watch a video in class, it is useful to be able to understand how the creator is trying to persuade you. But college is not the only place where an understanding of how rhetoric works is important. You will find yourself in many situations—from boardrooms to your children's classrooms or churches to city council meetings where you need to understand the heart of the arguments being presented.

One final example: in November 2000, Campbell's Soup Company launched a campaign to show that many of their soups were low in calories and showed pre-pubescent girls refusing to eat because they were "watching their weight." A very small organization called Dads and Daughters, a group that fights advertising that targets girls with negative body images, contacted Campbell's explaining the problems they saw in an ad that encouraged young girls to be self-conscious about their weight, and asked Campbell's to pull the ad. A few days later, Campbell's Vice President for Marketing and Corporate Communications called. One of the dads says, "the Vice President acknowledged he had received their letter, reviewed the ad again, saw their point, and was pulling the ad," responding to a "couple of guys writing a letter" ("Media"). Individuals who understand rhetorical analysis and act to make change can have a tremendous influence on their world.

DISCUSSION

1. What are examples of rhetoric that you see or hear on a daily basis?

2. What are some ways that you create rhetoric? What kinds of messages are you trying to communicate?

3. What is an example of a rhetorical situation that you have found yourself in? Discuss exigence, audience, and constraints.

Works Cited

"About Ad Council" *Ad Council.* Ad Council. n.d. Web. 11 March 2010. <http://www.adcouncil.org/default.aspx?id=68>.
"Arts Education." *Ad Council: Arts Education.* Ad Council. n.d. Web. 27 July 2009. <http://www.adcouncil.org/default.aspx?id=31>.
"Become an Ad Council Campaign." *Ad Council.* Ad Council. n.d. Web. 27 July 2009. <http://www.adcouncil.org/default.aspx?id=319>.
Bitzer, Lloyd. "The Rhetorical Situation." *Philosophy and Rhetoric* 1 (1968): 1–14. Rpt. in Martin J. Medhurst and Thomas W. Benson, eds. *Rhetorical Dimensions in Media.* Dubuque, IA: Kendall/Hunt, 1991. 300–10. Print.
Burke, Kenneth. *A Rhetoric of Motives.* Berkeley: U of California P, 1969. Print.
"Campaign for Real Beauty Mission." *Dove Campaign for Real Beauty.* 2008. Web. 27 July 2009. <http://www.dove.us/#/CFRB/arti_cfrb.aspx[cp-documentid=7049726]>.
Leonard, Annie. "Fact Sheet." *The Story of Stuff with Annie Leonard.* n.d. Web. 27 July 2009. <http://storyofstuff.com/resources.html>.
"The Media's Influence." *Perfect Illusions: Eating Disorders and the Family.* PBS. 2003. Web. 27 July 2009. <http://www.pbs.org/perfectillusions/eatingdisorders/preventing_media.html>.
"Why Some People Say 'D'oh' When You Say 'Homer.'" *Ad Council: Arts Education.* Ad Council. n.d. Web. 27 July 2009. <http://www.adcouncil.org/files/arts_home_mag.jpg>.

From Topic to Presentation: Making Choices to Develop Your Writing

Beth L. Hewett

Introduction

Every semester, I ask my students for topic ideas, and then I write an essay for them.[*] When we're in a traditional classroom, they watch me write the initial draft using a computer and projector; they comment on the writing, and I present revisions to them later. When we work online, they receive copies of all my drafts with changes tracked for their review and comments. My students like this exercise—partially because they don't have to do the writing, but mostly because they like to see what I can make of an assignment they give me. They tell me that they struggle with beginning the writing and that the model I offer teaches new ways of understanding writing and revision. I like this exercise for the same reasons.

This chapter addresses how to make decisions about essay development and revision. It pays particular attention to using feedback from peers, instructors, or other readers. While you've probably had a lot of instructor feedback and many opportunities to review other students' writing and to have them review yours, you may not have learned much about how to make revision choices related to such feedback. To help you learn about making choices, I present my own argumentative essay that I developed from my students' feedback, and I analyze my decision-making processes as a model for you.

In this chapter, you'll see various stages of an in-progress essay:

1. Choosing among topics

2. Brainstorming

3. Writing an initial, or "zero," draft

4. Writing a preliminary draft that is intended to be revised

5. Using student feedback to revise

6. Completing a presentation draft

7. Considering how to make these processes work for you

The drafts, feedback, and commentary demonstrate how you can develop an essay from early thinking to preliminary writing to presentation-quality writing. Although there are many other ways to write an essay, this model may give you some ideas for your own writing. In addition, don't be surprised if you need more drafts for your essays than you see presented here. This essay was a short one (for me), and so I was able to revise fairly thoroughly in one step. However, a longer project usually takes me many drafts and many feedback rounds to develop fully.

My essay was developed much like your essays are even though I'm a more experienced writer. My assignment was to write an argument, so I was constrained by the genre's requirements. The argument needed to state a position (my assertion or thesis) and had to support that position with good reasons and sufficient evidence to substantiate those reasons. I had a choice of topics, but I didn't have complete freedom to write about just anything I wanted. The topic I ultimately chose was one that I was interested in but knew little about, so I needed to do a lot of research. Because my class was taught in a completely online setting and because I was working from home, I didn't have a physical library to go to, so I used my university's library search engines and the Internet for my research. Finally, I had only four work days to begin and complete a preliminary draft for student review; the process took twelve solid work hours.

My Students' Suggested Writing Topics

To figure out what I would write about, I asked my students to suggest an assignment for me. As the example topics show, some them were pretty mundane—easy to do, but insubstantial and, frankly, boring. Other topics were substantial, but difficult to research and write about thoughtfully in just four days for the class. Finally, one student suggested a topic that captured my interest and that of other students; peers added their questions, and I knew this was the topic I wanted to address even though I knew little about it.

Students' Suggested Topics

- Write about a cell phone charger. I had a teacher in high school that would pick random things every class and make us write about it for 10 minutes to "warm up" our brains. I hated those assignments.
- Why are liquid laundry detergents superior to powdered detergents?
- Does modern technology make life better and more convenient?
- How will the recent election of President Barack Obama affect race relations in the U.S.?
- What are your thoughts and opinions on adoptions by homosexual couples?
- Nadya Suleman gave birth to octuplets. Should the doctors have advised her against in vitro fertilization since she's not financially stable to take care of all of those children? If she does end up on welfare should taxpayers be outraged? At what point or if at any should the government step-in in situations such as this?
  - One angle to look at this sort of story is whether humans should impregnate themselves with "litters" of babies.
  - Personally, I would also like to know what doctor would inseminate this woman without [who didn't have] the funds to do so. It makes me wonder if he/she just wanted part of the publicity.

When you find a topic that is interesting and challenging, you've probably got a good subject that will sustain your attention during the harder parts of the writing. In this case, I was fascinated by the idea of a woman giving birth to eight children and the moral questions that the students asked about this case. I wondered what the woman's motivation was for having more children when she already had six of them, was unmarried and without a supportive partner, and unemployed.

Notice that the interest level of the topic doesn't guarantee an easy one to research. I chose to do quite a bit of digging into the issue because I had an "itch to know"; my curiosity was sufficient reason for me to do this work. Although school assignments may not seem this way, the motive behind research is—or should be—the genuine need or desire to answer a question for which you don't have the answer but about which you really want to know more.

My topic choice also took into consideration that my students would be writing an essay that supports a position during the semester. I wanted to write a similar type of essay that would provide a model for them at that time in their writing development. Thus, choosing my topic was connected to the rhetorical situation of my teaching these students to write arguments that are designed to convince audiences.

Brainstorming

One way that writers can find ideas is commonly called "brainstorming." While there are many ways to find ideas, brainstorming is popular because writers often learn how to do it by such strategies as journaling, listing thoughts, and circling and connecting ideas.

To brainstorm my essay topic, I developed a series of questions that interested me. I also did some preliminary research. Although I didn't list where that research came from in my notes here, I did list them on my original notes so I could be sure to credit my sources with their ideas and words.

Brainstorming

- Octuplets = irresponsibility?
- Selfishness?
- Freak of non-nature?
- Potential for abuse of children
- How the children will/may grow up
- Include stats

- The increase in multiple births in the past 29 years clearly is due to supplemental fertilization methods like invitro fertilization (IVF). Increase of rates XYZ.
- Newborn octuplets have taken the world by surprise and gotten our attention: how were they conceived (IVF), who is the mother and why would she have asked to have so many embryos implanted (six other children, divorced and single, no job, on disability, lives with mother)—what about them?
    - Multiple birth children are exploited; humans not made to have litters; how do we care for all these children? Sensationalism: TV, movies, books, Quintland. Can we predict the ramifications for the children? Yes. Dionne quintuplets; Jon/Kate + 8
- Assertion? As the rate of multiple births increases due to various fertility treatments, we must be thoughtful about the possibility that children of such births will be exploited by their parents and a curious society. (curiosity, money, nurturing) (to insist on protecting these kids would be a persuasive paper)
- Assertion? As fertility treatments increase the rate of multiple births, the potential for both parents and society to exploit these children also increases.

Notice that while I just listed some ideas, my notes show that I also began my research. First, I needed to learn about the topic, which is to earn an "informed opinion," and then I could express that informed opinion through a thesis, or assertion. I wrote two possible assertions at this early stage. They helped me to narrow down what I believed I wanted to argue.

Initial, or Zero, Draft

After brainstorming, many people write an initial draft, which I am calling a zero draft. The zero draft gets the writing started and generally isn't going to be ready for others to see. This draft is a great way to begin because you don't have to be neat and tidy or super correct sentence-wise. Since this draft just begins to organize ideas, a zero draft should never be turned in as a completed draft for grading; trust me—these drafts just aren't ready for prime time. Zero drafts also tend to be fairly useless in a peer response session, so write a complete preliminary draft for that purpose. Unless your instructor asks you to provide it, this draft is yours alone. Return to it as you write your preliminary draft to keep track of how your earliest ideas are developing. You'll be interested in seeing whether your preliminary draft follows these early ideas or veers from them.

Zero Draft

The Exploitation of Multiple Birth Children

Two weeks ago, Nadya Suleman gave birth to octuplets in a California hospital. Although all eight babies lived, they were very small and some may die. Suleman now is the mother of fourteen children—six between the ages of 2 and 7. She is unemployed, without a husband or partner, and lives in her mother's home (she fights with her mother enough that her mom has said so publically). Suleman's babies and her own poverty are the talk of the tabloids and everyone seems to have an opinion. But people have always been excited when multiple children are born to women. But there will likely be more of these births because of in vitro fertilization. Both parents and society tend to exploit these children, but it is not acceptable because it is harmful to the children.

For demonstration purposes, I'm showing you only one paragraph of my zero draft. It provides the barest details of what the first paragraph of my preliminary draft would become. Don't worry if my zero draft looks stronger than one of yours might. I write professionally and I teach writing—it's natural that I would get a good start. When you look at the preliminary draft, however, you'll see that I can do much better! The assertion, which is the last sentence in both examples, is much more focused in the preliminary draft than it is in the zero draft

For people who really become stuck or "blocked" when beginning to write an essay, the combination of some brainstorming and a zero draft can get you started writing fairly painlessly. If you're really stuck, just take some of your brainstorming ideas and begin writing without looking at the paper or screen. Take time to begin developing your thinking before worrying about whether it makes much sense. As long as you take time for writing additional drafts, this zero draft process will be helpful.

Preliminary Draft

How does this first paragraph change in the preliminary draft? As we can see from the example preliminary draft that follows, the argument becomes more fully fleshed out. It contains more detail in general and it uses various source citations for authority. One of the reasons that I included these citations was to give my readers a sense that I had earned an informed opinion. My process before writing this next draft was to deepen my knowledge of the topic through more research and to try to express my informed opinion through a coherent assertion. Throughout the entire argumentative essay, I needed to support that opinion so that readers could be convinced that it is reasonable. Readers didn't have to agree with me or with each other for my argument to be successful. Because people argue only about those things for which there is no definite or single position, it isn't possible to get everyone in my audience to agree with me—which is why my readers only needed to find the argument reasonable.

Let's look now at the complete preliminary draft. After I finished this draft, I posted it for my students to review. Their feedback is shown in the right hand column. At various places in this draft, I make a break and respond to the comments to show my thinking and decision making process. Since I'm writing this chapter for you months after teaching this particular class, I provide you with some hindsight thinking as well.

Bold text shows what I added to the preliminary draft in response to student feedback and my own developing thinking. A strikethrough shows what I deleted in revision. If you can imagine that these changes were all accepted, then you have a good sense of what the presentation draft looked like. Notice that the revision was fairly substantial in that I addressed what I considered to be most important: content, organization, and sentence-level issues in that order.

Preliminary Draft and Tracked Changes

The Exploitation of Multiple Birth Children

~~Two weeks ago,~~ **On January 26, 2009,** Nadya Suleman gave birth to octuplets in a California hospital. To date, all eight babies are alive, but they weighed only between 1 pound, 8 ounces and 3 pounds, 4 ounces at birth, which means that they will be in the neonatal unit of the hospital for weeks to come. Suleman now has fourteen children—six between the ages of 2 and 7—all of them conceived by *in vitro* fertilization (IVF), but she also has no job, no husband or significant other, and no home of her own. She lives with her mother, who publicly has expressed disgust with her daughter's obsessive desire for multiple children ("Grandma," 2009).). ~~Although in the past she has subsisted with disability payments for a job-related injury, Suleman said she refuses Welfare money to support herself and her children (Celizic 2009). However, she has retained a publicist, who mentioned that she's looking at seven-figure offers for her "story" (Celizic 2009; Rochman 2009).~~ Suleman's babies and her own life circumstances are being discussed *ad nauseam* by the media, medical and mental health professionals, and everyday citizens alike. The flurry of interest in Suleman's situation is just a recent example of the excitement people tend to experience when multiple births occur. However, as fertility treatments increase the rate of multiple births, the potential for both parents and society to exploit these children also increases. Even though it might be understandable given the financial challenges of raising multiple children, such exploitation is unacceptable because it skews the children's experiences of family at best and it is emotionally harmful to the children at worst.

> **Comment [BLH1]:** Student 1: …future readers need a specific date to reference.

> **Comment [BLH2]:** Student 2: I did find it difficult to establish the thesis statement. Increase IVF & multiple births, health risks, publicity, family structure, single mother and time dedication were all mentioned as part of what I found to be the thesis.

The first revision change I made was in response to Student 1's comment, which was a good catch on his part. It's surprising that such a small change as adding a date to an event can contextualize an entire argument. In this case, I substituted the actual date of the octuplets' birth, which makes the piece understandable in the future.

Student 2's feedback clearly indicated that there was a potential misunderstanding of the thesis, or argumentative assertion. This argument opens with an anecdote about a mother of octuplets, which doesn't mean that this mother is necessarily its subject. The assertion appears in the last sentence of the opening paragraph, a common place for a thesis in a short essay. This essay's goal is to support the position that exploiting multiple children harms them by skewing their experience of family and emotionally harming them. Notice that the goal is broader than just Suleman's case, as indicated by the word "example" in the third from the last sentence. In order to further help readers to understand that Suleman isn't the topic, I deleted detailed information about her that might have caused some readers to think the argument is all about her. I moved that information to later in the essay when I talk about Suleman as an example of an exploitative parent.

~~How frequent are~~ **In order to understand the problems surrounding multiple births, it is useful to consider the general frequency of** multiple births.~~?~~ Because of fertility treatments that were not available more than twenty-five years ago, the rates have increased considerably. In 1980, the number of human spontaneous twin births, for example, was only 68,339 out of all the births in the United States that year (Fierro, 2008 & n.d.). In 2005, however, the twin birth rate was 133,325, nearly twice the number from 25 years previous (NOMOTC, 2009). The increase in multiple births in the past 29 years is due in part to fertilization treatments like IVF. 1980 marks a period when fertility methods and procedures became more readily available, if still costly. According to Fierro (2008 & n.d.) of About.com, the odds for having twins when pregnancy results from fertility treatments have increased nearly 60% since 1980. Triplets, which once occurred spontaneously in every 1 of 8,100 births, have increased in frequency by 400% since 1980, while quadruplets, which once occurred spontaneously in every 1 of 729,000 births, also have increased by orders of magnitude. Indeed, she estimates: "that 60% of the triplets are the result of fertility enhancing treatments; while 90% of quadruplets ... are due to reproductive technology" (2008). Although the author noted that these statistics are estimates gathered from several sources, the numbers seem reasonable given the increasing popularity of fertilization treatments among women in the later period of child-bearing years.

Comment [BLH3]: Student 3: At times the language seems too colloquial, beginning paragraphs with "Ah" or a question, and using phrases such as "the norm."

Comment [BLH4]: Student 4: I think that the part about the biology of the human towards having multiples is informative but too extensive.

Student 3 found my uses of language to be somewhat informal on various occasions. I didn't always agree with this reader's advice; for example, there's nothing wrong with beginning a paragraph with a question, but she was right that I was being informal in a way that she wasn't being taught to be informal in most of her college writing.

To that end, I eliminated the initial paragraph question and created a sentence that was somewhat more precise.

I had to agree with Student 1's remark that about.com wasn't a strong source. I knew that fact when I first used the source, and I searched the Internet and the library search engines for something more authoritative. I wasn't able to find a better source, but I think that if I had talked to a librarian about these statistics, I probably would have done better. My way of trying to mitigate possible problems from using this source was to make sure that I used the available statistics well from the preliminary draft onward; the rest of the paragraph demonstrates how I used this source.

On the whole, this paragraph seems out of place in the sense that it doesn't directly deal with the assertion. To some degree, I think that is what Student 4 was indicating. Yet, the information also seems necessary as context. In a longer essay, this paragraph (and even more contextual material) might come in a section called "Background." I thought a lot about the student's advice; I tried moving this material to another place in the argument, and I also tried deleting it altogether. Finally, I decided it was needed information and I left it where it was.

Despite advances in reproductive medicine, however, women's bodies have not evolved to give birth to spontaneous multiples, as evidenced by the rarity of natural multiple births. Thus, both the mothers' health and that of the babies are at risk in these pregnancies (Carroll, 2009). Infant early births, **which are common in multiple births,** give rise to dangerously low birth weights along with insufficiently developed lungs and other organs. It is not uncommon for such infants to have developmental problems and chronic illnesses **like cerebral palsy and others** that reveal themselves later in life. Pregnant mothers of multiples also experience challenges as they may be required to spend months in bed to reduce their physical risks and to avoid preterm births. **The mother may experience increased risks of gestational diabetes, preeclampsia, and the need for a Cesarean section, which carries its own dangers. Implanting only two or three fertilized eggs are one medically accepted way to avoid higher levels of multiple births particularly among women in their thirties and forties ("Octuplet's Mom," 2009).** Where more than three fetuses are involved, many doctors advocate "selective reduction" of the fetuses so that the living ones have more uterine space and nutrition to be carried to full term and to have healthy birth weights. Such selection can be a difficult choice dependent on the parents' moral values. Given the frequency of

> **Comment [BLH5]:** Student 1: Provide more specific details.

> **Comment [BLH6]:** Student 4: Connect your ideas.

> **Comment [BLH7]:** Student 5: I do wish that you would have given a statistic to represent the odds of that many babies surviving in the womb.

multiple births from IVF and other fertility treatments, beyond these obvious health issues involved, we have the responsibility to consider how multiple births potentially affect the children and their relationships to their parents and society as a whole.

It certainly is not the norm for a woman to give birth to more than one child at a time. While many mammals give birth to litters, humans typically give birth to only one child. Spontaneous multiple human births do occasionally occur in nature, just as rarely a cow will birth twin calves or a horse twin foals. That is why people delight in seeing twins, whether fraternal or identical. The relative rarity of twins may cause typically respectful, yet curious people to become intrusive, asking questions about the twins' sizes, hair and eye coloring, emotional dispositions, personality traits, and even bathroom habits. Not only is this intrusion off-putting, but it also can make the children feel abnormal when children usually want nothing more than to be considered normal. Indeed, both the parents and the twins themselves experience their lives as more public than parents of singles and their children typically do. Naturally, our interest levels increase when triplets and quadruplets are born, and they go sky high when higher numbers of multiple birth children arrive. But our interests can be dangerous to the emotional well being of the children.

> **Comment [BLH8]: Studen t 5:** The essay goes on to speculate as to why people pay close attention to multiple births, but does not provide evidence that the public actually does pay attention or why this is the case.

These two paragraphs are fairly intimately connected in terms of content, so let's look at them together. I added the information about the challenges of multiple births here and in paragraphs found below to satisfy readers like Students 1 and 4, who needed more information and wanted better transitions. Throughout the revised essay, I used their advice and added more detailed material wherever it seemed useful. Pointing me to the need for strong transitions was especially good advice. When I write early drafts, I don't worry much about transitions because I know that my organization of certain material will change and that I'll insert appropriate transitional later. I like it when students notice that the "glue" that holds an essay together is missing.

Student 5 really wanted some statistics and other evidence of my argument's main points. I agreed that I needed to find more statistical proof to support a point about the unnatural nature of multiple births. Doing so would have helped to show why people are so interested in them. This paragraph also has background material that I used to get to the heart of my thesis: that there's disruptiveness about multiple birth children's and parents' lives. It provides a reason for why people respond so intrusively to multiple births. But the feedback is well-taken. This material needed authoritative support—not statistics necessarily—but pertinent thoughts about human behavior around multiple birth children.

The final sentence of the second paragraph takes the background information and links it to the assertion. Unfortunately, this technique didn't work for some of my student readers who were already confused about the thesis—wrongly believing it was about Suleman alone. I left this sentence intact because I believed that the other changes to the essay would make this thesis link more obvious in the presentation draft.

For those who are curious about methods for arguing an assertion like this one, at the end of this second paragraph, I reasoned from the lesser to the greater: if something is true at a smaller number (twins, triplets), it also will be true at a higher number (sextuplets, octuplets). I'll say more about such reasoning later in this chapter.

Although Student 6 believed that opening the next paragraph with the words "an historical example" was unnecessary, I thought the idea of history was quite important because I also used two contemporary examples. Instead of deleting the sentence as advised, I added material to help make that connection: "because it demonstrates that multiple births can be problematic even when they arise from natural causes."

It's helpful to remember that "positive" criticism like that from Student 5 can be useful to writers by reinforcing what they are doing well. In this case, the example of the Dionne children is reasoning from past fact to future fact: what happened in the past will happen in the future. Some student readers, like Student 7, were unconvinced because the situation was a little different in the 1930s. Yet, the quintuplets from natural birth were just as much a curiosity in the 1930s as octuplets or sextuplets from IVF birth are in the twenty-first century. Additionally, the financial issues that the Dionne parents experienced are similar to the two main cases I cited. Finally, the "zoo" atmosphere of the Dionne quintuplets certainly can be compared to the television screen that gives the world a peek into the Gosselin sextuplets (discussed later in the essay) and the Suleman octuplets. For these reasons, I left the historical example intact and developed it even more.

In the second paragraph of this set, I restated the assertion. This paragraph and the following one directly support the thesis, which, as you recall, isn't about Suleman, but about the potential exploitation of all multiple birth children. These causes of death for the Dionne adults are suggestive evidence of the health problems I noted earlier in the essay about multiple birth children, for example.

This third paragraph particularly makes a transition from the past to the present. I made changes to address level of formality appropriate to what my students also were writing. But I also added material

An historical example will be useful here **because it demonstrates that multiple births can be problematic even when they arise from natural causes**. In 1934, in a small farming town in Ontario, Canada, quintuplet daughters were born to Olivia and Elzire Dionne, who already had six children and were economically quite poor. The world was fascinated and, even as the astounded parents began to absorb the shock of having five babies who each weighed less than 2 pounds at birth, their family doctor moved in, created a nursery out of the first floor of the family's farmhouse, and barred the parents from even holding their children (Kehoe, 1998). In short order, the parents were deprived of custody of the little girls, in part because the unlucky father had contracted to move the children to Chicago as an exhibit for the Chicago Century of Progress Exposition, which was a small world's fair. The Ontario government intervened and suspended the parents' parental rights, stating: "'The lives of children are a bigger concern in Canada than profits of an exploitation or promotional undertaking.'" Ironically, ~~they~~ **the government** proceeded to build a small theme park, Quintland, around the children across from the family farmhouse. Between 1935 and 1943, they were exhibited "two to three shows a day, seven days a week" and were viewed as they played by "more than three million people"; as many as "6000 people a day" walked through their observation galleries. By the age of five, the girls knew that they were being observed, just as they knew that they were unhappy when their parents had to leave them each day (Kehoe, 1998; see also Leroux, 2000). According to Kehoe (1998), the quintuplets were further exploited through commercial endorsements for food, soap, and likeness dolls, as well as movies and a song. They had an official photographer and biographer appointed by the State and even their parents were not allowed to take photographs of them. Interestingly, Ontario—but not the family—made money on this venture; the take was more than 11.5 million dollars in current dollars. The girls received a much smaller amount of money in a trust fund that was mismanaged and quickly depleted.

Comment [BLH9]: Student 6: ...it was unnecessary to include the part about it being "a historical example" because the reader may naturally be able to come to the conclusion based on the data you provide.

Comment [BLH10]: Student 5: Another strength your essay had was telling the story of the Dionne sisters....They grew up and noticed they were other people's entertainment and not actually living a "normal" life.

Comment [BLH11]: Student 7: However I'm not sure I'm convinced that the same exploitation will happen to the Gosselin's or the Suleman's because as a society we have evolved in ways that would not showcase multiple births as if the kids were like animals at the zoo to be observed. .... I'm sure there is much to be learned from the Dionne's sisters, especially after the letter they wrote explaining how their parents desire for money and fame destroyed their livelihood during the childhood and adult years, which really does convince me that constant exploitation of multiple births can really hinder the lives of children. However who's to say that the Gosselin or Suleman children will even be affected by their parents exploiting them to the public.

This exploitation took its toll on the Dionne sisters. Even after they were returned to their parents, there was emotional and physical discord. They left home as soon as they turned eighteen. In their adult lives, they entered (and exited) a convent school, refused all contact with their parents who they deemed as having abandoned them, married, divorced, and—**began to** ~~now~~ live together again on a **single** small monthly income under $800.00 ~~total~~. In recent years, three of the surviving quintuplets (one died from epilepsy and another of chronic ill health and alcoholism) accused their deceased father of sexual abuse. In 1995, they sued the government of Ontario for the mismanagement of their trust fund and their public life of emotional pain (Kehoe, 1998; Webb, 2008). In 1998, they won a settlement between two and four million dollars—the amount was determined after the government established that the children had earned more than $500 million dollars in current dollars for Ontario (Fennell, 1998).

~~Ah, but this would not happen today, some will assert. That was then—d~~ It may be difficult to relate an historically distant example like the Dionne children to what can occur in the twenty-first century. Yet, as multiple births become more common because of assisted pregnancies, the exploitation of the Dionne quintuplets can be seen as foreshadowing what can happen as mass media removes the need to drive hundreds of miles to see such "oddities." Human nature has not changed much in less than one hundred years. During the Great Depression years **and prior to World War II**, people needed the excitement of a miraculous birth to distract them from their problems. **People still are excited by the advent of multiple births—as evidenced by the exuberant coverage of the first born set of octuplets in 1998 and the expressed sorrow at the death of one of the eight. The Chukwu octuplets are now ten years old and, by all accounts, seem to be living relatively normal lives with their parents and grandparents (Inbar, 2009). Their stability might make us think that n~~N~~ow, in 2009, such an** exploitative situation **as the Dionne quintuplets experienced** could not happen.

> **Comment [BLH12]: Stud ent 3:** This sentence is too colloquial.

about another set of multiple birth children that may not be as famous because they are not always in the public eye. Despite the major excitement of their birth as the first set of octuplets ever recorded (one died shortly after birth), the Chukwu octuplets appear to be living fairly normal lives. It is here that I use an argumentative strategy of providing a counterargument. A counterargument is an acknowledgment that there are valid points of view other than the one I argue; acknowledging (and sometimes refuting) counterarguments can increase my ethos, or believability, as a writer. I needed to provide evidence that I've considered assertions other than my own and that my position still is the most reasonable. This brief material about the Chukwu family (and later the McCaughey septuplets) counterargues that multiple birth children don't have to be exploited. After admitting this fact, however, I return to my argument in the next paragraph and reveal yet another example of exploited famous multiples: the Gosselins.

But, ~~it~~ **exploitation** does happen daily for eight children born to Jon and Kate Gosselin. Their television show reveals the day-to-day lives of their twin eight-year old daughters and sextuplet four-year olds. Their program "Jon & Kate Plus Eight" is in its fourth season on TLC and it its most popular show (Bane, 2008). The family plays together on the show, the parents bicker in friendly (and occasionally angry) ways, and the world sees a "real-life" family of multiples make it on their own. That is, they are on their own if we consider the fact that the reality show enabled Jon to leave his job and become a consultant and that it funds their existence. They also make money from sales of "DVDs, a book, speaking engagements and endorsements"; it is a "lucrative" job (Bane, 2008). When asked what the children think of being followed by cameras for about five hours a day, Kate responds: "'We call it the family job,' explains Kate. She has asked her kids if they would rather be a 'normal family' with parents who worked while their kids were in day care. 'Unanimously, they all say they would rather have the family job'" (Bane, 2008).

We must ask whether it really is possible that six toddlers who have been raised on camera and eight-year old twins can make a thoughtful decision about whether to be exposed to television cameras daily. ~~Apparently they do not~~ **Clearly they cannot** understand the potential ramifications of being offered up **as entertainment** to millions of gaping viewers. Indeed, when given the choice of a "normal" family at daycare and an exciting "family job" where the parents are home with them, what little child would choose day care? **The question is rhetorical at best with the response the children offered being the one the parents could have expected. Nonetheless,** ~~Yet,~~ the parents **do** admit that while the sextuplets have been raised on camera and are used to it, the twin girls may be finding fame a little more difficult: "'Sometimes their classmates make comments,' reveals Kate. 'Cara doesn't care, but Mady doesn't like to talk about it'" (Bane, 2008). If this is not exploitation, what is?

Comment [BLH13]: Stud ent 8: If there is any more data on multiple birth exploitation in the past, where the children are now adults, I think it would help prove the argument....We are just unsure if the exploitation of the Gosselins will have a positive or negative effect because the children are still children.

The evidence provided in the next two paragraphs might be called arguing from anecdote (story), but really it's a continuation of argument from past (to present) to future fact. It can be a very convincing technique because people tend to believe that what was possible in the past is possible again in the present or future. Part of reasoning from past fact to future fact is bringing in recent and current examples. It's impossible to accurately predict the future, but it's possible to suggest how the future might develop based on current events.

When I was writing this essay in early 2009, for example, the parents of the Gosselin children (Jon and Kate) appeared to be happily married. In the short months between writing my essay and using it to write this chapter for you, the Gosselin adults have become common faces in print and TV media tabloids as Jon has admitted to adultery and has taken on a playboy persona, and Kate has aired their problems publically and filed for divorce. Their children are sometimes photographed looking confused and sad. For all of that, the network has continued the television show for some time, suggesting that this divorce is just a normal part of the children's lives. Anecdotally, I think readers who are children of divorce would not have wanted television cameras filming their experiences and emotions as they adjusted to the new family situation. Similarly, in early 2010, Suleman contracted to begin a reality show with her currently-one year-old octuplets. If I were revising this essay today, I'd certainly be adding this material as proof of exploitation of the Gosselin children's painful home life and the Suleman children's lack of privacy.

Student 8 still wasn't convinced that the argument was reasonable. Fair enough. We can't convince everyone to take our position in an argument although we can present reasonable evidence. One student suggested that I use the case of child celebrities to show how innocent children can be ruined by exploitation and publicity. In a longer revised essay, I would seriously consider that argument from analogy.

Students 6 expressed a need for more direct connections among the past, present, and future. That was the difficulty of my argument from the outset because I was writing it only weeks after the Suleman octuplets were born. All I could do at this point was to predict, but my prediction wasn't a far stretch given that the infants already were on camera as a way to exonerate the mother's choice and to make money for her. Multiple sources revealed that she had received money to buy a much larger house and that she had daily outside assistance with

Returning full circle to Nadya Suleman's octuplets, it seems possible to predict the some of the ramifications for the children—both the octuplets and the six youngsters born previously. **In the past, she has subsisted with disability payments for a job-related injury and she currently receives $490 per month in food stamps and federal disability assistance for three of her first six children ("Octuplets' Mom," 2009); yet, Suleman has said that she refuses welfare money to support herself and her children (Celizic, 2009).** Asked how she will afford the children with no job and no other adult family member to help her pay her bills, she claims: "I know I'll be able to afford them when I'm done with my schooling" (Celizic, 2009). **Shortly after the birth, she retained a publicist, who offered her services pro-bono and mentioned that Suleman is looking at seven-figure offers for her "story," as well as offers for photographs, interviews, books, and other commercial enterprises (Celizic, 2009; Rochman, 2009).** If she were to get them, those offers would come in handy. Her hospital delivery bill for eight premies alone may cost upwards of one million dollars; forty six physicians and staff attended the births ("Grandma," 2009). Further, she will need to feed, diaper, clothe, and provide appropriate medical care for children who likely will have significant medical conditions. Additionally, it is important not to forget the six children that she has at home; each of them has similar needs. **While such offers of commercial assistance have not yet been revealed (perhaps because of recent negative press surrounding Suleman's situation), Suleman has set up a website where she will accept donations payable by PayPal, MasterCard, Visa, and other credit card options ("Welcome to," 2009).** Undoubtedly, ~~Hence,~~ while Suleman will need **both commercial ~~those~~ offers and private donations**, they represent the kind of exploitation suffered by the Dionne and Gosselin children.

Beyond those physical needs are emotional ones, as well. The Suleman children are not likely to be met by a mother with sufficient time to spend. She recently proudly stated that "she holds each child 45 minutes a day"

> **Comment [BLH14]: Student 6:** Common sense drives me toward your argument that any exploitation is grounds for an unstable upbringing, but facts can't be drawn on these two families (the Gosselin's and Suleman's) until the kids are able to draw their own conclusions.

> **Comment [BLH15]: Student 1:** The only apparent weakness is the lack of an expert opinion on the long term potential damage to the children.

(Celizic, 2009); while it is unclear whether by "each child" she meant the six at home or the eight premature infants, it seems ~~unlikely~~ **certain** that she will **not** have upwards of eight free hours a day to hold one child at a time. Her life will be as hectic as the Gosselins' but without the advantage of two parents. In fact, since Suleman, who has a degree in childhood and adolescent development ("Grandma," 2009), claimed that she will return to graduate school in the fall for a master's degree in counseling, one has to wonder how she will take care of the children and still complete her school work.

~~While it is true that~~ **The** first of Suleman's interviews has ~~not yet~~ aired **and information** about her is becoming more **available. It is true that she gives an appearance of sincerity, calm thoughtfulness, and tender love for her children. However, there remain signs** ~~about her is sketchy, there are signs~~ of trouble in the future for the octuplets and their siblings. First, their grandmother is not supportive of her daughter's actions and does not express confidence in her emotional balance ("Grandma," 2009). Hers is a case where a family member's help would be extraordinarily helpful and it is unclear whether the grandmother actually will be available to the family. Second, financial offers may yet pour in, and they would be enticing to a woman with fourteen children and no other income besides government subsidies. The odds of not exploiting the children are low. Sadly, one psychoanalyst interviewed about this situation found nothing wrong with such exploitation: "'And even if she was looking ahead to financial gain: What is so wrong with that? She's got a commodity that grabs the attention of the world and she's going to get rewarded. Why are we so morally outraged?'" (Carroll, 2009). With ~~that kind of~~ **such** public support **that would accept her children as an economic bargaining chip**, it seems unlikely that Suleman will seek enough reasons to avoid exploiting her children for the money that they will engender. Finally, Suleman herself may be far less prepared to raise her fourteen children than she realizes. In an interview with the TODAY Show's Ann Curry, she indicated that she believed her childhood as an only child was "dysfunctional" and that she lacked a "feeling of self and identity": "I just didn't feel

Comment [BLH16]: Student 9: We are finally presented with some 'authorities' on the subject: A psychologist, who is external to the situation, has believable scholarly authority, and out and out refutes your point.

as though, when I was a child, I had much control of my
environment. I felt powerless. And that gave me a sense of
predictability" (Celizic, 2009). It seems odd—and a little
frightening—that someone with ~~her~~ **an** undergraduate
degree in childhood development would not understand
that it is the nature of childhood to be somewhat
powerless and not in control of one's environment;
parents are supposed to support children in these areas. In
fact, the predictability that she complained of can be very
positive for children. Her lack of understanding of these
basic childhood needs suggests that Suleman **selfishly** may
try to correct her own childhood issues by giving her own
children too much power, which can lead to an unhealthy
and an unpredictable environment. Sadly, in all ways
possible, the Suleman octuplets and their siblings are at
risk of parental and public exploitation, **which can twist
their sense of family life and harm them emotionally.**

the children. Contemporary sources confirm those facts and certainly
much more evidence could be provided now that the babies are more
than one-year old.

Recall that my major thesis regards the emotional well-being of
multiple birth children, of which the Suleman octuplets were an example. According to Student 1, this argument would have benefited from
psychological predictions from experts or authorities. I didn't find any
such psychological predictions in my initial research, but my readers
have convinced me that I would need to do that research for any future
revisions of this argument. They simply need more evidence that my
reasoning is sound and probable.

In the third paragraph of this set, I used a psychologist's statement
about Suleman's likely exploitation of the children for money as a way
of showing irony. To me, it was clear that calling the octuplets a "commodity that grabs the attention of the world" and stating that "she's
going to get rewarded" for it, was disturbing in that the psychologist
herself wasn't showing appropriate concern for the babies' welfare. In
the preliminary draft, I assumed that all readers would understand
the import of this psychologist's statement. But as I thought about
the feedback I was getting—Student 9, for example—I realized this
point needed sharper language in the presentation draft to indicate the
bargaining power of children viewed as a "commodity" to be bought
and sold.

In a cautionary letter to parents of newly born ~~septuplets~~ McCaughey **septuplets** born in 1997, Annette, Cecile, and Yvonne Dionne—the surviving quintuplets—urged thoughtfulness and respect toward the children. They said:

> We hope your children receive more respect than we did. Their fate should be no different from that of other children. Multiple births should not be confused with entertainment, nor should they be an opportunity to sell products.
>
> Our lives have been ruined by the exploitation we suffered at the hands of the government of Ontario, our place of birth. We were displayed as a curiosity three times a day for millions of tourists. To this day we receive letters from all over the world. To all those who have expressed their support in light of the abuse we have endured, we thank you. And to those who would seek to exploit the growing fame of these children, we say beware.

Comment [BLH17]: Student 10: The letter from the Dionne's sisters was a powerful statement and supported your position perfectly. The paper did convince me that you had a reasonable position.

I used this cautionary letter from the Dionne adults to the McCaughey family as a way to prove that the quintuplets were sufficiently damaged by their exploitative upbringing that they felt a need to help other multiple birth children. Although my research did not reveal specifically how the letter affected the parents of the septuplets, it seemed possible to speculate in the essay's final paragraph that they took these words to heart. Student 10 commented that she found this letter to be convincing evidence of my assertion.

The second to last sentence of the argument restates the assertion. Why did I choose this kind of assertion instead of talking about Suleman alone? I did so because there was no way I could prove convincingly what has not yet happened in the babies' lives. But I could build on past and present fact and published anecdotes to strongly suggest that the futures of these infants' and others like them are in danger. Overall, I think I accomplished this goal. In the process, my students and I had a good opportunity to study one writer's processes in depth.

Conclusion

This is a useful time to say that even the best advice cannot always be put into effect in an essay revision. Sometimes it just doesn't fit the current plan for the essay. Thoughtful choice about using feedback for revision is always necessary. Try to be able to explain your choices, as I have in this chapter, if you are questioned about your revision choices by your instructor or peers.

As my comments throughout this essay suggest, there are various areas for continued research before deciding that this piece (or any essay) is finished. Additionally, it's important to remember that any revised draft needs a final set of actions before it's ready for "publication" to an instructor or other audience. Accepting revision changes, spellchecking, and proofreading are all necessary editing steps to create a presentation draft. At that point, in a school setting, this essay would be ready for grading. In a more public setting, such as a "letter to the editor" of a newspaper or magazine, it would be ready for mailing. In both cases, readers might suggest additional changes before it would be assessed.

To teach you how to make similar decisions with the same kinds of resources, this chapter shows how I made many of my writing and revision decisions in an argumentative essay. Although my comments indicate that additional revisions could make the argument stronger, all writers must stop writing at some point and call the writing "done," even if it feels only semi-finished. Hopefully, however, before calling the piece done, you've learned that putting focused hours into the writing can help to develop a strong essay that conveys thoughtfully developed meaning. As you begin your next essay, apply whatever version of this brainstorming, zero draft, research, preliminary draft, feedback, revision, and presentation draft approach that may fit your own writing process. I think you'll find yourself working hard while enjoying your writing more!

DISCUSSION

1. How do you use brainstorming, other prewriting, and/or initial/zero drafts in your writing?

2. What are the main differences between a preliminary and a presentation draft? With these terms in mind, how would you describe your own drafting process?

3. What have you learned about making writing and revision choices based on your own thinking? What have you learned about acting on feedback from readers like your peers or your instructor?

4. What have you learned about giving feedback to other writers? How will you apply it the next time you give feedback to another writer?

5. This chapter uses the American Psychological Association (APA) style for formatting in-text citations and bibliographic entries. Compare it to the Modern Language Association (MLA) style that you have seen in other Writing Spaces' chapters. Discuss how APA in-text citations compare to MLA. How are the bibliographic references on an APA References page different from those on a MLA Works Cited page?

References

Bane, V. (2008, Oct 13). The Gosselins get real. *People, 70*(15), 70–75.

Carroll, L. (2009, Feb 6). Octuplet backlash: Are we just jealous? *msnbc. com*. Retrieved on February 6, 2009, from http://www.msnbc.msn.com/id/29039266/

Celizic, M. (2009, Feb 6). Octuplet mom defends "unconventional" choices. *TODAY*. Retrieved on February 6, 2009, http://www.msnbc.msn.com/id/29038814/

Fennell, T. (1998, Mar 16). Justice at long last. *Maclean's, 111*(11), 26.

Fierro, P. P. (2008, Aug 18). What are the odds? *About.com, Twins and multiples*. Retrieved February 6, 2009, from http://multiples.about.com/cs/funfacts/a/oddsoftwins.htm

Fierro, P. P. (n. d.). Twin and multiple birth rate. *About.com, Twins and multiples*. Retrieved February 6, 2009, http://multiples.about.com/od/funfacts/a/twinbirthrate.htm

Grandma: Octuplets' mom obsessed with kids. (2009, Jan 31). *msnbc.com*. Retrieved on February 6, 2009, from http://www.msnbc.msn.com/id/28943010/

Inbar, Michael. (2009). First U.S. octuplets offer advice to parents of 8. *TODAY*. Retrieved February 14, 2009, from http://www.msnbc.msn.com/id/28891400/

Kehoe, J. (1998, Jun). Growing up behind glass. *Biography, 2*(6), 96.

Leroux, Y. (2000, Jan 1). Tragedy of the young Dionnes. *Maclean's, 112*(52), 113.

National Organization of Mothers of Twins Club, Inc. (NOMOTC). (n.d.). Multiple birth statistics. Retrieved February 7, 2009, from http://www.nomotc.org/index.php?Itemid=55&id=66&option=com_content&task=view

Octuplets' mom on welfare, spokesman confirms. (2009, February 10). *FoxNews.com*. Retrieved on February 14, 2009, from http://www.foxnews.com/story/0,2933,490269,00.html

Rochman, B. (2009, Feb 5). The ethics of octuplets. *Time.com*. Retrieved on February 6, 2009, from http://www.time.com/time/magazine/article/0,9171,1877396,00.html

Webb, C. (2008, Aug/Sep). Canada's miracle babies. *Beaver, 88*(4), 26.

Welcome to the Nadya Suleman family website. (2009). Retrieved on February 14, 2009, from http://www.thenadyasulemanfamily.com/.

Taking Flight: Connecting Inner and Outer Realities during Invention

Susan E. Antlitz

One of the toughest challenges beginning writers face is figuring out what to write about.* Connecting personal identity and purpose to more public contexts and subjects can play a significant role in helping people to write confidently. Also, since writing anxiety is a common cause of difficulty getting started, strategies for reducing anxiety including movement, sound, intentional distraction, role playing, journaling, and prayer and meditation can help the invention process to unfold more smoothly. Electronic media such as email, messaging or texting, and presentation software also provide avenues for generating ideas. By exploring these methods, you can also increase your satisfaction with writing, and you can find new ways to build bridges between the ideas and purposes that are meaningful to you and the writing you produce for others.

Understanding the Connection between the Personal and the Social

Some college writers see the writing that is done for classes as separate or different from one's personal goals and interests. It can be easy to slip into the mindset that those personal activities, commitments, and convictions are off-topic or not relevant to class-work. But it doesn't have to be that way.

Instead of writing being driven either by individual identity or by outside criteria, both of these facets of identity are interwoven, and used in conjunction with one another, these influences act as the two wings that can help get a writing project off the ground. The sense of personal identity and having one's own goals when writing (something that waits to take flight) can play a significant role in a writer's motivation and ability to write confidently. However, a text also needs to connect with the rest of the world in ways the audience can understand if it is to be effective.

That which makes us unique also connects us to others. Our DNA is our individual blueprint, and except for the case of identical twins or clones, each person has his or her own unique combination of genes. Yet, those genes come to us through a long heritage, stretching back countless generations, and have been passed down to us by our ancestors. Much like DNA, the social world of ideas and experiences we are born into both forms the basis of our individuality and deeply connects us to larger contexts in the world around us.

The individual and the collective are not mutually exclusive; in fact, they complement and reinforce one another. The inner world and the outer world are in constant flux, shaping, reinforcing, and challenging one another into new awareness. This matters in writing because it's easy for people to think of writing as more one or the other—as being about personal expression, creativity, inspiration and communicating one's ideas, or as being a task that is required by and for teachers, supervisors, or other audiences. Neither fully captures what writing is, and indeed, these two aspects can work together in many ways.

Trying to divide the personal from the social is ultimately a futile task because they overlap and influence one another so much, but as human beings, we have a tendency to think in terms of categories, porous as they may be. The categories are an illusion, but they can be helpful as a way to get started.

The Two Wings: An Exercise

While thinking about an idea and devising a way to write about it, you may find the following exercise helpful. We can call this exercise

Taking Flight, or finding the two wings of your ideas. Since there is a personal as well as an inter-personal, or social, aspect to any idea, this is a way of mapping out those aspects of the idea.

1. Sketch out a blank diagram like the one I've drawn below.

2. Think about your interests, thoughts, activities, goals, and questions.

3. List the ideas that are mostly personal under one wing (leave the corresponding space under the opposite wing blank until step 5).

4. List the ideas that are connected to larger contexts, communities, or issues under the other wing.

5. Once you have your initial list, go back and fill in information relating to each idea under the opposite column, so that each idea now lists both a personal and a social component.

In Figure 1, I've outlined some key areas that will generally fall under each category. You might think of other key areas to include. Figure 2 shows an example of what your actual diagram might look like.

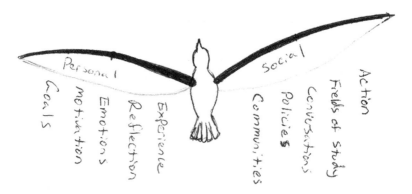

Figure 1. Diagram of Personal and Social Topical Aspects

This diagram can be used with either a list of interests you are using to try to find an idea, or it can be used to focus or develop an idea once you have a general direction.

Here is the diagram I made that lists several possible ideas:

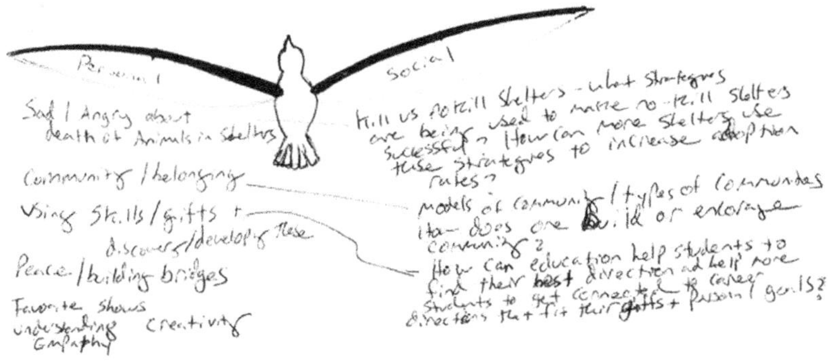

Figure 2. Diagram of Personal Interests and Social Components.

Here, I listed a few of the ideas or causes that are personally important to me, and then tried to pair those with the issues in the outside
world by asking questions that I could explore in the process of building an essay. For example, an issue that I have a strong personal and
emotional response to is the killing of healthy and potentially adopt-
able animals in shelters and animal control facilities. To link this to a
context beyond myself, I listed the issue of kill versus no-kill shelters
in the right-hand column, and in the left-hand column, I asked how
the strategies used by no-kill shelters could also help other shelters to
increase adoption rates and reduce euthanasia. I now have a question I
can research and write about.

Look for Unexpected Connections

Another way to build possibilities for writing is to look over your list
of ideas and create connections between options that are not deliber-
ately paired. For example, since I already had three potential ideas and
their social aspects listed in the diagram, I didn't put anything in the
social column for the last few ideas I had in the personal column. One
of these was "Favorite shows." If I had gone into more detail, I might
have listed the titles of some of my favorite television series, and then
connected that to the social aspects I had listed for other items. In this
case, one that would work would be "models or types of community.
How does one build or encourage community?" I could write an essay
that looks at how the relationships form and change over time between
the characters in my favorite shows, and then even do some research
into models of community building and community formation and

see how well fiction mirrors what the relationship/community scholars have theorized.

Alternately, I could connect the subject of TV programs to the animal shelter idea. It's unlikely I'd find a direct connection, but if I alter the idea of the animal shelter to something like how animals are portrayed on screen, I could also build on that idea, or even write about the different ways our society views or treats animals.

Remember that your diagram and your list of ideas are meant to be a jumping-off place, so you can change them as needed if you think of new ideas or find a new direction you want to explore.

The openness to creating connections where you may not expect to find them can be very useful. Cultivating creativity and connection-building is a very healthy habit that can have unforeseen benefits for your writing.

Random Words

Here is a game you can use to help develop your creative flexibility. It's one of my favorites.

1. Take a sheet of paper and fold it in half.

2. On one half write a list of random words, one per line.

3. Then, with the page still folded down the middle, give the paper to someone else, with your list facing down so the other person can't see it.

4.   On the other half of the paper, ask the other person to write a list of random words that he or she thinks of.

5. Then unfold the paper. You should have, on each line, a word you wrote and a word someone else wrote. These words will hopefully have nothing to do with one another.

6. And this is where the game begins: Try to find the connection between the two words on each line. Write a sentence that uses both of them in a logical and believable way.

This exercise can help to build your mental agility and help to make you more alert to forming connections that may not be immediately obvious to other people.

For example, I have picked a word, tree, and using a Facebook status update, asked one of my friends to give me a random word, which has turned out to be svelte. The sentence I created from these two words was, "The svelte tree waved its branchy arms like an ecstatic dancer." I used the metaphor of the dancer to make it more of a challenge, but the sentence could have been simply, "The svelte tree waved its branches."

Half of the game is the sense of anticipation before you know what word or words the other person will give you. It lightly mirrors the anxiety you may feel before you know what to write about. However, since, it's also a game and the stakes are low, it begins to build an association between the anticipation of the unknown and your amusement or enjoyment. The game usually turns out to not be as hard as one anticipates. An element of play can take the edge off of writing anxiety.

Another friend gave me the word bongo. I admit this was slightly harder, but I came up with, "As the tree stood drinking in the sun with its verdant leaves, it had no awareness that its life would soon change forever, and that it was destined to become the frame of a pair of bongo drums for young Sally." I saw a connection between the tree and the word bongo because a bongo is a type of drum, and drum frames are usually made of wood. I've embellished my sentence just to play with the language, but "The wood from the tree was used to make bongo drums" would have also sufficed. Simple or complex, poetic or plain, no sentence that connects the two words is wrong. This is also fun to do with a group of people, where everyone can share what they came up with. It's neat to see the sorts of things people can create out of this.

Build Ideas through Compound Topics

An important part of invention is the ability to make connections. One strategy that I find myself using is to think of my topics not as single ideas, but rather pairs of related ideas. It can be helpful to phrase your topic in such a way that it includes "and," "or," "but," or other connecting words because that can shift your focus to the relationships between parts of the subject. You are more likely to end up with a more specific focus or direction that way.

An example might be to take a broad subject such as the Internet and combine it with another subject, such as the workplace, to focus on the Internet in the workplace. Bringing the two subjects together makes me think of the following questions. How has the workplace changed as a result of the Internet? How has email changed the way a company is run? What do employees or managers need to know about digital communications technologies? What problems might they encounter, and how can those be resolved or prevented? From there, I can keep asking questions until I find one I want to learn more about and eventually write about.

The advantage of focusing your essay around a compound idea is that it will tend to make the subject and focus of what you are writing about more complex. For example, if I make up a pair of subjects like "Animals and the Elderly," "Doctor Who and identity," or "work as spiritual growth," I could then build on each of these ideas and try to think of what sorts of things might be in a resulting essay.

EMBRACING THE PERSONAL

Prayer and Meditation

You may be surprised to find a reference to personal spirituality in an essay of this kind, but when you are doing the invention work for writing, you need to be who you are. If you have your own faith, embrace it as part of your thinking and writing process, and that openness can help to keep your creativity flowing. It's much harder to be creative and generate ideas while closing off a part of yourself. Therefore, love and accept all aspects of yourself as you are in the process of creating a text.

I worked for a time at a private, religious institution, and the classes I taught there were like most writing classes in terms of the content of the class and the use of well known invention techniques for writing such as freewriting, looping, concept mapping, etc. (if you are unfamiliar with these, ask your teacher to explain them to you or look them up online). However, since it was a religious school, I had the freedom and even the institutional support to bring faith into the work the class did.

One day at the beginning of the semester after we had been discussing various aspects of our individual writing processes, I asked the students if they ever included prayer as part of their writing process, and I was surprised when no one in the class had previously thought to do that, even though prayer was a part of their lives in other ways. This demonstrates that using one's personal and even spiritual resources is not always an obvious strategy in a formal class setting, even when it would be welcomed. Sometimes we have to bring those options out into the open and talk about them because it might not automatically occur to us that we can make those connections.

If you belong to a religion or spiritual tradition that uses prayer or meditation, then I encourage you to also include that as part of your writing process and as part of how you generate ideas to write about. Pray for insight and ideas, if that fits with your belief system, or meditate to free up your awareness. These activities may lead to becoming aware of an idea that you had not considered before, and they may help with exploring and developing an idea once you have one. These practices can also lessen anxiety since anxiety is partly about being alone when facing an overwhelming task. If you are a spiritual person who believes in a deity, then use that to remind yourself that you are not alone, even when confronted with a challenging writing task. Or, if you meditate, that can help you to relax your mind and body and let go of stress, which usually increases intellectual and creative performance. Let those parts of your life be part of your writing process as well.

I often pray for insight when I am working on a writing project. There is a certain amount of trust involved—I am generally confident that I will be able to think of something, and I always do, even if I am not sure at first what I am going to come up with. That sort of confidence helps to limit my worrying about what I am going to write, and it puts me more in the frame of mind that discovering possible ideas is an exciting adventure. Then I can't wait to see what happens. If you are a person who prays about other aspects of your life, try doing so with your writing assignments, and see how it turns out. Remember, let all of who you are be part of your inventing. What other aspects of your identity might inform your writing process?

During invention, no aspect of who you are is off limits, though you need to decide for yourself how much of that process you are willing to share publicly, and how much is appropriate to include in the final draft. The final draft should be adjusted to fit the needs and expectations of your audience and to suit the purpose of your writing. The behind-the-scenes work you do, however, is yours to do with as you will, unless an assignment also asks you to try specific invention or pre-writing strategies as part of your work.

Feelings and Ideas

I have learned that feelings and ideas are very closely related during invention, and so it's a good idea to pay attention to them. One of my hobbies is collecting gemstones and crystals, which are to me an inspiring form of natural artwork. Part of what gives me such a sense of delight when looking at stones comes from seeing them through an artist's eye. Consider, for instance, a polished stone made from polychromatic jasper and how my observations led me to think about writing.

Figure 3. Polychromatic Jasper.

One day, I picked up this stone and took a careful look at it. The bands of color reminded me of the seashore and a beach of pink sand. Since it was late at night, I imagined what it would be like to stand on such a beach, silhouetted by the twilight, and stare out to sea, an endless dark sky stretching into the distance with a single bright star illuminating the silent silvery waves. The scene, if one could touch it, would be soft and even soothing, like velvet. The meaning of this scene to me is one of potential waiting to be explored. It felt like standing on the shores of a world that was waiting to be created, imagined into being. And I thought about people who write stories, and how they create, in their imagination, the worlds they write into being—which in some sense is always what we do when we write. We are creating a picture of the world for our audience, and it is colored and stylized by how it emerges from our own perspectives.

The artist in me also wanted to try to paint this scene. And this is one of the most natural forms of invention of all—we see something and our imagination responds. We feel a desire to create something in response to what we have seen, whether that creation is a painting, a poem, or an essay. Often in a writing class, we are responding to texts, but our response could really be to anything.

Figure 4. Landscape Painting Inspired by Polychromatic Jasper.

My quick painting is far from photorealistic, and if you saw the painting by itself, I very much doubt that "polychromatic jasper" would spring to mind. But that is the beauty of invention. As an artist, photorealism is not, and likely never will be, my style. I accept that about myself, and instead of seeing it as a limitation, I choose to celebrate my own unique style. One of my art teachers back in high school once told the class that if a perfect recreation of reality was the goal, then one might as well take a photograph, because painting is more about interpreting the world through the artist's vision and way of seeing. I'd like to suggest the same principle to you: your writing is not about trying to recreate what is out there in the world, or to write what someone else—some imaginary perfect writer—could write, but rather to see the subject of your writing through your own vision of it. Even when we write non-fiction, we are recreating a vision of the world with our words and putting that portrayal out there to share with our audience. As my art teacher told the class that day, what you create will be unique because you are unique.

Creativity and Play

Having an attitude of play can help writers to be more open to creativity, and increased creativity means that ideas are likely to flow more easily. Reflective activities, such as journaling, can also lead to creative new insights. While taking time to play with words or reflect on ideas may seem like a distraction from the work of writing a paper, building one's creative fluency tends to save time in the long run.

An example of how taking the time to do some reflective writing can lead to new ideas is illustrated in the following journal entry:

July 4, 2009

Invention is more than a set of techniques—it's an attitude and an openness to inviting new ideas and experiences into our lives. A willingness to approach writing playfully, without allowing concerns about grades and even the final outcome to intrude into the time and space set aside for that thinking and play is ironically an important practical step in the work of writing. Writing certainly can be hard work, and while that may make having an open and exploratory approach to writing challenging, the play really is part of the work. This is a paradox, but the key to accepting it, I think, is often a matter of giving ourselves permission to be less than serious during the process of creating a serious outcome. Cultivating play is basically practicing generating ideas and trying out new approaches and ways of thinking, which is what is most needed when trying to get a piece of writing started.

Play, and giving oneself the permission to play, is also part of lessening anxiety, since worry about how a text will or will not turn out in the end, or how it will be evaluated, can lead one to second-guess one's work. I often feel like writing is like building a house of cards—when I'm focused on putting one card on top of the others, the house gets built, but when I start worrying about whether it is good enough, whether readers will like it or not, how long it needs to be, or whether I can finish or not, it's like the wind that comes along and blows the house of cards apart, all collapsing in on itself. Some patterns of thinking are not helpful during the early phases of a writing project. It's important to catch these negative patterns and purposefully move oneself back into the mindset of building the house.

What I did when writing these last few paragraphs was to think of the first sentence, and then write to elaborate on it. Be open to the possibility that a text, especially during its generative moments, does not need to conform to a traditional format. Give yourself permission to write an early draft that is a combination of prose, snippets of thoughts, images, or even audio or video, if you have access to those technologies.

It might be helpful to think of your early work on a text as a collection of all sorts of documents and items. Don't limit yourself just to paper. Let your thinking grow, without regard to traditional formats. Once you have a grasp on the ideas and direction for your writing, you can make the final draft fit the guidelines you have been given and the expectations of your audience. Working with non-traditional formats can be helpful when generating ideas for a traditional paper assignment.

Writing Anxiety

The idea-based play writers engage in can serve a dual purpose. It helps to generate ideas and possibilities for writing, and it can also help to alleviate writing anxiety. Even for experienced writers, the pressure to produce something substantial can be intimidating. I think one's expectations for oneself grow proportionately to one's abilities—as human beings, I think we tend to always be looking ahead, envisioning the level we would like to be at.

I know for myself, I can imagine what I want a text or a painting to be, and the way I picture it often exceeds what I know how to produce. It's not a weakness, per se, but rather, a tendency that shows how we are always growing into something new. I'd be more concerned if my ideas never pushed the limits of my current abilities. So, if you get frustrated because your writing is never quite how you want it to be, just accept it as a sign of your potential to grow. I think over time, we move ourselves closer to what we envision.

One can be a successful writer and still experience moments of anxiety or frustration. I have known students who were very anxious writers, but produced wonderful texts despite those feelings. Feeling stressed or overwhelmed when faced with a writing assignment does not mean that you are a bad writer. It means that you are a writer who needs to learn, and can learn, ways to overcome those challenges. The strategies in the following sections can help you to work around any writing anxiety you may have; however, these strategies can be used by any writer as part of his or her invention process.

Anxiety and Procrastination

Anxiety can be a cause for procrastination for me. I don't panic, really. I get just nervy enough to not be able to concentrate. And so I'll put off writing. I have, however learned something along the way: whether I write a text weeks in advance or the night before, it still takes the same number of hours to write it. If you find you tend to procrastinate, it may be possible (though not optimal) to write a paper the day before it is due. But make sure you block out the hours you will need, say about eight hours for a five-to-seven page paper. And make sure you have access to sources and other people to talk to and get feedback from if you can—the conversation helps to break up the time, and other people can help keep you motivated if they are there to help.

A very common recommended strategy is to put a draft away for at least a few days and then reread it and make changes. Keep in mind that you will miss out on that if you do wait until the last day. But if it can't be helped, and you find yourself having put off the paper until the end, then at least make sure you have enough hours available to put a solid effort into the paper. I'll confess to having put papers off to the last day before, but I will also admit that I always ended up wishing that I had more time to work over the finished draft than what I ended up with. Planning ahead can spare you some anxiety if you don't respond well to feeling rushed.

INVENTION AND ANXIETY REDUCING ACTIVITIES

Journaling as a Way to Reflect on Writing (and to discover new ideas)

The following is a brief journal entry I wrote while gathering my ideas for this essay that reflects on the connection between feelings of anxiety and other related emotions that can affect one's writing processes:

Notes: April 18, 2009 (Visual Feelings)

When I think about starting to write, I feel both an excitement about the possibilities, but also some uncertainty as well—some anxiety about creating an actual text that resembles the one I can imagine. The feeling of potential often comes to me as a vague sense impression of a visual image. For example, around 2:00 A.M. yesterday as I was thinking about writing this, what I felt was an image of a starlit midnight with crickets chirping and perhaps a moon in the sky, or a streetlight. And I suppose that image makes sense as a way to think about the feeling of anticipation that comes with starting to write—the very early morning hours tend to be cool and crisp, and one tingles a bit as a result of that coolness. Anticipation or the sense that one is on the verge of creating a text that is somewhat stirring or artistic has the same kind of tingle to it. Sometimes, creativity feels like an eagle soaring or like a bright, warm sun. These feelings and faint visual impressions are almost always part of what's going on in my mind and spirit when I am planning a piece of writing. Once, when I found myself with only two hours to write a seven-page paper, my feeling was that of being like a racecar driver, with the keyboard as my steering wheel. (Incidentally, my limited time wasn't because I procrastinated—it was because I had thought so much about the topic that I couldn't get the ideas organized, and so, even though I had put a lot of hours into the paper, I found myself running out of time.)

I had little idea what I would I write in that journal entry when I first touched pen to paper, but while writing, I became consciously aware of the way anticipation and excitement feel very similar to anxiety. And that gave me an idea—what if there was a way to turn one emotion into another? Essentially, this is what many of the activities I use to reduce stress do—redirect the emotions into a more constructive direction.

Just as it did for me, taking the time to journal about your thoughts and feelings related to the activity of writing and to specific writing assignments can help you to gain insight and find new ideas and directions.

Be a Star

Even though you may not think of writing as fun, try to enjoy it and role-play having a positive attitude. The following role-playing activity may help you:

1. Pretend you are an established writer, that everyone loves your work, and that your audience is eager to read your next exciting publication, which they will love simply because they adore you. You have to do the work of writing eventually anyway, and optimism yields better results than worrying. Staying positive gives you the best chance of doing your best. So, imagine an audience that will be delighted with everything and anything you write.

2. If this is hard to imagine, ask a friend or two to role-play your adoring public and make the whole thing a game.

3. Pretend you're giving them the press release about what your next book will be about. Let them ask questions, and let it become a conversation.

4. Let yourself be over-the-top with the ideas you share, and have a good time.

5. Dress up in pretentious or obnoxious clothing and pretend to be more eccentric than you actually are if this helps to create the mood and make you feel more outgoing.

If you are anything like me, you and your friends will likely find yourselves laughing at some point during this activity. Laughter is a great way to beat anxiety and build a positive attitude. You'll be re-training your gut response to writing tasks, and you may even find yourself looking forward to these sorts of fun interactions with your friends or classmates during the early stages of writing. Take turns being the star and audience. A more serious peer review can be done later, after you actually have a completed draft.

If You Can't Avoid Distractions, Use Them

I find that being slightly distracted helps with invention, and that sometimes, it's helpful to watch TV or a movie while thinking about a writing project. Doing so lets me take micro breaks and keeps anxiety to a minimum. It can be counterproductive to see all distractions as a problem—rather, use and even create distractions to consciously adjust the emotions you feel when trying to get started with writing. It may help to have a couple of fun objects within reach. Items that light up and make sounds are great for this. Small puzzles can also help, especially the kind where you try to fit different plastic geometric shapes together to form a particular outline. A glass of water to drink or a healthy snack can serve as a brief distraction.

I do find that activities involving sound can help. I have a Bodhran, which is an Irish frame drum, and a singing bowl. If I seriously need to de-stress, I go and bang on my drum. Both of these instruments require movement to produce the sound. The drum has to be stuck with fast, rhythmic movements using a stick called a cipin or beater, and the singing bowl is made to sing, or produce harmonic tones, by rubbing the outside rim of the bowl with a suede covered striking tool or mallet. Listening to the drumbeat or whirring of the bowl is calming, giving the mind one thing to focus on, and the arm movement releases tension by using up excess adrenaline.

Figure 5. Bodhran

Figure 6. Singing Bowl

Once you've indulged in a few of these methods of intentional distraction, bring yourself back to the page or screen. I have found that it is important to make the very small step of writing something, even if it is not much. Even if it is only a word or two, or one sentence, write it down. Take a break, and come back in five minutes and write down another few words or another line. Eventually, you'll find you have more to say.

Movement

Movement helps. With as much work as I often to do, it is very easy to be sedentary, and sitting for long periods of time each day can lead to sluggishness and fatigue. Students with a full load of classes and the accompanying hours of studying are likely to face similar issues. Getting up and moving gets the circulation and adrenaline going and can sometimes build enjoyment. I find that I become more excited about my writing projects—usually because I will have had a mini-epiphany by then—after I take some time to engage in some type of physical activity, whether it is taking a walk or doing some manual labor around the house. If you feel nervous, physical activity like lifting weights or taking a walk can help. I like to go for a walk or a drive and listen to music just to unwind and think. Getting the circulation moving improves thinking for me. When writing, I often feel the urge to get up and pace for a few minutes before getting back to work. It's both a way to release excess energy as well as to celebrate the energy that writing tends to generate for me. Keeping the adrenaline regulated can help you to avoid getting too worked up, or feeling too overwhelmed.

Change of Scenery or Method

Another strategy that I find helpful is periodically moving to a new location. If I am writing at the table downstairs and start to get stuck, I'll take the laptop upstairs, or take it to the office and work there instead. Changing the scenery every few hours helps. Also, even though my composing primarily takes place on the computer, I do switch back and forth between the computer and paper if I am at a sticking point. Usually, the change is all I need to get going again.

Describe Your Plans—Even if You Don't Have Any Yet

One strategy that I often use is to write a brief summation of what I plan to do with an essay I am starting to work on. I am someone who usually doesn't have more than a vague idea of what I will write until I actually start writing. The activity of writing a plan jumpstarts that process. I make up my plan as I start to put it down in writing. I recommend that you try this and write a paragraph or so about what you plan to put in your paper, even if you aren't sure where you are going with your general idea yet. At first, this may sound like a paradox, but for some people this will get the ideas flowing. Some writers are more comfortable with paradox than others, but it can't hurt to give it a try.

ELECTRONIC STRATEGIES

Email and Messaging

Email or instant messaging can be used as part of this planning and reflecting. I have even used my Facebook wall in this way. The exchange that follows was prompted by a document I wrote while just playing around with ideas. I wrote my 1400 word essay because I thought my sister and sister-in-law would find it amusing, and I am aware that other people in my field have presented conference papers that link science fiction or fantasy programs to theoretical concepts. You might try to pair one of your own favorite programs to theories from psychology, sociology, or from your major area of study for one of your papers, if your instructor allows you to develop your own topics for class papers.

> Susan Antlitz
>
> Wrote 1400+ words on the spiritual aspects of technology in Torchwood and Doctor Who yesterday evening. Starting a new status here for comments from the readers. I must say that I really enjoyed exploring the theme of the interplay between technology and humanity.

Laurel Antltiz at 11:09am April 21

I read the whole paper and it is very inspirational

Susan Antlitz at 12:26pm April 21

Tell me more about how it inspired you. I want to develop it some more and maybe turn it into something.

Laurel Antltiz at 1:00pm April 21

Let's see what inspired me. I need to think about this some then I will give you an answer

Laurel Antltiz at 3:15pm April 21

I have thought and thought about this. I like the way that you described each show and the technology that goes into what each character portrays. I am also inspired by the fact that you outline certain show in detail and especially the characters role in each show

Debbie Antlitz at 5:30pm April 21

My feeling on RTDs stuff is he is never talking so much about what the technology makes us do or not. And in many instances it is not the *technilogy* but the concept behind the technology which is just a carrier (a magic potion would fit the same bill if he were writing Harry Potter). For example, Cybermen are not about ear buds, but about emotionless conformity.

The bliss patch that killed the senate in [the episode Gridlock] was not about drug abuse, but about mood-motivation detached from a community sense. The general gist of RTD is that humans are/should be responsible for their own actions—never say the technology, or the Devil, or the Doctor made you do it . . .

Susan Antlitz at 5:34pm April 21

well, what you said is pretty much what I was saying.
The technology brings the human tendencies to the
surface and amplifies them.

Susan Antlitz at 5:35pm April 21

it doesn't cause them, but rather creates the occasion.

Debbie Antlitz at 5:44pm April 21

Yeah, but the technology is also a distraction. It's like
writing a thesis on "uses of muscle mass in Spirit Stal-
lion of the Cimeron"

Laurel Antltiz at 5:45pm April 21

True the technology does bring the human tendencies to the surface but it also shows how each character is portrayed in their role

Susan Antlitz at 6:04pm April 21

But I think I am most interested, as I said earlier,
in how shows, as a technology in themselves, present ways of thinking and imagining the human. I'd
probably be most interested in the cohesion and dis-
integration of group identity and identification.

Laurel Antltiz at 6:05pm April 21

write about group identity and identification of technology in shows.

Susan Antlitz at 9:18am April 22

The group dynamics are interesting.

Debbie Antlitz at 6:33pm April 24

Like at the end of *Journey's End* you have a very happy
and dynamic family group bringing the Earth Home.
Then they peel off one by one leaving him alone,
like the whole group was "about" him but not about
"him" Except for the one with Wilfred at the end. At
the end, community comes down to the resonance of
the person.

I began with the idea about the way the technology relates to humanity, but by the end of the Facebook thread, I realized what I was really
interested in was the social dynamics among the characters. Exchanges
like this can happen through message boards, Instant Messenger, text
messages, email, Twitter, or other social networking tools.

When I was a graduate student, I used to use instant messaging to
talk with one of my friends from my undergraduate years after she had
moved away to Tennessee. I would message her about my work, and we
would chat about it online. In addition to the feedback, it really helped
me to put my plans into words. Usually, by the time I had finished explaining to her what I was writing, I had a much clearer idea about it. I
find I can get a lot more done than I think I can by taking a little time
to explain to myself or someone else, in writing, where I am at with
my work. Usually, in the process of explaining it, the next idea or next
step will occur to me, and then I can move forward with the writing.

Another strategy I use is to send my notes to myself on email. I
will write just a short paragraph or so of the ideas I have so far, and hit
send. Then, later when I've had more time to think about my project,
I'll reply to my message with additional notes and ideas, and I'll do
that several times over the course of a few days. The paper begins to
emerge from my collection of notes and reflections. It's kind of like a
journal, only it's on email.

Using PowerPoint as an Invention Space

Presentation software such as PowerPoint can also be used as a space
for invention. If you find you have a vague idea of what to write about,
or if you have many ideas but aren't sure how to bring them together
into enough focus for a rough draft, creating a slide show presentation
of your ideas may help.

- Put each main idea as a heading on a slide
- List your thoughts about each point, using more than one slide per point when needed.
- Add images, audio, or video when these capture an idea you haven't yet put into words but want to eventually address in your rough draft.
- Add Web links to your slides if there is online content you think you may want to eventually cite within your document. Since school libraries often provide students with free access to full-text databases for professional journals and other periodicals, you are likely to find that a good many of your sources can be linked to. This way, you will be able to find them quickly when you need to.
- If you aren't sure what order to put the points in, or which points should be main or sub-points, that's okay for now. PowerPoint makes it easy to reorder slides and move the content around later.
- While not directly related to the content of your writing, choosing a slide design template or color scheme can make your presentation-draft look more visually appealing and help to reinforce a certain tone or mood while you are generating your ideas and sense of direction.
- Making your ideas literally look good on the screen may help to boost confidence for anxious writers or provide a welcome change from the typical black text on a white screen.
- While the traditional background and text color will be required in the final draft that you turn in to your instructor (unless your assignment guidelines specify otherwise), your behind-scenes invention work can be much more flexible.

PowerPoint or other software designed for presentation has potential as an invention tool because it helps us to work with the overall points or ideas in a text rather than becoming focused on the minute details. If you haven't used PowerPoint before, or if you are unfamiliar with some of its features, there are several free tutorial videos available on YouTube.

Growth and Change

While I enjoy concept maps and am very good at creating them, they aren't one of my primary invention strategies anymore. I used to love them. When I was in high school, I once made a concept map that was an arm span wide and an arm span tall, filled with intricate detail. I filled the entire page with miniscule writing, ovals, squares, and webbed lines. I even wrote all of the connections on the lines between the bubbles. It was an exquisite masterpiece, and it helped me to write a very detailed paper. However, over the years, the techniques I use have changed, and now my invention work typically includes listing, journaling, prayer and reflection, and instant messaging. I don't think the methods I used to use have lost any of their value, but rather, the ways of thinking and connecting ideas they represent have become second nature, making it easier to make intuitive leaps. When one uses a particular strategy frequently, it can become intuitively ingrained and become instinctual.

When I am inventing, I don't try to make my notes fit into any particular form, and I allow them to switch form as I feel moved to do so. I often do still use a form of freewriting. I also use other ways of keeping the ideas flowing, like taking a short break, getting up and moving around, taking a sip of water, rereading what I have written and then adding more, or switching from writing on the computer or writing on paper or vice-versa. If you use a variety of strategies and write regularly, over time, your fluency and ability to keep generating text will grow. And as it does, you are likely to find that the strategies you use also change over time, and you'll probably even develop some of your own.

Discussion

1. Name something in your environment that inspires you. What thoughts and feelings come to mind when you look at it or think about it? What objects do you encounter throughout a usual day that are meaningful to you? Take some time to describe them and their significance.

2. What emotions do you experience when you begin to write? One a scale of 1–10, how much anxiety do you tend to have about writing? What aspect of the writing concerns you the

most? What additional strategies can you think of that might help to lessen or redirect nervous energy?

3. What strategies have you used to generate ideas in the past? What has worked or not worked for you? Try several of the strategies discussed in this essay. Which ones appeal to you most, and why?

Reinventing Invention: Discovery and Investment in Writing

Michelle D. Trim and Megan Lynn Isaac

PART 1: WHAT IS INVENTION AND WHY DO WE CARE?

Invention can be understood as a process of discovery (Conley 317) and creation (Welch 169).* This can mean that you will discover something new about an existing idea or create a new way of looking at something. That seems pretty straightforward on the surface. Writers invent texts the way engineers invent new gadgets. But invention in the rhetorical sense is about a lot more than just coming up with ideas. Invention is also a way to describe what happens when a writer searches for a topic, develops a specific idea about that topic, and then strategizes a plan for fitting that specific idea to the writing situation at hand. In other words, invention is about coming up with something shiny, new, and unique, but it is also about brainstorming, synthesizing, and learning.

You use invention without realizing it every time you solve a problem. When presented with the dilemma of how to complete an assignment after spilling cola all over her new laptop, a student might engage in the following thought process.

She could begin by brainstorming ideas for actions she could take. Some of those might include:

- Call tech support for help.
- Go use a public terminal.
- Handwrite the essay.
- Ask a friend to loan his computer.
- Request an extension from the professor.

Once she has several possible ideas to work with, she has to evaluate her options to see which might best fit the situation. Her evaluation process might go something like this:

- Call tech support for help. "Not enough time; the assignment is due tomorrow."
- Go use a public terminal. "The nearest lab closes in two hours; that is not enough time to begin again and complete the essay."
- Handwrite the essay. "This is possible, but the syllabus says the professor accepts only typed work."
- Ask a friend to loan his computer. "This might work; Sam is next door and enrolled in a different English class."
- Request an extension from the professor. "This might work, but the professor has a strict policy on late work."

Now that she has evaluated her options, she can refine the selection to reflect new ideas. That refinement process might result in the following results:

- Sam loaned his computer, but it did not have the same word processing software on it.
- In discussing the problem with Sam, he suggested combining two ideas by handwriting the essay and submitting it while also requesting an extension.

As with this example, invention activities can and do occur at any stage of the writing process. Writers can brainstorm ideas, hone in on a topic, and refine that topic continually, no matter how much drafting, researching, or revising has already occurred.

The first two aspects of invention—brainstorming ideas and developing a workable topic—seem to be the areas of invention that challenge students the most. Unless the professor assigns a specific writing prompt, college students most likely will be expected to develop writing that reflects their—not their teacher's—ideas. This can be scary. Students in our first year writing classes remarked that they liked knowing what the teacher wanted. For example, Alice[1] writes, " . . . I never know whether the teacher is going to like the topic I chose, which scares me a lot." Jared indicates that developing topics from scratch seems too challenging: "I have trouble thinking of my own ideas but when I am given ideas and examples it is a lot easier . . . ."

It has been suggested that part of the reason why first year college students struggle with invention may be due to widespread standardized testing practices that require students to respond to a pre-formed writing topic in limited ways (Hillocks 64). Such experiences rarely offer students the opportunity to develop a writing topic, let alone forefront their own interests in that topic. They also do not challenge students to think about how one kind of approach to a topic fits some writing situations better than others. For instance, a student wanting to write about date-rape prevention would likely formulate a very different means of constructing his argument for his sociology professor than for his fraternity newsletter. Likewise, a student writing to local businesses about why they should support Autism research would construct a personal essay on the subject very differently.

Without practice doing invention, you may find yourself struggling to meet the demands of your college writing assignments. More than half of the students in our composition classes remarked that they didn't have much experience devising topics in high school. For example, Liz writes, " . . . we did not have a choice about what to write about." Josh explains, "Oftentimes we would have a list of a few topics that everyone had to choose from." With similar past experiences, students may feel antagonized by a professor's resistance to such tried and true topics as "steroid use" or "stem-cell research." A student may perceive herself as reliable and responsible when she chooses a standard topic, but her professor may label it trite and tired. Learning to reimagine writing as an opportunity to create something original rather than as a duty to respond predictably can be challenging. Students are often accustomed to being rewarded for following directions precisely, and thus are conditioned to fear breaking the rules. When college instructors introduce changes to the set of expectations student writers have about the composition process, it is not unusual for them to react with disbelief and dismay.

Even more perplexing, professors may insist you develop more than one workable topic for a particular assignment. For students accustomed to responding to a single prompt or who expect to be rewarded for producing the right answer, the idea that invention is a process including experimenting with and refining ideas can be frustrating. Instructors hope students will think broadly, creatively, and playfully as they craft approaches to a writing assignment—in part because they believe that investing time in invention helps prevent problems during the later stages of the writing process. Students are busy and often value efficiency. They often want to hone in on a topic immediately, proceeding directly to the drafting stage of the writing process. The problem is that the lack of a "Plan B" may lead to various forms of collapse as the project develops. Just as avid hikers spend time studying a topographical map and evaluating several different routes to the summit before they hit the trails, you will find that energy invested in the invisible stages of writing pays dividends later on.

Lack of experience selecting writing topics isn't the only challenge you may face when it comes to invention. Not being excited by one's writing often results in less successful writing (or as writing process researcher Janet Emig argues, less successful learning). Once the opportunity presents itself, invention is the key to identifying writing topics that both satisfy the writing situation and reflect your interest and investment. That is just one reason why many professors disallow those tried and true paper topics; they want their students to write about something that interests them now, not something they have written about since high school. Furthermore, professors want students to learn from their writing rather than circumvent new learning by rehashing a comfortable topic.

While invention skills may be rusty for some, the good news is that they only require practice to become just another part of everyday writing. In order to help our writing students practice their invention skills, we have developed some invention exercises that work well for different kinds of invention tasks and at different stages of the writing process.

PART 2: PRACTICING INVENTION

Writers can engage in a variety of invention activities when confronted with a writing task. The key is to develop a practice of invention that works, not to wait for inspiration to strike while staring at a blank screen until the wee hours of the morning. Some writers become so accustomed to writing first drafts that are "good enough," that they may skip aspects of the invention process beyond selecting their first idea for a topic. Others rely on ancillary sources to provide topics, such as a teacher's example or a list of common debate questions and oral presentation topics on the WWW. One of our students stated that she often relied on Facebook quiz topics for ideas. In a pinch, these methods might help a writer squeeze by, but in the long run, writers need to trust themselves to generate topics of importance to them with whatever resources are available.

It is not that teachers mind students working together to develop ideas or to use television, the Internet, or even the lyrics of their favorite song as inspiration for a writing topic. In fact, teachers would likely applaud these activities. Many writers have in their minds an image of the inventor—someone like Thomas Edison, for example—who toils alone until that great idea hits him like an act of nature. This image is a romantic one, but it isn't very realistic. Invention, as writing scholar Karen LeFevre argues, is "a social act: one in which individuals interact with society and culture in a distinctive way to create something" (121). It is not a solitary experience. In terms of invention, this means that writers should not see invention as something they go off and do by themselves, free of the influence of the world around them. Writers' ideas are always already impacted by the context and the culture in which they live. The key is not to try to develop an idea that is perfectly unique, but rather to uniquely develop a topic in response to a specific rhetorical situation—that is, for a specific audience and with a specific purpose. Think of how a music lover might build her playlist on her computer. She might have all the same songs as her best friend, but his process for surveying an album, evaluating choices, and selecting tracks to include will be very different. Both friends are part of the culture that decides what music is good, which songs are worth buying and listening to, but they also have their own tastes and their own way of enjoying the music they decide to play. Some songs are perfect for working out while others can only be appreciated after a particularly unpleasant break-up. While listeners might agree about the genres of these kinds of songs, their own choices in similar situations may be very different.

When students ask what they should write about, writing teachers often respond by asking about their interests. Teachers might ask you, "What do you care about?" or "What makes you mad?" Traditionally, teachers might guide you in a prewriting activity like freewriting or clustering. These approaches can help you generate that first initial idea for a topic, but they may not work for everyone. Sometimes writers need help remembering what areas of study they find exciting and what issues stimulate their thinking. More often, writers can feel constricted by the academic setting and automatically eliminate ideas or approaches that don't seem conventional. You may expect a teacher to value a dry piece of writing because it fits the assignment, despite the fact that you have no interest in producing or reading it. In fact, some of you may never expect to enjoy the topics of their writing. It does not have to be this way. What seems like a dull and prescribed research assignment, or even specific prompt, can actually be an opportunity for creativity. And, if writers find the results of writing about an uninteresting topic to be boring, readers will likely agree.

Considering your individual interests while also engaging with others in a group environment can make for a fun and dynamic invention experience. The following activity builds on this idea by beginning with individual responses before juxtaposing them with those of classmates. The goal is both to spark interesting ideas that might not have been considered otherwise, while also learning how different people, with different experiences can resolve invention activities in unexpected ways.

Classroom Activity 1: Brainstorming as a Group

While on the surface the following activity may appear like a survey for finding the perfect blind date, it works best if you try to take the questions seriously. The questions can be modified to fit a specific writing situation or left more general, as we suggest, to fit a more open-ended writing task. One of the important elements of this activity is to share your responses with others—a friend, your writing group, a Writing Center consultant, etc.

Step 1

Respond in writing to the following questions.

1. What new place would you most like to visit?
2. What form of technology or invention do you value most?
3. What famous person (alive or dead) would you most like to meet?
4. What is your favorite astral body? (planet, moon, star, etc.)
5. What hands on skill would you like to learn (sailing a boat, making stained glass windows, etc.)?
6. What two qualities do you admire most in a leader?
7. What profession is the most rewarding?
8. What law would you change and why?
9. What one thing should all children learn?
10. What is the most unjust event in history?
11. What historical incident would you most like to witness?
12. What is the most important book written in your lifetime?
13. What is the highest honor a person can achieve?
14. What difference in people do you find most troubling?
15. What product would you take off the market if you could?

(You can add other questions to this list, because the exact formulation of the questions is less important than their potential for stimulating your thinking in unexpected ways.)

Step 2

You should individually compose answers to the questions being careful not to share your ideas with others (yet).

Step 3

You should share your responses to at least three or four of the queries that you found most provocative, paying attention to the responses of others. (Recording the answers as lists helps you focus on the range of your peers' responses).

Step 4

Writers should spend a few minutes listing what top five answers particularly grabbed their attention or seemed most compelling.

Step 5

With others, discuss the individual lists.

Step 6

With others, generate a list of ten possible paper topics based on either the individual lists generated in step 4 or the discussion of the lists in step 5. (It is a good idea to generate more than ten rather than discarding ones that group members find especially exciting.)

Step 7

You may select one topic from the list or lists to develop for the writing assignment or use the topics as a jumping off point for inventing another topic idea altogether.

Responses to Invention Activity 1: "Brainstorming as a Group"

Although our writing students generally found this activity to be interesting and new to them, the same invention activity will not work the same way for every writer. If we return to the original description of invention from Part 1, we see that invention incorporates both discovery and creation. Discovery in this instance is a singular experience since it depends on what writers already know about themselves. In other words, when we discover an idea that we want to explore further, what we are really discovering is our interest in that idea—not the subject matter itself. You create a topic when you fit that interest to the writing task at hand. Since every writer encounters a writing task with a unique set of attitudes and experiences, it makes sense that he or she would generate different topic ideas even when applying the same invention tool.

Unsurprisingly, since we did this as a class activity, the "Brainstorming as a Group" invention activity did not generate a paper topic idea in the same way for every one of our students. Some students commented that they found the questions too random and couldn't see how they fit with the paper assignment. Their comments imply that they expected the activity to entirely lead them to a topic that was already preformed to fit their interests and the writing assignment. But, here's the thing: this activity was designed to do exactly the opposite. Its goal is not to ask a random question with an ideal writing topic as its answer. The objective of this activity is to remind you of your own passions, interests, and opinions on a variety of real life subjects. That is the discovery part of the process. In jogging that part of our your memories, we seek to pull you out of school mode and into everyday life mode where you can bring one of your interests from life outside of school into the classroom via your writing assignments. As one student writes:

> The activity was a great start to open our minds on what topic to write about. It didn't give me a topic but rather sparked certain areas to think about. My answers showed what I was passionate about, things that are important to me, and things I want to do in my life. My own answers showed me personal beliefs and opinions on certain topics. Then listening to other people's answers sparked a whole new way of thinking. Hearing other people's interpretations of the questions and their answers allowed me to broaden my thinking. Different answers sparked different reactions that allowed for topics to debate about. Someone's answer to a question might prompt me to say, "Oh really? That's surprising to me. I thought about it a completely different way," and thus a conversation could ensue. The activity allowed for us to gain our own opinions and then react to other people's opinions. (Cabbie)

Other students amiably completed the questions but did not initially realize that they were inventing a paper topic by doing so. For example, one group of students found that they all enjoyed answering the question about their favorite astral body. Discussing their answers to this question led them to a debate on space exploration. That then led them to a debate on funding such space-related projects—the pros and cons of which formed the nexus of their group argument project. They formed a topic that explored the funding of agencies like NASA, arguing for continued monetary support while acknowledging the unavoidable economic constraints. Despite the seeming lack of successful

topic generation by the invention activity, this group used the activity
to arrive at a topic that they probably would not have selected otherwise. They discovered their shared interest and conflicting views on
funding for space exploration and shaped that interest to fit their writing assignment.

Similarly, Emily writes that the activity,

> " . . . encouraged my creativity, and sparked my cu-
> riosity, but it did not help me to select a topic . . . .
> It did however guide my entire group to the decision
> to write about something with a more objective feel.
> We immediately all decided we wanted an issue with
> concrete sides and arguments that could be supported
> by evidence instead of opinions (like which invention
> is the most important). The activity also steered us to
> choose a broader topic, instead of concentrating so
> much on the answer. For example, in response to my
> answer about which law I would change we thought
> of immigration from Cuba as a possible topic."

Like many other aspects of the writing process, the success of invention strategies cannot always be measured by the 'product' (in this
case a clearly stated topic for a writing assignment). Sometimes, the
most successful invention activity is the one that gets you thinking so
that ideas are more accessible and easier to formulate. As Mary states,
"[b]ecause this activity asked such broad questions, we were able to get
ideas from our classmates' answers and from other ideas that occurred
as a result of the questions of the activity."

Individual Activity: Brainstorming Based on Interests

While Activity 1 asks you to interact with others about your ideas and
responses, answering the same set of questions can be equally helpful
when you are working on your own to generate a writing topic. In this
case, writers can work entirely alone by looking at their responses and
then spending time freewriting or clustering in response to any one
given answer. You may also interrogate a specific answer to flesh out
your revealed interests more fully. Using the reporter's 5 W's and an H
is one way to do this. See the following fictional example.

Oscar decided that he wanted to develop a paper idea based on
his answer to the question about a leader's qualities. He believed that

a leader should be open-minded and have integrity. In order to try to
see how these ideas could become a topic, he had to ask himself the
following questions:

1. Who did he have in mind when naming these qualities? Oscar
    did not have a specific person in mind when generating this
    answer.

2. What kind of leader needed these qualities? These qualities
    might have applied to any leadership position, but Oscar was
    thinking of the recent undergraduate student government
    meeting he had attended.

3. When would these qualities matter the most? There had been
    some student protesting lately over the school's policies regard-
    ing its observation of certain religious holidays. That kind of
    conflict seemed to need leadership from a person with these
    qualities.

4. Where would a leader like this exist? Oscar did not have a
    specific place in mind, but he wasn't thinking of someplace
    unknown or unfamiliar.

5. Why this answer? Oscar assumed that the recent happenings
    on his campus combined with the discussion at the last student
    government meeting had triggered this response. The current
    president was stepping down due to problems with academic
    achievement, and the representatives had to decide if the cur-
    rent vice president would take her place or if there would be an
    election. Oscar was concerned that the vice president seemed
    to see only one side to the current problem and tended to make
    fun publically of the opposition.

6. How would these qualities take shape? Oscar believed that an
    open-minded leader would listen to all sides before respond-
    ing and that a sign of integrity would be when she/he treated
    constituents with respect, no matter her/his side on an issue.

In this instance, Oscar discovered that he wanted to write about
the need for a leader to be open-minded and have integrity. The assignment had asked students to make an argument that was supported
by examples or reasons. Specifically, after the above exercise, he dis-

covered that he wanted to argue for the importance of these two qualities above all else and connect that argument to times of conflict and
disagreement. He decided he would use examples from the current undergraduate student government dilemma in order to make his points
clear to his readers.

Group Activity 2: Inventing for Genre, Audience, and Purpose

Although we think strong writing often develops out of a writer's own
interests, we also like invention activities that help writers think about
the rhetorical context of a writing task. Good writers, whether generating a text about how to fund NASA or the most significant qualities
demanded of a candidate for student government, also think about
who will be reading their text, why, and what kind or genre of text will
best communicate the necessary information. Some college writing
assignments state the audience, genre and purpose of the task absolv-
ing you from having to make too many decisions, but others don't.
Invention activities that encourage writers to think about rhetorical
context are helpful because they forefront these concerns and remind
writers that the invention process goes beyond selecting a topic—it
includes developing that topic according to the writing situation.

Inventing an Audience

This activity works well either in a group or as an individual writing
activity. Begin by reading the following scenario:

> Imagine a friend asked you to move his car for him
> from one side of campus to the other. He had just
> discovered that the parking lot where it was located
> was being closed for a special event, but since he had
> class, he did not have time to move it himself. While
> moving the car, you leaned over to adjust the sound
> system and didn't notice that you were coming up
> on one of the college's many pedestrian crosswalks.
> You hit a pedestrian as he entered the walkway. The
> man's leg was broken. The man also happened to be
> the college president. The police cite you for reck-
> less driving, and in two weeks, you will be called to
> appear before the campus Honor Board for possible
> further sanctioning.

Develop a plan for responding to each of the following five writing activities:

- Write a letter to your parents informing them about the situation.
- Write a letter to a close friend from high school informing him or her about the situation.
- Write a letter to the college president about the situation.
- Write a letter to the Honor Board about the situation in preparation for the upcoming hearing.
- Write a letter to your insurance agent explaining the situation.

Then, select one plan to follow and write the letter using the plan you devised.

Next, you might join a small group and share your different approaches with each other, discussing the following topics:

- What strategies did the writer employ to make this letter appropriate to the audience?
- What purpose does this letter serve?
- What strategies does the writer employ to further its specific purpose?
- How does each writer portray himself or herself?
- Which letter seems most likely to be successful?

Finally, each group might analyze the writing strategies that enabled each writer to address her/his audience and purpose effectively.

Inventing a Genre

Like the previous activity, this exercise asks you to work in a group from a shared prompt to develop a range of different texts geared toward varying rhetorical contexts, but this activity asks writers to complicate the task a bit more by writing not only to different audiences with different purposes, but in a variety of short genres.

Consider the following scenario:

> On the first Monday of every month at 7:00 p.m., the campus residence halls test their fire alarms. No one is required to exit the building during these regularly scheduled tests. Last Monday (the third Monday

of the month) at about 7:15, a candle was left unat-
tended on the sill of an open window in a residence
hall. Apparently, a billowing curtain was ignited,
and the fire quickly spread. When the two students
who shared the room returned and discovered the
fire, they pulled the alarm in the hallway, but almost no one in the residence hall paid any attention,
mistaking the alarm for the monthly test. The fire
department arrived quickly but was forced to spend
significant time helping to evacuate the building before they could turn their full attention to controlling the fire. No one was injured, but damage to the
building was significant.

Develop a plan for how you might craft one of the following:

- Write the text for a new college brochure on fire safety to be
  distributed to all occupants of the campus residence halls.
- Write a news article for the college paper.
- Write an email from a student whose room was destroyed by
  fire to a faculty member requesting an extension on a research
  paper.
- Write a letter from the President of the university to alumni
  asking for emergency contributions to repair and refurbish the
  residence hall.
- Write a letter from the Fire Chief to the Director of the campus
  residence halls.

Next, share your plans with others and discuss the following questions about each of the five writing assignments' situations:

- What purposes does this text serve?
- How does the intended audience for this text affect the strate-
  gies that the writer should employ?
- What constraints does the genre of this text impose on the
  writer?
- What kinds of information does this genre convey best?

In generating plans for these writing situations, you can perhaps
see more clearly some of the ways that genre, audience, and purpose

affect how a topic can best be articulated. In this exercise, writers had to decide basic things like length, style of writing (informal versus scholarly), and use of support (reasons or examples). They also had to have an idea of what information, or message, they wanted to convey, what ideas worked to their best advantage, and what ones could be left out. When the audience, purpose, and genre of a text are taken into account at any stage of writing, invention takes place.

Classroom Activity 3: Refining Topics for Research

The following invention activity also aids in finding an initial idea for a research paper, but then goes further by using group work to aid you in developing that idea into a workable paper topic. This activity is especially useful if you are nervous about researching in a subject area new to you.

Writers embarking on a research writing project sometimes encounter two different problems. Either, like one recent student interested in the cognitive skills developed by multiple-player on-line games, they are so deeply invested in their topic, that they have trouble imagining an audience less schooled and enthusiastic than themselves. Or, despite a genuine interest in a topic, like another recent student excited about exploring biofuel alternatives, they have no idea how to begin writing about a subject they know virtually nothing about. These situations are complicated when writers don't have a clear idea of who they are writing for (other than their teacher) or what purpose their writing is intended to serve (other than fulfilling a requirement for a grade.) Are they writing to educate an audience unfamiliar with their topic or are they writing for a community of insiders who are deeply invested in it?

This exercise can help illustrate how writing can be one avenue toward learning and how peers are often a valuable audience.

Step 1

Join together with other students to share a potential research paper topic and a typed paragraph of at least 200 words describing why this topic appeals to you, what kind of text you would like to create, and who would be most interested in reading/seeing it. (One purpose of this step is to ensure that you have the opportunity to engage in some advanced preparation rather than feeling like you are grasping at straws once you arrive in class. A general rule of thumb says that if writers cannot sustain interest in a topic long enough to write 200 words about it, then it is not the best choice for an extended project.)

Step 2

With others, very briefly share your topic, audience, and text ideas. Afterwards, each member of the group should answer in writing the following set of questions about the topics being proposed by all the other group members. You should expect to spend around ten minutes writing about each of the topics introduced by your fellow writers.

1. What do you already know about this topic? (Simply make a list of facts or claims brainstorming as quickly as possible.)

2. Where have you seen information about this topic in the past? (What kinds of texts have you seen that discuss it?)

3. What should a writer exploring this topic do to make it interesting to you as a potential audience member? (Be as specific as possible and provide as many possibilities as you can think of.)

4. What background information, questions, or facts should someone exploring this topic make sure to cover for an audience already interested in the topic? For an audience unfamiliar with the topic?

5. What kinds of sources or authorities do you think the author should consult while researching this topic?

Step 4

Have everyone in the group give their responses back to the original authors of the topics. Then have everyone spend a few minutes reading the responses they received for their topic.

Step 5

With others, discuss your topics with the goal of helping each other understand how to refine each topic, shape it to appeal to the selected audience, develop research strategies, and account for differences in background knowledge between the writer and the chosen audience.

Step 6

Thinking about the experience of your group, you should reflect on what you have learned about the kinds of things that writers should take into account when developing a topic for a specific audience. You should invite other writers to discuss the activity further, focusing on what aspects of topic generation you found most challenging and/or surprising.

Student Response to "Refining Topics for Research"

As with all group work, classes using this invention activity will experience the occasional hiccup. You might become frustrated with your topic and toss it out. Although you may perceive the exercise as a failure since it eliminated your topic instead of enriching it, invention is, among other things, a sorting process and figuring out what won't work is a very practical use of time. Even those students who find themselves without a topic when the exercise is completed will have a much clearer idea of what kind of topic might work based on those they have helped their peers develop.

Students who do manage to keep their topic intact over the course of the exercise may have a very different idea of how to approach it after it has been vetted and discussed by their peers. In one recent class, Jessica[2] began her research assignment intending to write about post-partum depression. Initially, she was frustrated by the responses provided to the four questions by one of her group members, Kyle, because he claimed he did not know anything at all about post-partum depression and answered the four questions with ideas that she perceived to be ridiculously basic and simplistic. Since she had written thoughtfully and at length about his topic, new developments in artificial intelligence, she believed Kyle was being lazy and irresponsible by not providing her with similar feedback. During the small group discussion, however, Jessica realized that Kyle was being honest. Aside from having a vague idea that post-partum depression had something to do with pregnancy, the concept was foreign to him, and he had no idea why it should concern him. Since Jessica had originally intended to write for an audience unfamiliar with her topic, she not only devoted more of her paper to educating her audience about her topic than she had expected, she also shifted her approach to include arguments about why a phenomenon that only affects women should be of interest to men, even those men who are not themselves fathers.

Group discussion of the topic development exercise also helped our students to see each other as resources. After one student discussed her interest in writing about increased diagnoses of celiac disease, another student volunteered the information that her mother struggled with the condition, and the two students began to discuss the possibility of arranging an interview with the mother. Students also helped narrow each other's topics by pointing out what aspects of a broad field intrigued them the most. Kaleigh's group realized that her topic, animal rights, was horribly large when they recognized how diverse their written responses to her topic were. It clearly would not be possible for her to use the topic without further refinement. So they helped her consider and eliminate different aspects of animal rights (in the food industry, in drug experimentation, and in puppy mills) until they hit upon a focal point that intrigued Kaleigh—the treatment of captive wild animals in zoos and circuses.

Finally, using group work as part of the invention process serves a larger goal in any writing class—it sets you up to be invested readers and editors of each other's work as the writing process progresses. Kyle was a much more enthusiastic peer reviewer of Jessica's paper because it included issues he had raised, and he now saw himself as a genuine audience for the work. Similarly, other students took pride in noticing how their ideas had been incorporated or were able to make very concrete suggestions for revision by reminding their peers of issues that had been raised in the initial invention session.

CONCLUSION

Invention, like every other aspect of the writing process, is neither a single-faceted nor a static skill. Each new writing situation brings a different set of rhetorical challenges that vary from writer to writer. Experienced writers expect that they will have to wrestle and play with ideas before they begin writing. You should remember that the mental calisthenics that precede the production of a string of words are not a waste of time or indicative of the absence of writing talent; they are instead utterly normal and wonderfully useful. Making choices among ideas is a significant aspect of writing. And making choices is important—whether the decision is as frivolous as picking which flavor of ice cream to order from a store with dozens of options or deciding which college to attend. But making choices can be fun, too. When you focus on invention by using activities like the ones discussed above, you are able to break down stereotypes about "appropriate topics," forefront your interests and areas of expertise, and craft texts that speak to an intended audience while accomplishing an intended purpose.

Discussion

1. How would you describe the invention process? In other words, what are writers doing when they are inventing?

2. Why might some students find generating their own writing topics to be stressful or challenging? List as many reasons as you can.

3. What are the goals of the group-based invention activities? In other words, what are they trying to help students learn about invention?

Notes

1. Direct quotes from student work are cited using students' first names according to the students' stated directives to use their actual first names or pseudonyms.
2. References to student conversations use pseudonyms only.

Works Cited

Conley, Thomas M. *Rhetoric in the European Tradition*. Chicago: U of Chicago P, 1990.

Emig, Janet. "Writing as a Mode of Learning." *College Composition and Communication* 28.2 (1977): 122–28.

Hillocks, George, Jr. "Fighting Back: Assessing the Assessments." *English Journal* 92.4 (2003): 63–70.

LeFevre, Karen Burke. *Invention as a Social Act*. Carbondale and Edwardsville: Southern Illinois UP, 1987.

Welch, Kathleen E. *The Contemporary Reception of Classical Rhetoric: Appropriations of Ancient Discourse*. Hillsdale: Erlbaum, 1990.

"Finding Your Way In": Invention as Inquiry Based Learning in First Year Writing

Steven Lessner and Collin Craig

Imagine the initial meeting of your first year writing course.[*] After welcoming you to the course and going over the basics, your writing instructor prompts you and the other students to reflect on how you typically begin to think about approaching a writing assignment. Several hands raise and you listen as students begin answering. One student hesitantly states that he normally waits until the last minute to think about it and stays up all night before it's due, working away. Another student asserts that she often has trouble choosing and then narrowing down a topic. Disagreeing about this shared response, a student sitting near you asserts that he has trouble generating more supporting ideas once he has chosen a topic to explore. Still someone else states that she tries to get ideas from the readings she is supposed to write about in essays—often without success. After hearing from these students, your writing instructor tells the class that this is a good time to start talking about invention and helpful activities to use when approaching and starting a writing assignment.

Your first year college writing course often becomes a primary place where new writing techniques and tools are presented to help smoothen your transition into college-level writing. We hope this chapter will encourage you to see the diverse invention possibilities available when beginning a writing assignment. For instance, have you ever felt a blank sheet of paper or empty word processing screen intently staring at you while you decide what to say? Learning potential invention activities for writing can help you feel more comfortable as a writer in college by giving you many more places to begin. As college writing teachers, we know that first year writing students have plenty of generative ideas to share and many insightful connections to make in their writing. Knowing that a wide range of invention activities are available to try out may be all you need to begin approaching writing assignments with more effectiveness, clarity and creativity.

In his piece entitled "Inventing Invention" from *Writing Inventions: Identities, Technologies, Pedagogies,* college writing professor Scott Lloyd DeWitt makes a comparison between the inventing space his father used as an engineer and the multitude of invention activities open to writers (17–19). DeWitt describes his father's garage as a generative place where "wires, tool handles, broken toys, thermometers, an ice bucket, lamp switches, an intercom system, the first microwave oven ever manufactured . . ." are drawn on as invention tools that his father selects depending on what project he is starting and what tool will ultimately help him the most (17). Similarly, as a writer in college with many different writing assignments, you will need to think about what invention activity best helps you not only to begin specific papers most effectively, but also to generate new ideas and arguments during the writing process.

In considering your previous experiences, you may have been taught that invention "is a single art form, or a single act of creativity" (DeWitt 23). When taught in this way, readers and writers may be misled to understand invention as something that takes place in one definite moment that can't be revisited while in the middle of writing. Viewing invention as a one time, hit or miss event does not allow the construction and development of ideas to be seen as a continuing process a writer employs throughout the act of writing. In looking at invention as a "single act," you might miss how helpful invention can really be as an ongoing developmental practice that allows new ideas and exciting connections to be made.

The invention activities we offer in this chapter will help you begin to see invention as more than formulaic correct or incorrect approaches for producing writing. We want these invention activities to be ones that you can try out and, ultimately, make your own as college readers and writers. Let us be clear in stating that no one invention activity may work for all writers. Some of these approaches for beginning your writing assignments will be more useful than others. However, each invention activity has been crafted with you in mind and as a generative way for you to begin thinking about your writing assignments. Through the invention strategies of reading rhetorically, freewriting, focused freewriting, critical freewriting, flexible outlining, bulleting, visual outlining and auditory/dialogic generative outlining, you will begin inventing in ways that stretch your writerly muscles. You will see how beginning papers can be a process that invites you as a participant to share and build on your experiences and knowledge in productive ways. And much like Professor DeWitt's engineering father with his tools in a garage, you will learn to choose your invention tools with care when starting to write.

READING RHETORICALLY

As a college reader, finding an author's intent is a commonly learned critical thinking strategy that works for analyzing texts. But engaged reading can also be about discovering how the writing strategies of authors are working to build an essay and convey a message. A good start towards transitioning into college-level writing is discovering what you can stand to gain as a writer from the reading process. Through directed reading, you can learn strategies for building structure and argument in your own texts. Moreover, as part of your successful development as a writer, you'll need ample opportunity and space for creativity in your writing process. Reading with a purpose teaches you how to use creativity to generate multiple approaches to building arguments and making connections between ideas.

Rhetorical reading is our approach for understanding the tools that writers use to persuade or effectively communicate ideas. This critical reading approach will have you analyze, interpret, and reflect on choices that writers make to convey a thought or argument. Reading rhetorically develops critical thinking skills that not only interrogate ideas but also situates them within a rhetorical situation (context) and works towards determining how the message, intended audience, and method of delivery work together for the purpose of persuasion and effective communication. For example, when reading a New York Times op-ed about the war in Iraq, you might consider the traditional political stance the newspaper has taken on the war in the Middle East and how this might determine how Iraqi citizens are spoken for, or how visual images are used to invoke an emotion about the Muslim faith in times of war. You will find that the ability to perform specific analytical moves in your reading can make you

- more aware of your own intentions as a writer;
- more specific in developing methods of delivery;
- and, more cognizant of how you want your intended audience to respond to your ideas.

This critical reading exercise encourages you to think about reading as a social interaction with the writer. Take a look at an assigned reading by an author for your course. What questions might you ask the author about the writing moves that he/she makes to draw readers in?

Here are some sample questions to get you started towards reading rhetorically.

- How does the author organize events, evidence, or arguments throughout the text?
- What stylistic moves does the text do to draw readers in?
- Does the author rely on experts, personal experience, statistics, etc. to develop an argument or communicate an idea? Is this rhetorical approach effective?
- Who might we suggest is the intended audience? How does the author make appeals or cater her message to this audience specifically?

In a writing situation that asks you to effectively communicate a specific idea to a target audience, knowing how to respond will develop your critical reading skills and provide you with effective strategies for writing in multiple genres. Having a rhetorical knowledge of how genres of writing work will also prepare you with tools for generating inquiry-based writing for multiple audiences.

A Rhetorical Reading Activity

Below is an excerpt from Gloria Anzaldua's "How to Tame a Wild Tongue," an autobiographic text that demonstrates how the author finds her identity as Chicana, shaped by multiple language practices and responses.

> I remember being caught speaking Spanish at recess—that was good for three licks on the knuckles with a sharp ruler. I remember being sent to the corner of the classoom for "talking back" to the Anglo teacher when all I was trying to do was tell her how to pronounce my name. "If you want to be American, speak 'American.' If you don't like it, go back to Mexico where you belong."

> "I want you to speak English. Pa' hallar buen trabajo tienes que saber hablar el ingles bien. Que vale toda tu educacion si todavia hablas ingles con un 'accent,'" my mother would say, mortified that I spoke English like a Mexican. At Pan American University, I and all Chicano students were required to take two speech classes. Their purpose: to get rid of our accents.

> Attacks on one's form of expression with the intent to censor are a violation of the First Amendment. El Anglo con cara de inocente nos arranco la lengua. Wild tongues can't be tamed, they can only be cut out.

Asking Rhetorical Questions

Here are a few rhetorical questions you might consider asking:

- What is the rhetorical situation in which Anzaldua finds herself using different language forms? (Rhetorical situation refers to the context, intended audience, and purpose for writing.)

- Does Anzaldua's writing attempt to invoke an emotional response from its readers?
- What makes Anzaldua credible to speak about language practices as a condition of access into a community?
- Does the author make any logical appeals to persuade readers?
- What assumptions about culture can we make based on the content of Anzaldua's text?

Asking rhetorical questions provokes a process of inquiry-based thinking that is useful for learning how to participate in academic conversations in a way that investigates the decisions writers make when they compose and arrange compositions. As you read, get in the habit of asking rhetorical questions about the composition of texts. This will further guide your prewriting process of brainstorming and frame decisions for how you might compose your own texts. Freewriting can be an initial invention exercise that begins your composing process.

ENTERING CONVERSATIONS AS A WRITER

Freewriting

Freewriting is a warmup exercise that is designed to jumpstart the writing process. Writing professor Peter Elbow, well-known for promoting the practice of freewriting, describes freewriting as private writing without stopping (4). Freewriting is an effective prewriting strategy that allows you to explore an idea without worrying about grammar errors or coherence. This form of writing is not about developing a finished product or performing "good writing." Many writers might use this exercise to get their brains into gear when developing ideas about a topic. If you are struggling with pinning down ideas that are at the back of your mind, freewriting enables you to explore the field of thoughts in your mind and get words down on paper that can trigger connections between meaningful ideas.

Here is an exercise to get you started:

Exercise 1

Take about ten minutes to write about anything that comes to mind. The goal is to keep writing without stopping. If you are coming up blank and nothing comes to mind, then write "nothing comes to mind" until something does. Do not worry about the quality of the writing, grammar, or what to write. Just write!

Focused Freewriting

Focused freewriting asks you to write about a specific topic. It is more concentrated and allows writers opportunities to develop continuity and connections between ideas while exploring all that you might know about a subject. Focused freewriting can be useful in sorting through what you know about a topic that might be useful for outlining a writing project.

Exercise 2

Take about ten minutes to focus freewrite on one of the topics below. As with initial freewriting, write without stopping. But this time, pay closer attention to maintaining a focus and developing continuity while building upon and connecting ideas.

- What writing moves can you learn from a close rhetorical reading of Anzaldua's text to compose your own text?
- Write about an important language practice that you participated in or experienced that is not school related.

Kelsey, a first year writer on the university basketball team, offers an example of a focused freewrite she performed in her college writing course about learning how to talk to her baby sister.

> I'm not really sure what he wants us to exactly write. Like speaking a different language? Talking in different tones? Language like Amy Tan described? Well since I'm not sure, I guess that I'll just guess and see how this works. When Mackenzie was first learning to speak, she obviously didn't produce full sentences. She used a lot of touching, showing, and pointing. When speaking to her, it was important to emphasize certain words (that she would pick up on or understand), to make them clear to her and not allow an entire sentence or phrase to confuse her. And, when she spoke to us, it was important to not only pay at-

tention to the word that she was saying (often not comprehendible), but watch her facial expression, and notice how she used her hand to point, gesture, etc. It was truly fascinating to watch how her language developed and grew over such a short period of time. She went from shouting out short, one syllable words, to formulating her own sentences (although often without correct tenses or order), to speaking in such a way that little observation from me or my family was needed. She continued to occasionally sometimes mix up her words, or even mispronounce them, but it is still astounding to me that she learned what so many things are, how to say them, and how to describe them, without ever attending any school. I know that this is pretty much how everyone learns to speak, but the power of simple acquisition still is fascinating. Ok so now im all out of what I wanted to say.

Kelsey begins her focused freewrite with questions that help her create a framework for making sense of non-school language practices. Using personal narrative, she is able to explore the concept of acquisition in how her baby sister learns how to communicate. She also takes moments throughout her freewrite to reflect on the literacy issues implied in her recounted story. During interpretive moments of her freewriting, Kelsey can formulate ideas she might further explore about literacy as a social practice, such as the influences of both formal education and the mundane experiences of family social life.

Critical Freewriting

Critical freewriting asks writers to think more analytically about a topic or subject for writing. When we say "critical," we do not mean it simply as an analytical approach focused solely on creating an opposing viewpoint. We use the term critical to define a reflection process during freewriting that includes

- asking questions
- responding
- engaging with opposing points of view

- developing new perspectives and then asking more questions

Critical freewriting gives you permission to grapple with an idea and even explore the basis for your own beliefs about a topic. It involves going beyond writing freely about a subject, and placing it in relationship to larger existing conversations. For example, you might ask, "How does my stance on teenage pregnancy align with existing viewpoints on abortion?" or "What are the consequences for sex education in high schools?" Critical freewriting provides you the opportunity to use reflection and inquiry as inventive strategies towards exploring multiple angles into a writing topic.

Below is an example of critical freewriting on the benefits and possible consequences of other forms of writing, such as text messaging.

> Text messaging is a kind of writing that I do to keep in touch with friends and family back home and on campus. I use it everyday after class or when I get bored with studying homework. It's a lot like instant messaging in my opinion because it allows you to communicate without having to worry about weird silences that can happen when you run out of things to say. On the other hand I wonder about how it will affect my ability to communicate in formal settings, such as a phone interview for a job when I graduate. Often times for example when I receive a phone call I will ignore it and send a text message instead of calling back. I would say that I text message more than I actually talk on the phone. I wonder how such indirect communication might create bad habits of passivity that might cause me to miss out on all the benefits of human interaction. I feel the same way about online instant messaging. Though it is a great way to maintain contact with friends that are going to college in another state, I wonder if it makes me less inclined to initiate face-to-face communication with others on campus. Some might say that digital communication is more efficient and that you can say whatever you feel without the pressure of being embarrassed by someone's response. I would agree but

> meaning in words can be understood better when
> hearing emotions in someone's audible voice, right?
> Meh, this probably won't change my habits of typing
> up a quick text over calling someone. LOL.

Here the writer takes an inconclusive stance on the pros and cons
of text messaging as a form of everyday communication. Her assignment might ask her to either make an argumentative stance or to take
an open-ended approach in exploring instant messaging as a language
practice. In either case, she engages in a recursive (ongoing) process
of questioning and answering that invents scenarios and raises issues
she might explore in order to develop a working knowledge on trendy
forms of technological communication.

Exercise 3

Spend ten minutes critical freewriting on one of the following topics.

- What is a type of writing that you do that is not school related?
  How does your knowledge about the context (people, place, or
  occasion) of writing determine how you communicate in this
  writing situation?
- How has writing contributed to your experiences as a member of an online community (ex. Facebook, Twitter, writing
  emails)?

Critical freewriting encourages recursive thinking that enables
you to create a body of ideas and to further decide which ones might
be worth researching and which themes might work together in constructing a coherent, yet flexible pattern of ideas. We value flexibility
because we believe it complements how ideas are never final and can
always be revised or strengthened. Flexible outlining enables this process of ongoing revision, no matter what writing stage you are in.

Flexible Outlining

Once you have engaged in freewriting, you may find it useful to use a
process called flexible outlining that can help you arrange your ideas
into more complex, thought provoking material. First year writing
students and their comments about outlining inspired the kind of
flexible outlining we encourage in the exercises below. Summing up

many students' needs to begin writing a paper in some kind of outline format, first year writer Valencia Cooper writes, "The way I start a paper usually is to organize or outline the topic whatever it may be." Valencia used a variety of bullets and indenting when beginning her work, which suggests that flexible outlining could be more effective in terms of organizing generative thoughts for papers. Similarly using a form of flexible outlining, first year writing student Tommy Brooks conveyed that he "makes an outline and fills in the blanks." These examples encourage you as a writer to remember that there is no right or wrong way to engage in outlining ideas as you start thinking about what directions to take your paper. We encourage you to visualize, hear, and talk through important information generated from your critical freewriting using the techniques of bulleting, drawing, and dialoguing that we detail below.

Bulleting

After generating a body of ideas from freewriting, bulleting your ideas can be the next step towards conceptualizing a map of your writing project. Organizing your thoughts in bullets can generate possibilities for how you might sequence coherent streams of ideas, such as main points, examples, or themes. For instance, if you chose to critically freewrite about writing that is not school related as prompted in Exercise 3 above, itemizing the ideas in your response through bulleting allows you to isolate prospective themes and decide if they are worth exploring. Below is an example bulleted list generated from the above critical freewriting demonstration about text messaging as an alternative writing practice.

- Text messaging allows me to keep in touch with those I am close to that live far away and nearby me as well.
- Text messaging is a kind of writing that I use everyday in situations, like when I'm bored with schoolwork.
- Text messaging is very similar to instant messaging in how it avoids weird silences that happen in face-to-face or phone conversations.
- Text messaging may create bad habits of passivity that might cause missing out on human interaction.
- Text messaging does not allow emotions to be fully understood like listening to someone's audible voice.

Visual Outlining

After locating common themes from your bullets, try to visually think about the best way to represent the arrangement of your ideas for what we call a visual outline. This exercise will require some drawing, but please understand that visual outlining does not require you to be an artist. The point of this exercise is for you to conceptualize your paper in a new way that helps generate new ideas. Peter Elbow points out in *Writing With Power* that drawings connected to your writing "have life, energy and experience in them" (324).

Take some time to consider how you visualize the arrangement of your paper. Is your central idea the trunk of a tree, with other ideas expanding outward as the branches, and with details hanging like leaves? Or is your beginning idea a tall skyscraper with many small windows on the outside and hallways and elevators on the inside underlying your ideas and claims?

For instance, if you wanted to visualize the above bullets concerning text messaging in the shape of a tree diagram, you might write text messaging in what you draw and label as the trunk. As you continue sketching in the branches on your tree, each one should represent an idea or other evidence that supports a main claim being made about text messaging. Below, we have created a conceptual tree from the previous critical freewriting excerpt as a visual example for outlining that can be both generative and flexible. But you don't have to imitate ours. Be stylistically creative in developing your own tree outline (see figure 1).

Developing a tree diagram as a way of outlining ideas prompts you to see that linear approaches to orchestrating ideas are not the only way of arranging a composition at this stage. While "Text Messaging As Alternative Writing" works as the foundational theme in Figure 1, having a variety of visually horizontal alignments in this outline can eliminate premature decisions about how you might arrange your composition and which topics can be best aligned in relationship to others. Use this type of spatial alignment to make more effective decisions about how to communicate your intended message.

Exercise 4

Take some time to draw your own visual outline using the ideas developed from your critical freewriting. Think about reoccurring cen-

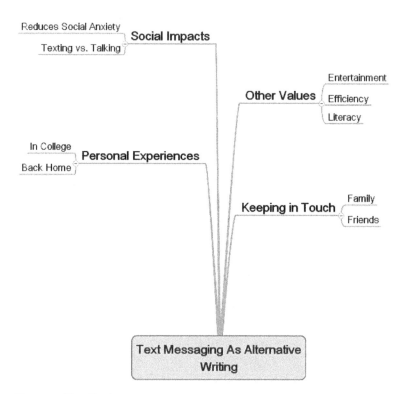

Figure 1. Tree Outline

tral theme(s) that surface. Decide which ones can be foundational in building supporting arguments or potential alternative perspectives.

Reflection
- From looking at your visual outline, what directions might you first consider pursuing in the process of developing and organizing an essay?
- In what ways did using an image as a medium for outlining allow you to think about how you might arrange your ideas?

Auditory/Dialogic Generative Outlining

We also want to suggest an interactive outlining process that allows you to get more immediate feedback from your peers about the directions you may want to take in your writing. In her work *Remembered Rapture: The Writer at Work*, author and cultural critic bell hooks writes about how her outlining process is improved through communication with others. When trying to write her autobiography, hooks recalls that memories "came in a rush, as though they were a sudden thunderstorm" (83). Often, she found that her remembering and categorizing process in recalling old memories of her younger life were best to "talk about" with others before she began writing (83).

For this exercise, you will want to return to the original bulleted list that you generated from your critical freewriting. If you find it helpful, you can use the example bullet list about text messaging we provided in the "Bulleting" section above.

Step #1

As you did with your visual outline, take some time to think about the central idea in your bulleted list that you created from critical freewriting. Highlight, underline or circle these main ideas in your bullets. You may want to use different color highlighters to differentiate between your starting, central idea and those that are supportive and expanding. Below, we have provided an example of coding in our created bulleted list by making starting, central ideas bold and expanding, supportive points italicized.

- **Text messaging allows me to keep in touch** with *those I am close to that live far away and nearby me as well.*
- **Text messaging is a kind of writing** *that I use everyday in situations like when I'm bored with schoolwork.*
- **Text messaging is very similar to instant messaging** in how *it avoids weird silences that happen in face-to-face or phone conversations.*
- **Text messaging may create bad habits of passivity** *that might cause missing out on human interaction.*
- **Text messaging does not allow emotions to be heard** *like in someone's audible voice.*

Please note that the distinctions between your central and supporting ideas do not have to be finalized. Some initial thoughts may be part of your supporting points. Or you may still be in the process of solidifying an idea. This is perfectly fine. Just do your best to make as many distinctions as you can.

Take some time to code the bulleted list you generated from your starting, central ideas and supporting ideas.

In Step #1 of Auditory/Dialogic Generative Outlining, separating main and supportive ideas by marking them differently (highlighting, underlining, circling), helps you see generative connections you are making with your topic of text messaging. In looking over this list, there are many ideas you can explore about text messaging and its relationship to something else (ability to keep in touch with others, writing, instant messaging, bad habits of passivity, and emotions). Having these diverse connections about text messaging listed pushes you to see that there is no one, right answer that you need to explore in your writing. Instead, this invention step opens up many different possible connections for you to consider as you begin writing.

Step #2

For the next piece of this outlining strategy, work with a peer. In discussing the interactive nature of writing and communication, Elbow points out "there is a deep and essential relationship between writing and the speaking voice" (22). In speaking face to face with another student in your class that is writing the same assignment, you may find a higher level of comfort in conveying your ideas. However, you could also choose to share your bullets with another individual outside your class, such as a friend or family member.

Instruction #1 for the Writer: Look closely at your central, starting point(s) (coded in bold in the example above). Find a partner in class. Give them your coded list.

Instruction #1 for the Reader/Recorder: Read aloud each of the writer's central starting points (coded in bold in the example above). Then frame a question for the writer that relates to their central points. An example question can be, "You have a lot of starting points that talk about text messaging and its relationship to something else (writing, instant messaging, bad habits of passivity, emotions). Why do these relationships to text messaging keep coming up in your ideas?"

Below is a list of three other example questions a reader/recorder might ask in relationship to the writer's central starting points about text messaging. These example questions are offered here to help you think about what types of questions you could ask as a reader/recorder to a writer.

1. The majority of your central starting points seem to express a strong point about text messaging with definite wording such as in "Text messaging allows me . . . ," "Text messaging is a kind of writing . . . ," "Text messaging is very similar . . . ," and "Text messaging does not allow . . ." However, you have one central starting point that does not express certainty, and that one is "Text messaging may create bad habits of passivity . . ." Why is the opinion in this idea not as strong as your other starting central points? Why do you choose to use the word "may" here?

2. In two of your central starting points, you seem to make a kind of comparison between text messaging and other forms of communication such as "writing" and "instant messaging." Are there any other forms of communication that you can compare text messaging to? If so, what are they?

3. Three of your central starting points ("Text messaging allows me to keep in touch . . . ," "Text messaging may create bad habits of passivity . . . ," "Text messaging does not allow emotions to be heard . . .") appear to deal with human emotions and their relationships to text messaging. Is this relationship between human emotions and text messaging something you find interesting and want to further explore? If so, how?

Instruction #2 for the Writer: After the reader asks you a question about your central, starting points, start talking. While you want to try to remember the supporting details (coded in the example above in italics), do not hesitate to speak on new thoughts that you are having.

Below, we have provided samples of what a writer might say in response to each of the above reader/recorder questions.

1. Well, I mean, text messaging may not definitely create bad habits that cause you to miss out on human interaction. At times, it could actually help you resolve something that might be tough to talk out with someone—like if you were in an argument with that person or something. Then, it might be easier for some people to text. But then again, text messag-

ing is passive in some ways and does not allow you to talk with that person face to face. However, text messaging could be something that two friends use who live apart as a way to stay in touch because they can't have human interaction due to geographical distance. So yea, I guess I used "may" to make sure I was not taking a decided stance on it. I'm still thinking through it, you know?

2. Well, I mean text messaging can also be considered a type of reading that is a form of communication as well. You have to be able to know what certain things like "lol" mean in order to understand what you are reading in texts. Otherwise, you will not be able to respond to the person sending you the text. The reading you have to do in instant messaging and text messaging is really similar—you have to know the codes to use, right? And you can just keep on texting or instant messaging without all the awkward silences.

3. Yea, I find that pretty interesting. I mean, text messaging can have certain inside jokes in it, but you don't get to hear someone's voice when texting. Also, you don't get to give someone a high five, handshake, or hug. But yet, texting does allow you to keep in touch with some people far away from you. And texting is so much easier to use when trying to communicate with some friends rather than calling or visiting, know what I mean?

Instruction #2 for the Reader/Recorder: Write down what the writer is telling you about the question you asked, recording as much as you can on a sheet of paper. After you have finished taking notes, look back over what the writer has given you as supporting points (coded in the example above in italics) in his/her highlighted bulleted list. Check off ones that are mentioned by the writer. Then hand back the original paper with your check marks.

If you look at the samples above (under subheading Instruction #2 for the Writer), you would most likely place check marks next to the following ideas that were original supporting points of the writer. While you would not have written everything the writer said word by word, your notes should be able to provide you with his/her original, supporting points. These are listed below from the sample, and you could place check marks by them.

1. missing out on human interaction

2. avoiding weird silences

3. you can't hear someone's voice when texting, but you can keep in touch with those that live far away

Instruction #3 for Writer: Look through the recorded notes your reader/recorder took about what you referred to in regards to the question the reader/recorder asked. Reflect on what you may have talked about that was originally not on your list.

Here, if you refer back to the samples above of the writer talking aloud (under subheading Instruction #2 for the Writer), you can see that much new information has been generated. Once again, the sample is not as detailed as what the reader/recorder would have written down. However, you should still be able to look through what the reader/recorder hands back and see new information that you generated while talking aloud. In our examples, this new information is listed below:

1. text messaging might help you resolve something with someone else such as an argument

2. reading is another form of text messaging communication, and you have to know the code of texting in order to read it

3. text messaging can have certain inside jokes in it between people that are close

Now make sure to switch your roles as writers and readers/recorders once so each of you can have the benefit of this exercise.

You will uncover more specific supportive details in this invention exercise. You also may find that talking freely about your starting, central idea(s) can push you towards encountering new supportive details that come about from physical dialogue with a peer who is asking questions about your ideas. As bell hooks points out in recalling salient moments of her past, you can ignite productive reflection on ideas through talking them over with someone else.

In openly dialoguing with and also listening to a partner during this process, you will actively invent new supporting ideas as well as reinforce ones you find important about your topic. Talking through the ideas that come to mind as you dialogue with your partner is a way to experience more spontaneous invention. On the other hand, in asking questions and listening to a partner as he/she speaks, you are helping someone else invent—much like the diverse tools did for DeWitt's father as he invented. In participating in invention that is collaborative, you are giving your writing peer support as he/she generates new ideas. This activity situates invention as a social, interactive process that can help you see many different directions you can take with a subject in your writing.

Reflection

In looking back over your experiences as both a writer and reader/recorder, it will be helpful to reflect on what you learned in your dialogue process. We have found it useful for students to spend time writing about their ideas after talking them over with someone. Here are some questions you might consider asking as a writer:

1. What did you learn from verbalizing your ideas?

2. How might dialogue enable you to conceptualize and organize the structure for an essay topic?

Conclusion

When student writers are given the space and tools to be critical thinkers and writers, we have learned that they have a greater stake in the knowledge that they produce, recognizing their value as contributing members of the university. Invention in the writing process is not just about exploring ways into your writing, it is about also developing new ideas within ongoing academic conversations in an intellectual community. The strategies we offer for writing invention are by no means to be seen as individual, exclusive exercises in and of themselves. We have arranged them in sequence so that you might understand invention as a process of taking practical steps that work collectively in developing your reading and writing skills. As a college writer, you will find that not all conversations are alike; some require you to use a repertoire of rhetorical moves that are less formulaic and more complex. We hope that this chapter has demonstrated writing as an ongoing process of discovery, where developing multiple approaches to analyzing texts in your reading process also provides you the opportunity to learn multiple invention strategies for writing effectively.

DISCUSSION

1. How have you generally started your own writing assignments? What worked and didn't work for you? Are there any ideas you have for invention in writing that are not in this chapter that you would like to add? What are they, and do you think they could help other students?

2. Out of the new invention strategies you have learned in this chapter, which do you think would be most helpful as you transition into writing in higher education? Why do you think the invention strategy you choose would work well and in what way do you see yourself using it?

WORKS CITED

Anzaldua, Gloria. *Borderlands/La Frontera: The New Mestiza*. Aunt Lute Books, 1999.

DeWitt, Scott Lloyd. *Writing Inventions: Identities, Technologies, Pedagogies*. New York: SUNY P, 2001.

Elbow, Peter. *Writing With Power: Techniques for Mastering the Writing Process*. NewYork: Oxford UP, 1981.

hooks, bell. *Remembered Rapture: The Writer at Work*. New York: Henry and Holt Co.,1999.

Why Visit Your Campus Writing Center?

Ben Rafoth

There is something about the experience of speaking with someone one-on-one—the facial expressions, enunciations, gestures—that makes us feel alive and energized.* Who we talk with can matter more than the topic itself, but either way most people love a good conversation. Among strangers traveling through an airport or waiting in a doctor's office, words seem to gather like stones in a pool. People gravitate to conversations so naturally that they make time and travel far to experience them. When time is short and travel impractical, people buy conversations by the minute.

Conversation is the key idea behind writing centers, and it's the number one reason why it pays to visit your campus writing center. Writing is too hard to do alone, and writing center tutors can help. I asked several tutors from different writing centers to tell me how students benefit from the writing center, and I hope you will find what they said as convincing as I did.

Talking It Up

Every day, tens of thousands of students across the U.S. and around the world walk into (or go online for) their campus writing center, many

---

* This work is licensed under the Creative Commons Attribution-Noncommercial-Share Alike 3.0 United States License and is subject to the Writing Spaces Terms of Use. To view a copy of this license, visit http://creativecommons.org/licenses/by-nc-sa/3.0/us/ or send a letter to Creative Commons, 171 Second Street, Suite 300, San Francisco, California, 94105, USA. To view the Writing Spaces Terms of Use, visit http://writingspaces.org/terms-of-use.

for the first time. They usually say something like, "I need someone to look at my paper." They don't literally mean they want someone to look at the paper and that's all. They want someone to spend time with them, read the paper carefully, show appreciation, and say what they think about it. They also don't merely want to hear what a tutor thinks about the paper. They want to ask questions, explain what they've written, and see how the tutor reacts. They want a conversation that revolves around questions such as:

> What do you think about my paper? Is it any good? What do you think my instructor and my classmates will think about it? Does it need to be improved? And how would I go about that?

A conversation develops around these and other questions, writer and tutor sitting in chairs or on a couch, pages fanned out on the table before them. The tutor might invite the writer to read the paper aloud, but that's not a requirement; tutors also like to read the paper silently and absorb its content, structure, and stylistic nuances.

Reflecting back on her senior year as a tutor at Niles West High School's Literacy Center in Chicago, Susan Borkowski told me,

> I quickly learned that a tutoring session is mostly about asking questions. Writing is a way to communicate thoughts. It follows naturally that in order to produce good writing, we have to start by stimulating our minds to think deeply about our topics. So often we *think* we've pushed our minds to the limit and can't see a way to make a thesis any deeper or more complex . . . until someone asks a question about it. We *think* we've explained ourselves as much as we can because we are only thinking about it in a limited way. But when someone else asks a question, we start talking out loud and soon we find that we're thinking in completely different ways about a concept we thought we had already flushed out completely.

Susan tutored her classmates in a place where every day, hundreds of students stop by on their own to write and read and talk and listen. Literacy Center tutors would be the first to acknowledge that not everyone leaves one hundred percent satisfied, but the many students who keep coming back for help says something about the good things that happen there. Could these students do as well by themselves, sitting alone in front of a computer and waiting for inspiration? I tell my students to try it sometime, and when that doesn't work, visit the writing center.

Tutors try to focus on things that are important to the writer: the challenge of the assignment, the ideas there seem to be no words for, the little editing stuff that attracts red ink. Tutors encourage writers to take notes and start writing when the ideas begin to flow. Tutors are usually paid by the hour, so they'll wait while you write. The important thing is to build enough momentum so that when you go home to finish the paper, you'll already be on a roll.

Anthony, a first-year undergraduate from Philadelphia, had been coming to the Writing Center at Indiana University of Pennsylvania, where I teach, three to four times per week to write a rhetorical analysis for his freshman writing class. At first, he only wanted help in finding examples to illustrate logos, ethos, and pathos in an article he was assigned to read. It was a good session, and Anthony got the examples he wanted. Then he told his tutor that this was a hard assignment because all of the examples in the article seemed to fit more than one element. This observation might have ended then and there, but his tutor urged him to say more about the overlap. They talked for another fifteen minutes or so, and on his next paper, Anthony focused on the overlap in his thesis, claiming that logos, ethos, and pathos are not distinct elements in persuasive writing. Anthony was one of the few students in the class who wrote about the overlap, and when the instructor read his paper aloud in class, he looked pretty smart. He thought of the overlap on his own, but it took a conversation with a tutor to see how he could go in that direction and still stay within guidelines of the assignment.

When I asked tutors why they believe students benefit from visiting the writing center, it would have been perfect if they had all said, "It's the quality of the conversations we have here" because that's my thesis. Instead, they gave richer and more interesting answers. One wrote to me from a pool where he was lifeguarding, another wrote during downtime while working at the writing center, and another used a mobile phone on the road. All responses exuded the passion that leaps out from people who are totally committed to what they do, whether they make any money at it or not.

Daniel Phillips tutors in the Writing Studio at the Fashion Institute of Technology in Manhattan. Anyone who has ever seriously considered a career with Armani or Chanel or Claiborne would soon find that FIT is the first step to landing a job with these top tier design houses, and while there they learn that fashion designers spend a lot of time writing. Daniel said:

> When I sit down with a student for the first time, there's always a brief and slightly awkward introduction, and then we talk for a few minutes about their major, what they do, their assignment, the food they're eating hurriedly ("I'm so sorry, but I never get time for lunch"). And then for me comes the challenge. This is a new person. I have no idea how they learn, what works for them, if I should speak more or sit and listen, if I should focus on their grammar or on making the subject of their essay more focused and apparent. For you the student, it is a game of expectation. You want us to help you with your writing, probably. For us, it is a matter of pedagogy, the way we can teach you what you're asking to learn, but without simply laying it out for you to gather up. Sometimes in a session, I make almost no statements. I simply ask questions. We are not so much tutors as we are a presence that encourages you to write, to question your own logic, to revise, to reconsider.

How does it happen, this conversation that leads to better writing? There are many ways, but it starts with getting ideas out of your head, through your lips, and into someone else's head. When you verbalize something you have been thinking, several things happen:

- You hear what you just said and how it sounds, as if you were hearing someone else say it.
- The tutor hears what you said, and you have to respect their need to make sense of it.
- Once you speak, you become motivated to listen to what the other person says—because you started it.

- Once you both speak, there is momentum to keep going and to influence what comes next, or not. You can sit back, or disengage. It's up to you.
- Both of you have fired neurons in your brains that change what is in your heads.

Each of these has consequences for thinking and writing. Erica Bazemore, a tutor at the University of Iowa, pinpoints some of the consequences when she says: "I have had numerous occasions when I couldn't quite put into words what I wanted to say, and it only took a conversation with a professor or a colleague in my department to help me put on to paper what I have been grappling with in my head." Founded in 1934 by a professor of Communications, Iowa's Writing Center may be the first center in the nation. Working at a place with such a long and distinguished history of helping students to write, Erica understands the relationship between conversation and writing.

FINDING CONFIDENCE

Students go to the writing center not only because they are looking for ways to put their thoughts into words but also because they want reassurance. Daniel Phillips, the FIT tutor, wrote, "Sometimes we are there to tell you how good your writing already is (and it probably is already pretty good) and that you don't need to change much at all. It's different with every student and every session." I've never met anyone who went to a writing center to feel bad about themselves; there's ninth grade for that. Hearing that your writing is good and that you don't need to change what you have written is actually quite valuable.

Yecca Zeng, at FIT, told me,

> I can see an instant confidence arise when students walk through the door and find other students with whom they may discuss any idea, any step, any type of writing that they may be having trouble with. When students realize their peers are the ones who are helping, it is easier for them to relax and be more outgoing and elaborate on exactly what they want to accomplish.

Sometimes tutors can cure a case of cold feet, as when students invest time in a topic and even write most of their paper before they decide to change the topic and write about something else. Such last-minute, impulsive topic changes are usually a mistake. Most students would be better off if they had had the confidence to keep what they had written and sought input from others about how to revise it. "I have not come near to outgrowing the need to share my writing with a responsive, receptive person who can provide feedback and engage me in a discussion about how to move forward with revision," said Sam Van Horne of the University of Iowa.

On the east coast, at Loyola University in Baltimore, Paige Godfrey put it this way:

> Ever since I started working in the writing center, I have had a student who always requests a consultation with me. Being that there are so many wonderful consultants in the writing center, I always questioned what it was that made this student a "regular." At the end of the semester, the student pulled me aside to thank me for all that I had done to help her throughout the year. She stated that the most helpful thing I had done for her was make her feel more confident about her writing. Rather than pointing out the areas that needed improvement, I like to focus on the areas full of strength and work off of them to improve the weaker areas. There is no doubt that many students need improvement with their papers—I am certainly not Shakespeare myself. However, if you show them their own potential, it allows them to look deeper inside themselves as writers and grow from it.

For many people, the hardest part is showing their writing to someone else.

According to a popular website for health information, WebMD (http://www.webmd.com/anxiety-panic/guide/mental-health-social-anxiety-disorder), the most common situations in which people feel anxiety due to potentially negative judgments from others are:

- Eating or drinking in front of others
- Being the center of attention

- Interacting with people, including dating or going to parties
- Asking questions or giving reports in groups
- Using public toilets
- Talking on the telephone
- Writing or working in front of others

Most people are okay with toilets and telephones, but who hasn't experienced writing anxiety? The important thing is to reduce the feeling of vulnerability. Here is the University of Iowa's Erica Bazemore again:

> The ability to share something as personal as a piece of writing can be a daunting task for some students, but getting into the habit of not only sharing writing, but having someone respond to it can help to make someone a more confident writer. In addition, face-to-face communication through writing and speaking can help people develop effective ways of self-expression and comfortable ways of communicating with each other. Our society is becoming increasingly less personal on the level of language and through our daily interactions, but writing centers have a built-in mechanism to counter this trend. The writing center is a place for taking the abstract and making it concrete. It is a place for collaboration, sharing, expression, and empowerment.

For a few students, visiting a writing center feels like admitting they are not good enough to be in the course they're taking. I spoke to one of the graduate student tutors in my writing center, Motasim Almwaja, an excellent writer from Jordan who is cautious about what he says and writes in front of his friends from the Middle East because he does not want to appear foolish. (He had to remind me that even in soccer, accepting defeat in his culture is not an option.) For him, strength vs. weakness is a matter of how you look at it. Motasim has worked very hard to perfect his English, constantly memorizing words and phrases and then using them when he speaks and writes. He points out that instead of admitting a weakness, going to the writing center shows strength and the resolve to work for what you want.

When you share your writing with a tutor, you can be pretty sure the tutor is not going to laugh at your writing (unless you write comedy) or criticize your paper. They've seen it all and are not interested in judging you or your ideas. They will help you to discover something good about your writing that you can build on. They want to see you succeed because helping students to write is their job.

A Sense of Audience

A writing center can help students to refine their sense of audience so that they better understand how readers will respond to their writing. Acquiring this sense of audience is a bit mysterious because it depends a lot on experience. When a comedian causes an audience to convulse in laughter about ordinary things that happen to everyone, it's the comedian's keen sense of audience and timing that makes the jokes so hilarious.

Great comedians make telling jokes only seem effortless; we don't see the hours of preparation, false starts, and flops that preceded it— all things they probably relied on teachers and coaches to overcome. Tutors seem to understand that writing a good paper is a team effort. The part that tutors contribute as readers is crucial because they draw writers outside of themselves to see the paper as others are likely to see it. This is a hard thing to do on one's own. We tend to steep in our own thoughts. But a tutor stands apart, reading the draft with fresh eyes and pointing out the gaps the writer needs to fill so that ideas flow smoothly. Over time, writers learn to read their writing from the perspective of their readers by internalizing the responses of tutors and replaying them in their heads when they write the next time. We all develop a sense of audience, but we never outgrow the need for someone else's fresh eyes. Mike Czajkowski, an undergraduate at Illinois Wesleyan University in Bloomington, Indiana, told me,

> I do think it is important to seek another pair of experienced eyes when writing a paper, especially an academic one. I generally go see a professor I'm comfortable discussing my writing with, who knows my style really well, or I see a friend whose writing and opinion I trust (generally in the same class as me). I think it's important because we need to realize we

aren't writing those papers for ourselves, so we should inherently seek anything that allows us to see a paper outside of our own bias toward it.

I also heard from Marisa Martin, whose writing center shares its mission with her college's Jesuit tradition. The mission states: "In the Jesuit tradition of working with others to reach a common goal, the Loyola Writing Center understands that writing requires input from others. The Loyola Writing Center offers consulting for the entire Loyola community of writers, including undergraduate and graduate students, as well as faculty and staff." Working with others to reach a common goal is also what Marisa wanted me to know: "We are sounding boards for the fears and anxiety of writing. We are there to give writers tools to work through these situations and to give them tips to work it out on their own next time." Working together improves the chances of working independently. Marisa and her colleagues believe they can help students enough that they will be able to succeed on their own.

Getting What You Need

So why visit the writing center? If I had to boil down what I have tried to convey here, I would say students should visit the writing center because:

- Writing isn't easy and tutors can help. (It's pretty basic.)
- Tutors are able to discuss writing in a way that moves you forward. They create idea-rich conversations.
- Writing centers instill confidence that you are on the right track, or help you get there if you're not.
- Writers need readers.

I think these are sound reasons, but some readers may wonder why it has to be a writing center tutor and not a roommate or a gym buddy. Listen to Kelly Ruth Anderson, a tutor at the University of Iowa. I asked her the same question I asked the others, "Why do you believe students should visit the writing center?" For her answer, she posed a slightly different question: "Why do students visit the writing center?" She pointed out that what people should do and what they actually do are often quite different. I like her answer because it demonstrates one of the ways that tutors are trained to help writers: when given an assignment, they turn it to the writer's advantage. Kelly told me:

> Why *do* students visit the Writing Center? For all the wonderful talk about "becoming a better writer," most of my tutees visit the WC—at least initially—out of a sense of real and tangible need. *My teacher said that I need better transitions. English isn't my first language, and I need help with grammar. I need an "A"—how can I get an A on this paper?* And I'm not sure that I can blame students for acting out of these specific needs—we seem to be a pretty results-driven society, and many students overlook the role that writing can play in their future lives. (So why bother with some lofty, perhaps seemingly insurmountable, goal like "becoming a better writer"?) In other words, I can give students the "real" reason to visit the Writing Center—to become a better writer—but I'm not sure that answer will *actually get them to visit the writing Center.*

Kelly eventually answered the question I had asked, but first she said something she felt was just as important. This was a wise move, one that elevated her idea and made it memorable. Kelly knew what I had asked, but first she told me what I needed to hear. Writing center tutors do the same thing, and Kelly's response is a reflection of this. Tutors and teachers know that everybody wants to receive good grades on their papers. But grades are the end product of what you do to earn them. If Kelly were your tutor and you didn't know what to write in response to a question on an assignment, she could help you to see the question in a different light that would show you a different path to take. She cannot give you the A you want, but she can give you the idea you need.

Learning to write is not a uniformly warm fuzzy experience, but it can lead to some of the best encounters you will have in school—with tutors in the writing center who are there just to help.

Finding the Good Argument OR
Why Bother With Logic?

Rebecca Jones

The word argument often means something negative.[*] In Nina Paley's cartoon (see Figure 1), the argument is literally a cat fight. Rather than envisioning argument as something productive and useful, we imagine intractable sides and use descriptors such as "bad," "heated," and "violent." We rarely say, "Great, argument. Thanks!" Even when we write an academic "argument paper," we imagine our own ideas battling others.

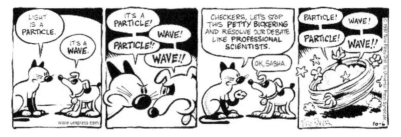

Figure 1. This cartoon demonstrates the absurdity of either/or arguments. (© 1997-1998 Nina Paley. Image available under a Creative Commons Attribution-Share Alike license.[1]

156

Linguists George Lakoff and Mark Johnson explain that the controlling metaphor we use for argument in western culture is war:

> It is important to see that we don't just *talk* about arguments in terms of war. We actually win or lose arguments. We see the person we are arguing with as an opponent. We attack his positions and we defend our own. We gain and lose ground. We plan and use strategies. If we find a position indefensible, we can abandon it and take a new line of attack. Many of the things we *do* in arguing are partially structured by the concept of war. (4)

If we follow the war metaphor along its path, we come across other notions such as, "all's fair in love and war." If all's fair, then the rules, principles, or ethics of an argument are up for grabs. While many warrior metaphors are about honor, the "all's fair" idea can lead us to arguments that result in propaganda, spin, and, dirty politics. The war metaphor offers many limiting assumptions: there are only two sides, someone must win decisively, and compromise means losing. The metaphor also creates a false opposition where argument (war) is action and its opposite is peace or inaction. Finding better arguments is not about finding peace—the opposite of antagonism. Quite frankly, getting mad can be productive. Ardent peace advocates, such as Jane Addams, Mahatma Gandhi, and Martin Luther King, Jr., offer some of the most compelling arguments of our time through concepts like civil disobedience that are hardly inactive. While "argument is war" may be the default mode for Americans, it is not the only way to argue. Lakoff and Johnson ask their readers to imagine something like "argument is dance" rather than "argument is war" (5). While we can imagine many alternatives to the war metaphor, concepts like argument as collaboration are more common even if they are not commonly used. Argument as collaboration would be more closely linked to words such as *dialogue* and *deliberation*, cornerstone concepts in the history of American democracy.

However, argument as collaboration is not the prevailing metaphor for public argumentation we see/hear in the mainstream media. One can hardly fault the average American for not being able to imagine argument beyond the war metaphor. Think back to the coverage of the last major election cycle in 2008. The opponents on either side (democrat/republican) dug in their heels and defended every position, even if it was unpopular or irrelevant to the conversation at hand. The political landscape divided into two sides with no alternatives. In addition to the entrenched positions, blogs and websites such as FactCheck.org flooded us with lists of inaccuracies, missteps, and plain old fallacies that riddled the debates. Unfortunately, the "debates" were more like speeches given to a camera than actual arguments deliberated before the public. These important moments that fail to offer good models lower the standards for public argumentation.

On an average news day, there are entire websites and blogs dedicated to noting ethical, factual, and legal problems with public arguments, especially on the news and radio talk shows. This is not to say that all public arguments set out to mislead their audiences, rather that the discussions they offer masquerading as arguments are often merely opinions or a spin on a particular topic and not carefully considered, quality arguments. What is often missing from these discussions is research, consideration of multiple vantage points, and, quite often, basic logic.

On news shows, we encounter a version of argument that seems more like a circus than a public discussion. Here's the visual we get of an "argument" between multiple sides on the average news show. In this example (see Figure 2), we have a four ring circus.

While all of the major networks use this visual format, multiple speakers in multiple windows like *The Brady Bunch* for the news, it is rarely used to promote ethical deliberation. These talking heads offer a simulation of an argument. The different windows and figures pictured in them are meant to represent different views on a topic, often "liberal" and "conservative." This is a good start because it sets up the possibility for thinking through serious issues in need of solutions. Unfortunately, the people in the windows never actually engage in an argument (see Thinking Outside the Text). As we will discuss below, one of the rules of good argument is that participants in an argument agree on the primary standpoint and that individuals are willing to concede if a point of view is proven wrong. If you watch one of these "arguments," you will see a spectacle where prepared speeches are hurled across the long distances that separate the participants. Rarely do the talking heads respond to the actual ideas/arguments given by the person pictured in the box next to them on the screen unless it is to contradict one statement with another of their own. Even more

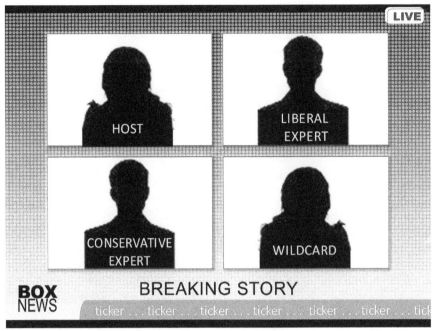

Figure 2. This mock up of a typical news show created by Colin Charlton offers a visual of the attempt to offer many "sides" of an argument.

troubling is the fact that participants do not even seem to agree about the point of disagreement. For example, one person might be arguing about the congressional vote on health care while another is discussing the problems with Medicaid. While these are related, they are different issues with different premises. This is not a good model for argumentation despite being the predominant model we encounter.

Activity: Thinking Outside the Text

Watch the famous video of Jon Stewart on the show Crossfire: (http://www.youtube.com/watch?v=vmj6JADOZ-8).

- What is Stewart's argument?
- How do the hosts of Crossfire respond to the very particular argument that Stewart makes?
- Why exactly are they missing the point?

These shallow public models can influence argumentation in the classroom. One of the ways we learn about argument is to think in

terms of pro and con arguments. This replicates the liberal/conserva-
tive dynamic we often see in the papers or on television (as if there
are only two sides to health care, the economy, war, the deficit). This
either/or fallacy of public argument is debilitating. You are either for
or against gun control, for or against abortion, for or against the environment, for or against everything. Put this way, the absurdity is more
obvious. For example, we assume that someone who claims to be an
"environmentalist" is pro every part of the green movement. However,
it is quite possible to develop an environmentally sensitive argument
that argues against a particular recycling program. While many pro
and con arguments are valid, they can erase nuance, negate the local
and particular, and shut down the very purpose of having an argument: the possibility that you might change your mind, learn something new, or solve a problem. This limited view of argument makes
argumentation a shallow process. When all angles are not explored or
fallacious or incorrect reasoning is used, we are left with ethically sus-
pect public discussions that cannot possibly get at the roots of an issue
or work toward solutions.

Activity: Finding Middle Ground

Outline the pro and con arguments for the following issues:

1. Gun Control
2. Cap and Trade
3. Free Universal Healthcare

In a group, develop an argument that finds a compromise or middle
ground between two positions.

Rather than an either/or proposition, argument is multiple and
complex. An argument can be logical, rational, emotional, fruitful,
useful, and even enjoyable. As a matter of fact, the idea that argument
is necessary (and therefore not always about war or even about winning) is an important notion in a culture that values democracy and
equity. In America, where nearly everyone you encounter has a different background and/or political or social view, skill in arguing seems
to be paramount, whether you are inventing an argument or recognizing a good one when you see it.

The remainder of this chapter takes up this challenge—inventing and recognizing good arguments (and bad ones). From classical

rhetoric, to Toulmin's model, to contemporary pragma-dialectics, this chapter presents models of argumentation beyond pro and con. Paying more addition to the details of an argument can offer a strategy for developing sound, ethically aware arguments.

What Can We Learn from Models of Argumentation?

So far, I have listed some obstacles to good argument. I would like to discuss one other. Let's call it the mystery factor. Many times I read an argument and it seems great on the surface, but I get a strange feeling that something is a bit off. Before studying argumentation, I did not have the vocabulary to name that strange feeling. Additionally, when an argument is solid, fair, and balanced, I could never quite put my finger on what distinguished it from other similar arguments. The models for argumentation below give us guidance in revealing the mystery factor and naming the qualities of a logical, ethical argument.

Classical Rhetoric

In James Murphy's translation of Quintilian's *Institutio Oratoria*, he explains that "Education for Quintilian begins in the cradle, and ends only when life itself ends" (xxi). The result of a life of learning, for Quintilian, is a perfect speech where "the student is given a statement of a problem and asked to prepare an appropriate speech giving his solution" (Murphy xxiii). In this version of the world, a good citizen is always a PUBLIC participant. This forces the good citizen to know the rigors of public argumentation: "Rhetoric, or the theory of effective communication, is for Quintilian merely the tool of the broadly educated citizen who is capable of analysis, reflection, and powerful action in public affairs" (Murphy xxvii). For Quintilian, learning to argue in public is a lifelong affair. He believed that the "perfect orator . . . cannot exist unless he is above all a good man" (6). Whether we agree with this or not, the hope for ethical behavior has been a part of public argumentation from the beginning.

The ancient model of rhetoric (or public argumentation) is complex. As a matter of fact, there is no single model of ancient argumentation. Plato claimed that the Sophists, such as Gorgias, were spin doctors weaving opinion and untruth for the delight of an audience

and to the detriment of their moral fiber. For Plato, at least in the
Phaedrus, public conversation was only useful if one applied it to the
search for truth. In the last decade, the work of the Sophists has been
redeemed. Rather than spin doctors, Sophists like Isocrates and even
Gorgias, to some degree, are viewed as arbiters of democracy because
they believed that many people, not just male, property holding, Athe-
nian citizens, could learn to use rhetoric effectively in public.

Aristotle gives us a slightly more systematic approach. He is very
concerned with logic. For this reason, much of what I discuss below
comes from his work. Aristotle explains that most men participate
in public argument in some fashion. It is important to note that by
"men," Aristotle means citizens of Athens: adult males with the right
to vote, not including women, foreigners, or slaves. Essentially this is a
homogenous group by race, gender, and religious affiliation. We have
to keep this in mind when adapting these strategies to our current het-
erogeneous culture. Aristotle explains,

> . . . for to a certain extent all men attempt to discuss
> statements and to maintain them, to defend them-
> selves and to attack others. Ordinary people do this
> either at random or through practice and from ac-
> quired habit. Both ways being possible, the subject
> can plainly be handled systematically, for it is pos-
> sible to inquire the reason why some speakers suc-
> ceed through practice and others spontaneously; and
> every one will at once agree that such an inquiry is
> the function of an art. (Honeycutt, "Aristotle's *Rheto-
> ric*" 1354a I i)

For Aristotle, inquiry into this field was artistic in nature. It
required both skill and practice (some needed more of one
than the other). Important here is the notion that public argument can be systematically learned.

Aristotle did not dwell on the ethics of an argument in *Rhetoric*
(he leaves this to other texts). He argued that "things that are true and
things that are just have a natural tendency to prevail over their op-
posites" and finally that " . . . things that are true and things that are
better are, by their nature, practically always easier to prove and easier
to believe in" (Honeycutt, "Aristotle's Rhetoric" 1355a I i). As a cul-

ture, we are skeptical of this kind of position, though I think that we do often believe it on a personal level. Aristotle admits in the next line that there are people who will use their skills at rhetoric for harm. As his job in this section is to defend the use of rhetoric itself, he claims that everything good can be used for harm, so rhetoric is no different from other fields. If this is true, there is even more need to educate the citizenry so that they will not be fooled by unethical and untruthful arguments.

For many, logic simply means reasoning. To understand a person's logic, we try to find the structure of their reasoning. Logic is not synonymous with fact or truth, though facts are part of evidence in logical argumentation. You can be logical without being truthful. This is why more logic is not the only answer to better public argument.

Our human brains are compelled to categorize the world as a survival mechanism. This survival mechanism allows for quicker thought. Two of the most basic logical strategies include inductive and deductive reasoning. **Deductive reasoning** (see Figure 3) starts from a premise that is a generalization about a large class of ideas, people, etc. and moves to a specific conclusion about a smaller category of ideas or things (All cats hate water; therefore, my neighbor's cat will not jump in our pool). While the first premise is the most general, the second premise is a more particular observation. So the argument is created through common beliefs/observations that are compared to create an argument. For example:

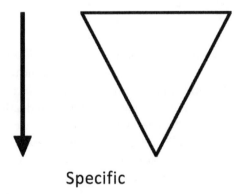

Figure 3. Deductive Reasoning

People who burn flags are unpatriotic. **Major Premise**
Sara burned a flag. **Minor Premise**
Sara is unpatriotic. **Conclusion**

The above is called a syllogism. As we can see in the example, the major premise offers a general belief held by some groups and the minor premise is a particular observation. The conclusion is drawn by comparing the premises and developing a conclusion. If you work hard enough, you can often take a complex argument and boil it down to a syllogism. This can reveal a great deal about the argument that is not apparent in the longer more complex version.

Stanley Fish, professor and *New York Times* columnist, offers the following syllogism in his July 22, 2007, blog entry titled "Democracy and Education": "The syllogism underlying these comments is (1) America is a democracy (2) Schools and universities are situated within that democracy (3) Therefore schools and universities should be ordered and administrated according to democratic principles."

Fish offered the syllogism as a way to summarize the responses to his argument that students do not, in fact, have the right to free speech in a university classroom. The responses to Fish's standpoint were vehemently opposed to his understanding of free speech rights and democracy. The responses are varied and complex. However, boiling them down to a single syllogism helps to summarize the primary rebuttal so that Fish could then offer his extended version of his standpoint (see link to argument in Question #1 at the end of the text).

Inductive reasoning moves in a different direction than deductive reasoning (see Figure 4). Inductive reasoning starts with a particular or local statement and moves to a more general conclusion. I think of inductive reasoning as a stacking of evidence. The more particular examples you give, the more it seems that your conclusion is correct.

Inductive reasoning is a common method for arguing, especially when the conclusion is an obvious probability. Inductive reasoning is the most common way that we move around in the world. If we experience something habitually, we reason that it will happen again. For example, if we walk down a city street and every person smiles, we might reason that this is a "nice town." This seems logical. We have taken many similar, particular experiences (smiles) and used them to make a general conclusion (the people in the town are nice). Most of the time,

Specific

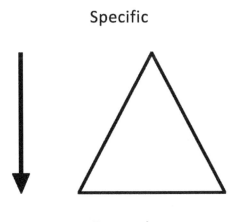

General

Figure 4. Inductive Reasoning

this reasoning works. However, we know that it can also lead us in the wrong direction. Perhaps the people were smiling because we were wearing inappropriate clothing (country togs in a metropolitan city), or perhaps only the people living on that particular street are "nice" and the rest of the town is unfriendly. Research papers sometimes rely too heavily on this logical method. Writers assume that finding ten versions of the same argument somehow prove that the point is true.

Here is another example. In Ann Coulter's most recent book, *Guilty: Liberal "Victims" and Their Assault on America*, she makes her (in)famous argument that single motherhood is the cause of many of America's ills. She creates this argument through a piling of evidence. She lists statistics by sociologists, she lists all the single moms who killed their children, she lists stories of single mothers who say outrageous things about their life, children, or marriage in general, and she ends with a list of celebrity single moms that most would agree are not good examples of motherhood. Through this list, she concludes, "Look at almost any societal problem and you will find it is really a problem of single mothers" (36). While she could argue, from this evidence, that being a single mother is difficult, the generalization that single motherhood is the root of social ills in America takes the inductive reasoning too far. Despite this example, we need inductive reasoning because it is the key to analytical thought (see Activity: Applying

Inductive and Deductive Reasoning). To write an "analysis paper" is to use inductive reasoning.

Activity: Applying Deductive and Inductive Reasoning

For each standpoint, create a deductive argument AND an inductive argument. When you are finished, share with your group members and decide which logical strategy offers a more successful, believable, and/or ethical argument for the particular standpoint. Feel free to modify the standpoint to find many possible arguments.

1. a. Affirmative Action should continue to be legal in the United States.

    b. Affirmative Action is no longer useful in the United States.

2. The arts should remain an essential part of public education.

3. Chose a very specific argument on your campus (parking, tuition, curriculum) and create deductive and inductive arguments to support the standpoint.

Most academic arguments in the humanities are inductive to some degree. When you study humanity, nothing is certain. When observing or making inductive arguments, it is important to get your evidence from many different areas, to judge it carefully, and acknowledge the flaws. Inductive arguments must be judged by the quality of the evidence since the conclusions are drawn directly from a body of compiled work.

THE APPEALS

"The appeals" offer a lesson in rhetoric that sticks with you long after the class has ended. Perhaps it is the rhythmic quality of the words (ethos, logos, pathos) or, simply, the usefulness of the concept. Aristotle imagined logos, ethos, and pathos as three kinds of artistic proof. Essentially, they highlight three ways to appeal to or persuade an audience: "(1) to reason logically, (2) to understand human character and goodness in its various forms, (3) to understand emotions" (Honeycutt, *Rhetoric* 1356a).

While Aristotle and others did not explicitly dismiss emotional and character appeals, they found the most value in logic. Contemporary rhetoricians and argumentation scholars, however, recognize the power of emotions to sway us. Even the most stoic individuals have some emotional threshold over which no logic can pass. For example, we can seldom be reasonable when faced with a crime against a loved one, a betrayal, or the face of an adorable baby.

The easiest way to differentiate the appeals is to imagine selling a product based on them. Until recently, car commercials offered a prolific source of logical, ethical, and emotional appeals.

Logos: Using logic as proof for an argument. For many students this takes the form of numerical evidence. But as we have discussed above, logical reasoning is a kind of argumentation.

> *Car Commercial:* (Syllogism) Americans love adventure—Ford Escape allows for off road adventure—Americans should buy a Ford Escape.
>
> OR
>
> The Ford Escape offers the best financial deal.

Ethos: Calling on particular shared values (patriotism), respected figures of authority (MLK), or one's own character as a method for appealing to an audience.

> *Car Commercial:* Eco-conscious Americans drive a Ford Escape.
>
> OR
>
> [Insert favorite movie star] drives a Ford Escape.

Pathos: Using emotionally driven images or language to sway your audience.

> *Car Commercial:* Images of a pregnant women being safely rushed to a hospital. Flash to two car seats in the back seat. Flash to family hopping out of their Ford Escape and witnessing the majesty of the Grand Canyon.
>
> OR

> After an image of a worried mother watching her six-
> teen year old daughter drive away: "Ford Escape takes
> the fear out of driving."

The appeals are part of everyday conversation, even if we do not use the Greek terminology (see Activity: Developing Audience Awareness). Understanding the appeals helps us to make better rhetorical choices in designing our arguments. If you think about the appeals as a choice, their value is clear.

Activity: Developing Audience Awareness

Imagine you have been commissioned by your school food service provider to create a presentation encouraging the consumption of healthier foods on campus.

1. How would you present this to your friends: consider the media you would use, how you present yourself, and how you would begin.

2. How would you present this same material to parents of incoming students?

3. Which appeal is most useful for each audience? Why?

Toulmin: Dissecting the Everyday Argument

Philosopher Stephen Toulmin studies the arguments we make in our everyday lives. He developed his method out of frustration with logicians (philosophers of argumentation) that studied argument in a vacuum or through mathematical formulations:

> All A are B.
> All B are C.

> Therefore, all A are C. (Eemeren, et al. 131)

Instead, Toulmin views argument as it appears in a conversation, in a letter, or some other context because real arguments are much more complex than the syllogisms that make up the bulk of Aristotle's logical program. Toulmin offers the contemporary writer/reader a way to map an argument. The result is a visualization of the argument process. This map comes complete with vocabulary for describing the parts of an argument. The vocabulary allows us to see the contours of the landscape—the winding rivers and gaping caverns. One way to think about a "good" argument is that it is a discussion that hangs together, a landscape that is cohesive (we can't have glaciers in our desert valley). Sometimes we miss the faults of an argument because it sounds good or appears to have clear connections between the statement and the evidence, when in truth the only thing holding the argument together is a lovely sentence or an artistic flourish.

For Toulmin, argumentation is an attempt to justify a statement or a set of statements. The better the demand is met, the higher the audience's appreciation. Toulmin's vocabulary for the study of argument offers labels for the parts of the argument to help us create our map.

> **Claim:** The basic standpoint presented by a writer/speaker.

> **Data:** The evidence which supports the claim.

> **Warrant:** The justification for connecting particular data to a particular claim. The warrant also makes clear the assumptions underlying the argument.

> **Backing:** Additional information required if the warrant is not clearly supported.

> **Rebuttal:** Conditions or standpoints that point out flaws in the claim or alternative positions.

> **Qualifiers:** Terminology that limits a standpoint. Examples include applying the following terms to any part of an argument: sometimes, seems, occasionally, none, always, never, etc.

The following paragraphs come from an article reprinted in UTNE magazine by Pamela Paxton and Jeremy Adam Smith titled: "Not Everyone Is Out to Get You." Charting this excerpt helps us to understand some of the underlying assumptions found in the article.

"Trust No One"

That was the slogan of *The X-Files,* the TV drama that followed two FBI agents on a quest to uncover a vast government conspiracy. A defining cultural phenomenon during its run from 1993–2002, the show captured a mood of growing distrust in America.

Since then, our trust in one another has declined even further. In fact, it seems that "Trust no one" could easily have been America's motto for the past 40 years—thanks to, among other things, Vietnam, Watergate, junk bonds, Monica Lewinsky, Enron, sex scandals in the Catholic Church, and the Iraq war.

The General Social Survey, a periodic assessment of Americans' moods and values, shows an 11-point decline from 1976–2008 in the number of Americans who believe other people can generally be trusted. Institutions haven't fared any better. Over the same period, trust has declined in the press (from 29 to 9 percent), education (38–29 percent), banks (41 percent to 20 percent), corporations (23–16 percent), and organized religion (33–20 percent). Gallup's 2008 governance survey showed that trust in the government was as low as it was during the Watergate era.

The news isn't all doom and gloom, however. A growing body of research hints that humans are hardwired to trust, which is why institutions, through reform and high performance, can still stoke feelings of loyalty, just as disasters and mismanagement can inhibit it. The catch is that while humans want, even need, to trust, they won't trust blindly and foolishly.

Figure 5 demonstrates one way to chart the argument that Paxton and Smith make in "Trust No One." The remainder of the article offers additional claims and data, including the final claim that there is hope for overcoming our collective trust issues. The chart helps us to see that some of the warrants, in a longer research project, might require additional support. For example, the warrant that TV mirrors real life is an argument and not a fact that would require evidence.

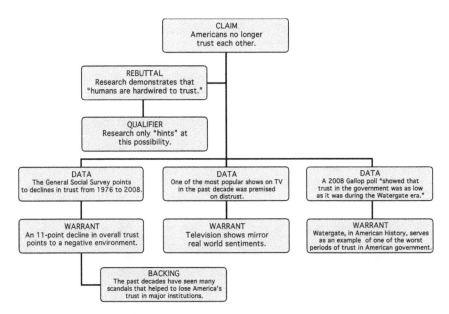

Figure 5. This chart demonstrates the utility of visualizing an argument.

Charting your own arguments and others helps you to visualize the meat of your discussion. All the flourishes are gone and the bones revealed. Even if you cannot fit an argument neatly into the boxes, the attempt forces you to ask important questions about your claim, your warrant, and possible rebuttals. By charting your argument you are forced to write your claim in a succinct manner and admit, for example, what you are using for evidence. Charted, you can see if your evidence is scanty, if it relies too much on one kind of evidence over another, and if it needs additional support. This charting might also reveal a disconnect between your claim and your warrant or cause you to reevaluate your claim altogether.

PRAGMA-DIALECTICS: A FANCY WORD FOR A CLOSE LOOK AT ARGUMENTATION

The field of rhetoric has always been interdisciplinary and so it has no problem including argumentation theory. Developed in the Speech Communication Department at the University of Amsterdam, pragma-dialectics is a study of argumentation that focuses on the ethics of one's logical choices in creating an argument. In *Fundamentals of Argumentation Theory: A Handbook of Historical Backgrounds and Contemporary Developments*, Frans H. van Eemeren and Rob Grootendorst describe argumentation, simply, as "characterized by the use of language for resolving a difference of opinion" (275). While much of this work quite literally looks at actual speech situations, the work can easily be applied to the classroom and to broader political situations.

While this version of argumentation deals with everything from ethics to arrangement, what this field adds to rhetorical studies is a new approach to argument fallacies. Fallacies are often the cause of the mystery feeling we get when we come across faulty logic or missteps in an argument.

What follows is an adaptation of Frans van Eemeren, Rob Grootendorst, and Francesca Snoeck Henkemans' "violations of the rules for critical engagement" from their book *Argumentation: Analysis, Evaluation, Presentation* (109). Rather than discuss rhetorical fallacies in a list (ad hominem, straw man, equivocation, etc.), they argue that there should be rules for proper argument to ensure fairness, logic, and a solution to the problem being addressed. Violating these rules causes a fallacious argument and can result in a standoff rather than a solution.

While fallacious arguments, if purposeful, pose real ethical problems, most people do not realize they are committing fallacies when they create an argument. To purposely attack someone's character rather than their argument (ad hominem) is not only unethical, but demonstrates lazy argumentation. However, confusing cause and effect might simply be a misstep that needs fixing. It is important to admit that many fallacies, though making an argument somewhat unsound, can be rhetorically savvy. While we know that appeals to pity (or going overboard on the emotional appeal) can often demonstrate a lack of knowledge or evidence, they often work. As such, these rules present argumentation as it would play out in a utopian world where everyone is calm and logical, where everyone cares about resolving the argument at hand, rather than winning the battle, and where everyone plays by the rules. Despite the utopian nature of the list, it offers valuable insight into argument flaws and offers hope for better methods of deliberation.

What follows is an adaptation of the approach to argumentation found in Chapters 7 and 8 of *Argumentation: Analysis, Evaluation, Pre-*

sentation (Eemeren, et al. 109-54). The rule is listed first, followed by an example of how the rule is often violated.

1. The Freedom Rule

"Parties must not prevent each other from putting forward standpoints or casting doubt on standpoints" (110).

There are many ways to stop an individual from giving her own argument. This can come in the form of a physical threat but most often takes the form of a misplaced critique. Instead of focusing on the argument, the focus is shifted to the character of the writer or speaker (ad hominem) or to making the argument (or author) seem absurd (straw man) rather than addressing its actual components. In the past decade, "Bush is stupid" became a common ad hominem attack that allowed policy to go unaddressed. To steer clear of the real issues of global warming, someone might claim "Only a fool would believe global warming is real" or "Trying to suck all of the CO_2 out of the atmosphere with giant greenhouse gas machines is mere science fiction, so we should look at abandoning all this green house gas nonsense."

2. The Burden-of-Proof Rule

"A party who puts forward a standpoint is obliged to defend it if asked to do so" (113).

This is one of my favorites. It is clear and simple. If you make an argument, you have to provide evidence to back it up. During the 2008 Presidential debates, Americans watched as all the candidates fumbled over the following question about healthcare: "How will this plan actually work?" If you are presenting a written argument, this requirement can be accommodated through quality, researched evidence applied to your standpoint.

3. The Standpoint Rule

"A party's attack on a standpoint must relate to the standpoint that has indeed been advanced by the other party" (116).

Your standpoint is simply your claim, your basic argument in a nutshell. If you disagree with another person's argument or they disagree with yours, the actual standpoint and not some related but more easily attacked issue must be addressed. For example, one person might argue that the rhetoric of global warming has created a multi-million dollar green industry benefiting from fears over climate change. This is an argument about the effects of global warming rhetoric, not global warming itself. It would break the standpoint rule to argue that the writer/speaker does not believe in global warming. This is not the issue at hand.

4. The Relevance Rule

"A party may defend his or her standpoint only by advancing argumentation related to that standpoint" (119).

Similar to #3, this rule assures that the evidence you use must actually relate to your standpoint. Let's stick with same argument: global warming has created a green industry benefiting from fears over climate change. Under this rule, your evidence would need to offer examples of the rhetoric and the resulting businesses that have developed since the introduction of green industries. It would break the rules to simply offer attacks on businesses who sell "eco-friendly" products.

5. The Unexpressed Premise Rule

"A party may not falsely present something as a premise that has been left unexpressed by the other party or deny a premise that he or she has left implicit" (121).

This one sounds a bit complex, though it happens nearly every day. If you have been talking to another person and feel the need to say, "That's NOT what I meant," then you have experienced a violation of the unexpressed premise rule. Overall, the rule attempts to keep the argument on track and not let it stray into irrelevant territory. The first violation of the rule, to falsely present what has been left unexpressed, is to rephrase someone's standpoint in a way that redirects the argument. One person might argue, "I love to go to the beach," and another might respond by saying "So you don't have any appreciation for mountain living." The other aspect of this rule is to camouflage an unpopular idea and deny that it is part of your argument. For example, you might argue that "I have nothing against my neighbors. I just think that there should be a noise ordinance in this part of town to help cut down on crime." This clearly shows that the writer does believe her neighbors to be criminals but won't admit it.

6. The Starting Point Rule

"No party may falsely present a premise as an accepted starting point, or deny a premise representing an accepted starting point" (128).

Part of quality argumentation is to agree on the opening stand-point. According to this theory, argument is pointless without this kind of agreement. It is well known that arguing about abortion is nearly pointless as long as one side is arguing about the rights of the unborn and the other about the rights of women. These are two different starting points.

7. The Argument Scheme Rule

"A standpoint may not be regarded as conclusively defended if the defense does not take place by means of an appropriate argument scheme that is correctly applied" (130).

This rule is about argument strategy. Argument schemes could take up another paper altogether. Suffice it to say that schemes are ways of approaching an argument, your primary strategy. For example, you might choose emotional rather than logical appeals to present your position. This rule highlights the fact that some argument strategies are simply better than others. For example, if you choose to create an argument based largely on attacking the character of your opponent rather than the issues at hand, the argument is moot.

Argument by analogy is a popular and well worn argument strategy (or scheme). Essentially, you compare your position to a more commonly known one and make your argument through the comparison. For example, in the "Trust No One" argument above, the author equates the Watergate and Monica Lewinsky scandals. Since it is common knowledge that Watergate was a serious scandal, including Monica Lewinsky in the list offers a strong argument by analogy: the Lewinsky scandal did as much damage as Watergate. To break this rule, you might make an analogy that does not hold up, such as comparing a minor scandal involving a local school board to Watergate. This would be an exaggeration, in most cases.

8. The Validity Rule

"The reasoning in the argumentation must be logically valid or must be capable of being made valid by making explicit one or more unexpressed premises" (132).

This rule is about traditional logics. Violating this rule means that the parts of your argument do not match up. For example, your cause and effect might be off: If you swim in the ocean today you will get stung by a jelly fish and need medical care. Joe went to the doctor today. He must have been stung by a jelly fish. While this example is obvious (we do not know that Joe went swimming), many argument problems are caused by violating this rule.

9. The Closure Rule

"A failed defense of a standpoint must result in the protagonist retracting the standpoint, and a successful defense of a standpoint must result in the antagonist retracting his or her doubts" (134).

This seems the most obvious rule, yet it is one that most public arguments ignore. If your argument does not cut it, admit the faults and move on. If another writer/speaker offers a rebuttal and you clearly counter it, admit that the original argument is sound. Seems simple, but it's not in our public culture. This would mean that George W. Bush would have to have a press conference and say, "My apologies, I was wrong about WMD," or for someone who argued fervently that Americans want a single payer option for healthcare to instead argue something like, "The polls show that American's want to change healthcare, but not through the single payer option. My argument was based on my opinion that single payer is the best way and not on public opinion." Academics are more accustomed to retraction because our arguments are explicitly part of particular conversations. Rebuttals and renegotiations are the norm. That does not make them any easier to stomach in an "argument is war" culture.

10. The Usage Rule

"Parties must not use any formulations that are insufficiently clear or confusingly ambiguous, and they must interpret the formulations of the other party as carefully and accurately as possible" (136).

While academics are perhaps the worst violators of this rule, it is an important one to discuss. Be clear. I notice in both student and professional academic writing that a confusing concept often means confusing prose, longer sentences, and more letters in a word. If you cannot say it/write it clearly, the concept might not yet be clear to you. Keep working. Ethical violations of this rule happen when someone is purposefully ambiguous so as to confuse the issue. We can see this on all the "law" shows on television or though deliberate propaganda.

Activity: Following the Rules

1. Choose a topic to discuss in class or as a group (ex. organic farming, campus parking, gun control).

   a. Choose one of the rules above and write a short argument (a sentence) that clearly violates the rule. Be prepared to explain WHY it violates the rule.

   b. Take the fallacious argument you just created in exercise a) and correct it. Write a solid argument that conforms to the rule.

Food for thought: The above rules offer one way to think about shaping an argument paper. Imagine that the argument for your next paper is a dialogue between those who disagree about your topic. After doing research, write out the primary standpoint for your paper. For example: organic farming is a sustainable practice that should be used more broadly. Next, write out a standpoint that might offer a refutation of the argument. For example: organic farming cannot supply all of the food needed by the world's population. Once you have a sense of your own argument and possible refutations, go through the rules and imagine how you might ethically and clearly provide arguments that support your point without ignoring the opposition.

Even though our current media and political climate do not call for good argumentation, the guidelines for finding and creating it abound. There are many organizations such as America Speaks (www.americaspeaks.org) that are attempting to revive quality, ethical deliberation. On the personal level, each writer can be more deliberate in their argumentation by choosing to follow some of these methodical approaches to ensure the soundness and general quality of their argument. The above models offer the possibility that we can imagine modes of argumentation other than war. The final model, pragma-dialectics, especially, seems to consider argument as a conversation that requires constant vigilance and interaction by participants. Argument as conversation, as new metaphor for public deliberation, has possibilities.

Additional Activities

1. Read Stanley Fish's blog entry titled "Democracy and Education" (http://fish.blogs.nytimes.com/2007/07/22/democracy-and-education/#more-57). Choose at least two of the responses to Fish's argument that students are not entitled to free speech rights in the classroom and compare them using the different argumentation models listed above.

2. Following the pragma-dialectic rules, create a fair and balanced rebuttal to Fish's argument in his "Democracy and Education" blog entry.

3. Use Toulmin's vocabulary to build an argument. Start with a claim and then fill in the chart with your own research, warrants, qualifiers, and rebuttals.

Note

1. I would like to extend a special thanks to Nina Paley for giving permission to use this cartoon under Creative Commons licensing, free of charge. Please see Paley's great work at www.ninapaley.com.

Works Cited

Coulter, Ann. *Guilty: Liberal "Victims" and Their Assault on America*. New York: Crown Forum, 2009. Print.
Crowley, Sharon, and Debra Hawhee. *Ancient Rhetorics for Contemporary Students*. 4th ed. New York: Pearson/Longman, 2009. Print.

Eemeren, Frans H. van, and Rob Grootendorst. *Fundamentals of Argumentation Theory: A Handbook of Historical Backgrounds and Contemporary Developments.* Mahwah, NJ: Erlbaum, 1996. Print.

Eemeren, Frans H. van, Rob Grootendorst, and Francesca Snoeck Henkemans. *Argumentation: Analysis, Evaluation, Presentation.* Mahwah: Erlbaum, NJ: 2002. Print.

Fish, Stanley. "Democracy and Education." *New York Times* 22 July 2007: n. pag. Web. 5 May 2010. <http://fish.blogs.nytimes.com/2007/07/22/democracy-and-education/>.

Honeycutt, Lee. "Aristotle's Rhetoric: A Hypertextual Resource Compiled by Lee Honeycutt." 21 June 2004. Web. 5 May 2010. <http://www2.iastate.edu/~honeyl/Rhetoric/index.html>.

Lakoff, George, and Mark Johnson. *Metaphors We Live By.* Chicago: U of Chicago P, 1980. Print.

Murphy, James. *Quintilian On the Teaching and Speaking of Writing.* Carbondale: Southern Illinois UP, 1987. Print.

Paxton, Pamela, and Jeremy Adam Smith. "Not Everyone Is Out to Get You." *UTNE Reader* Sept.-Oct. 2009: 44-45. Print.

"Plato, *The Dialogues of Plato, vol. 1* [387 AD]." Online Library of Liberty, n. d. Web. 5 May 2010. <http://oll.libertyfund.org/index.php?option=com_staticxt&staticfile=show.php%3Ftitle=111&layout=html#chapter_39482>.

"I need you to say 'I'": Why First Person Is Important in College Writing

Kate McKinney Maddalena

At this point in your development as a writer, you may have learned to write "I-less" prose, without first person.[*] I-less-ness is fine; writing habits, like all habits, are best simplified when first learned or re-learned. Jazz pianists learn strict scales before they are allowed to improvise. Someone might go on a strict diet and then return to a modified menu after the desired weight is lost, and the bad eating habits are broken. Constructing arguments without using "I" is good practice for formal "improvisation" at higher levels of thinking and writing. Avoiding personal pronouns forces you to be objective. It also "sounds" more formal; you're more likely to maintain an appropriate tone if you stay away from the personal.

But writing in various academic and professional contexts needs to be more flexible, sophisticated, and subtle than writing for high school English classes. In college, you should start using first-person pronouns in your formal academic writing, where appropriate. First person has an important place—an irreplaceable place—in texts that report research and engage scholarship. Your choices about where you place yourself as subject are largely determined by context and the

---

[*] This work is licensed under the Creative Commons Attribution-Noncommercial-Share Alike 3.0 United States License and is subject to the Writing Spaces Terms of Use. To view a copy of this license, visit http://creativecommons.org/licenses/by-nc-sa/3.0/us/ or send a letter to Creative Commons, 171 Second Street, Suite 300, San Francisco, California, 94105, USA. To view the Writing Spaces Terms of Use, visit http://writingspaces.org/terms-of-use.

conventions of the field in which you're writing. The key is making sure that your choices are appropriate for the context of your paper—whom you're writing it for, and the kind of information it's meant to communicate. Here I'll list some ways in which first person improves written argument and show you some examples of the ways scholars use first person, and then I'll propose places where it might be used appropriately in your own writing.

Why "I"?

First person can support the following characteristics of good written argument (and good writing in general).

1. Objectivity and Integrity

The main reason most teachers give for the discipline of I-less-ness is that it keeps your writing "objective." They want to make sure that you don't rely on personal experiences or perspectives where you should be providing concrete, researched support for your arguments. Your best friend at summer camp doesn't "prove" a sociological theory. Your memory of a "fact"—the average rainfall in a town, the actions of a character in a film, the tendencies of groups of people to behave in certain ways, or the population of Kenya—is not a reliable source in academic contexts. You shouldn't write, "because I think so," or "I know that . . ." But if you consider some of the higher-level implications of perspective's effects on argument, there are some well-chosen places where "I" can give your argument more objectivity and intellectual integrity.

Take scientific writing, for example. Up until very recently, when writing observational and experimental reports, scientists, as a rule, avoided first person. Methodology was (and is still, in many cases) described in the passive voice. That is, instead of writing, "We took measurements of ice thickness on the first and 15th day of every month," scientists wrote, "Measurements of ice thickness were taken on the first and 15th day of every month." Taking out the "we" focuses the reader's attention on the phenomenon (object) being observed, not the observer taking the readings (subject). Or at least that was the reasoning behind passive voice in science writing.

But during the last half of the last century, mostly because of developments in physics, scientists have talked a lot about a thing called the "observer effect": while observing or experimenting with a social or even physical system, the scientist watching can affect the system's behavior. When particle physicists try to measure the motion of something as tiny as an electron, their very observation almost certainly changes that motion. Because of the observer effect, the passive voice convention I've described above has been called into question. Is it really honest to act like "measurements are taken" by some invisible hand? Is the picture minus the researcher the whole picture? Not really. The fact is, someone took the measurements, and those measurements might reflect that observer's involvement. It's more truthful, complete, and objective, then, to put the researchers in the picture. These days, it's much more common to "see" the researchers as subjects—"We measured ice thickness . . ."—in methodology sections.

That same kind of "whole picture" honesty applies to you making written claims, too. When you first learned to write an essay, you were probably taught to make claims as though they were true; write "The sky is blue," not "I think that the sky is blue." That second claim isn't arguable—who can disprove that you think something? But a much more sophisticated claim includes your perspective and implies the effect it may have on your stance: "From my position standing on the earth's surface in the daytime, I see the sky as blue." You can make that claim without using first person, of course, and in some contexts (i.e. for a scientific argument), you probably should. When you're taking a stance on an issue, though, first person just makes sense. Defining your perspective gives your reader context for your stance: "As a volunteer at a bilingual preschool, I can see that both language immersion and individualized language instruction have benefits," or "As a principal at an elementary school with a limited budget, I would argue that language immersion makes the most sense." Consider those two positions; without the "whole picture" that the statement of perspective implies, you might assume that the two claims disagree. The subtlety of the subject—who the writer is—lets you see quite a bit about why the claim is being made. If you asked the second writer to take a stance on the immersion/bilingual instruction issue with only learning objectives in mind, she might agree with the first writer. The "truth" might not be different, but the position it's observed from can certainly cast a different light on it.

2. Clarifying Who's Saying What

A clear description of your perspective becomes even more important when your stance has to incorporate or respond to someone else's. As you move into more advanced college writing, the claims you respond to will usually belong to scholars. Some papers may require you to spend almost as much time summarizing a scholarly conversation as they do presenting points of your own. By "signification," I mean little phrases that tell the reader, "This is my opinion," "This is my interpretation." You need them for two big reasons.

First of all, the more "voices" you add to the conversation, the more confusing it gets. You must separate your own interpretations of scholars' claims, the claims themselves, and your argument so as not to misrepresent any of them. If you've just paraphrased a scholar, making your own claim without quite literally claiming it might make the reader think that the scholar said it. Consider these two sentences: "Wagstaff et al. (2007) conclude that the demand for practical science writing that the layperson can understand is on the rise. But there is a need for laypeople people to increase their science literacy, as well." Is that second claim part of Wagstaff's conclusion, or is it your own reflection on the implications of Wagstaff's argument? By writing something like, "Wagstaff et al. (2007) conclude that the demand for practical science that the layperson can understand is on the rise. I maintain that there is a need for laypeople to increase their science literacy, as well," you avoid the ambiguity. First person can help you express, very simply, who "says" what.

Secondly, your perceptions, and therefore your interpretations, are not always perfect. Science writing can help me illustrate this idea, as well. In the imaginary observation report I refer to above, the researchers may or may not use first person in their methodology section out of respect for the observer effect, but they are very likely to use first person in the discussion/conclusion section. The discussion section involves interpretation of the data—that is, the researchers must say what they think the data means. The importance of perspective is compounded, here. They might not be right. And even if they are mostly right, the systems scientists study are usually incredibly complex; one observation report is not the whole picture. Scientists, therefore, often mark their own interpretations with first person pronouns. "We interpret these data to imply . . ." they might say, or, "We believe

these findings indicate . . . ," and then they go on to list questions for
further research. Even the experts know that their understanding is
almost always incomplete.

3. Ownership, Intellectual Involvement, and Exigency

Citing scholarship contextualizes and strengthens your argument; you
want to defer to "experts" for evidence of your claims when you can.
As a student, you might feel like an outsider—unable to comment
with authority on the concepts you're reading and writing about. But
outsider status doesn't only mean a lack of expertise. Your own, well-
defined viewpoint might shed new light on a topic that the experts
haven't considered (or that your classmates haven't considered, or that
your professor hasn't mentioned in class, or even, quite simply, that
you hadn't thought of and so you're excited about). In that case, you
want to say, "This is mine, it's a new way of looking at the issue, and
I'm proud of it."

Those kinds of claims are usually synthetic ones—you've put information and/or interpretations from several sources together, and
you've actually got something to say. Whether your new spin has to do
with a cure for cancer or an interpretation of Batman comics, pride in
your own intellectual work is important on many levels. As a student,
you should care; such investment can help you learn. Your school community should also care; good teachers are always looking for what we
call "critical thinking," and when students form new ideas from existing ones, we know it's happening. On the larger scale, the scholarly
community should care. Having something new to say increases the
exigency of your argument in the larger, intellectual exchange of ideas.
A scholarly reader should want to pay attention, because what you say
may be a key to some puzzle (a cure for cancer) or way of thinking
about the topic (interpreting Batman). That's the way scholars work
together to form large bodies of knowledge: we communicate about
our research and ideas, and we try to combine them when we can.

An emphatic statement like "Much discussion has addressed the
topic of carbon emissions' relationship to climate change, but I would
like to ask a question from a new perspective," will make your reader
sit up and take notice. In I-less form, that might look like: "Much
discussion has addressed the topic of carbon emissions' relationship
to climate change, but some questions remain unconsidered." In this

case, second sentence still sounds like summary—the writer is telling us that research is incomplete, but isn't giving us a strong clue that his or her (new! fresh!) argument is coming up next. Be careful, of course, not to sound arrogant. If the writer of the sentences above was worried about his or her lack of expertise in an assignment involving scholarly sources, he or she could write: "What scholarly discussion I have read so far has addressed the topic of carbon emissions' relationship to climate change, but I would like to ask a question from a new perspective." He or she can use first person to employ both deference and ownership/involvement in the same sentence.

4. Rhetorical Sophistication

Some writing assignments focus on one simple task at a time: "Summarize the following . . ." "Compare the readings . . ." "analyze," or "argue." When you write a simple five-paragraph essay, your mode rarely changes—you can write an introduction, thesis, body, and conclusion without explaining too many shifts in what the paper is "doing." Writing at the college level and beyond often has to "do" a few things in the same text. Most involved writing assignments expect you to do at least two things. You may need to summarize/report and respond, or (more likely) you'll need to summarize/report, synthesize, and respond. A good introduction, as you've learned, needs to anticipate all of it so the reader knows what to expect. Anticipating the structure of a complex argument in I-less mode is tricky. Often, it comes out as a summary of the document that follows and is redundant. First person can clear that problem right up. Consider the introduction to this article; when I come to the part where I need to tell you what I'm going to do, I just . . . tell you what I'm going to do! My writing students usually find this rhetorical trick (or is it an un-trick?) refreshing and liberating. The same concept can be applied to transitions between sections and ideas: "Now that I've done this thing, I'd like to move into this other part of my argument . . ." I'll use this type of transition, myself, when I move into the section of this text called, "When, and When not?"

Academic Examples

The fact is, using first person for rhetorical clarity and to ease transitions isn't just easier—it's common in many academic contexts. It's accepted, even expected, in some cases, for scholarly writing such as abstracts, position papers, theses, and dissertations in many fields to employ first person in the ways I've just described. In almost all genres, formats, and fields, the scholarly writer is expected to describe the research done thus far by her peers and then make her own claims—a structure that lends itself to first person.

Robert Terrill, a cultural studies scholar, begins his article, "Put on a Happy Face: Batman as Schizophrenic Savior," with an evaluation of Tim Burton's movie's box office success, and then spends several paragraphs discussing other scholars' applications of psychological frameworks to film studies. Throughout the literature review section, Terrill's own voice stays remote; he uses third person. But look at what happens when he is ready to begin his own argument:

> Because much of my analysis is grounded in the theories of Carl C. Jung, I will begin by outlining relevant aspects of that theory. Then I suggest that Gotham City is a dream world, a representative projection of image-centered dreams. Within the framework of Jung's model, I show the principal characters to be archetypal manifestations that erupt from Gotham's unconscious. Wayne/Batman is a splintered manifestation of a potential whole; his condition represents the schizophrenia required of a hero dedicated to preservation of the shattered psyche of Gotham. (321)

Terrill's move to first person separates his own claims from the scholars he's summarized in his introduction, and it allows him to take ownership of his main claim. The way he "maps out" his article is also typical of academic argument.

First person is used similarly in the sciences. Unlike Terrill, who argues for a certain interpretation of a text, psychologists Jennifer Kraemer and David Marquez report research findings in their article, "Psychosocial Correlates and Outcomes of Yoga or Walking Among Older Adults." Much like Terrill, however, their introduction consists of a review of literature in the third person. For almost three pages, Kraemer and Marquez describe studies which have explored health and injury patterns in old age, as well as studies which have investigated various fitness programs for the elderly. When it comes time for

Kraemer and Marquez to describe their own study, they shift into first person:

> We hypothesized that an acute bout of yoga would be more effective at improving mood and reducing state anxiety among older adults when compared with acute bouts of walking. We further hypothesized that older adults who practice yoga would have lower levels of depression and higher quality of life when compared with those who walk for exercise. We did not make direct hypotheses for exercise barriers and barriers self-efficacy because, to date, there is no research that has examined those variables in this population. (393)

Kraemer and Marquez continue in first person as they describe their methodology. "We recruited a total of 51 participants (8 men, 43 women)" they write, "through classes at local yoga studios and mall walking groups" (393). The researchers themselves, in first person, are the subjects who "do" every action in the methods: "We asked questions on . . . We measured state anxiety by . . . We measured mood using . . ."(393–4). By putting themselves in the picture, Kraemer and Marquez acknowledge themselves as variables in their own study—a key aspect of any scientific methodology, and especially those which involve human subjects and use interviews to collect data.

On the other hand, some academic communities and genres stay away from first person. Susan Clark, a professor at Yale who writes about the communication and implementation of sustainable forestry practices, describes her study without putting herself in the picture. Where Kraemer and Marquez describe themselves "doing" the methods of their study, Clark has her article as the agent in her description of analysis:

> This article (a) describes the intelligence function in conceptual terms, including its sequential phases (as described by McDougal, Lasswell, & Reisman, 1981); (b) uses examples to illustrate the intelligence activity from Reading and Miller (2000), *Endangered Animals: A Reference Guide to Conflicting Issues,* which gives 70 cases by 34 authors in 55 countries

that focus on species, ecosystem, and sustainability
challenges; and employs a "problem-oriented" look at
intelligence activities across all these cases (Lasswell,
1971). It does so by asking and answering five questions . . . (637)

Clark's methods are to analyze others' processes—hers, then, is meta-
analysis. It's appropriate for her to remove herself rhetorically as she
deals with many actions and many, diverse actors. She is more a de-
scriber than a "do-er."

At the very end of her article, in a "call to action" that directly applies her findings, Clark does finally use first person. "We can increase
the possibility of better biodiversity and ecosystem conservation, and
better sustainability overall," she writes, "if we choose to use an effective intelligence activity. Success is more likely if we increase the
rationality of our own directed behavior" (659). Clark's "we" is different from Kraemer and Marquez's "we," though. It refers to Clark's
audience—the community of sustainable forestry as a whole—and
predicts future action in which she will be active.

When (and When Not) to Use First Person?

Now that I've convinced you to try first person in some of your academic writing, I should talk about how to use it appropriately. (See?
I just used "I" for a clear transition to a new idea.) The key is: don't
go "I" crazy. Remember the self-discipline you practiced with I-less
writing.

Probably the best way to approach first person in an academic context is this: use it to make yourself clear. You'll need "I" for clarity
when one of the ideals I described above is in question. Either 1) you'll
need to describe an aspect of your personal perspective that will help
the reader see (your) whole picture; 2) you'll need to make the divide between your voice and the scholars' as clear as possible in order
to avoid misrepresenting the scholars' claims; 3) your own claim will
need to stand apart from the other perspectives you've presented as
something new; or 4) you'll need to guide your reader through the
organization of your text in some way.

Below, I've listed a few common writing situations/assignments
that first person can potentially support.

Try "I" when . . .

. . . the assignment asks you to. Personal position papers, personal narratives, and assignments that say "tell what you did/read and provide your reaction," all explicitly ask you to use first person.

. . . you're asked to "Summarize and respond." You might transition into the response part of the paper with "I."

. . . you're introducing a paper with a complicated structure: "I will summarize Wagstaff's argument, and then respond to a few key points with my own interpretation."

. . . you are proud of and intellectually invested in what you have to say, and you want to arrange it in reference to others' voices: "Many scholars have used psychological frameworks to interpret the Batman movies, but I would argue that a historical perspective is more productive . . ."

. . . you are unsure of your interpretation of a source, or you feel that the claim you're making may be bigger than your level of expertise: "If I read Wagstaff correctly, her conclusions imply . . ."

"I" Is a Bad Idea When . . .

. . . you use it only once. You don't want to overuse the first person, but if you're going to assert your position or make a transition with "I," give the reader a hint of your voice in the introduction. An introduction that anticipates structure with "I will," for instance, works well with transitions that use "I" as well. If you use first person only once, the tone shift will jar the reader.

. . . The assignment is a simple summary. In that case, you need only report; you are "eye," not "I."

. . . you're writing a lab report for a science class, as a general rule. But you might ask your teacher about the issues of objectivity I've addressed above, especially in terms of objective methodology.

Discussion

1. Can you remember a writing task during which you struggled to avoid using the first person? What about the nature of the content made "I" hard to avoid? Can you link the difficulty to

one of the four values that first person "supports," according
to this essay?

2. McKinney Maddalena claims that scientists use "I" more of-
    ten in research reports, nowadays. Find a scientific article in
    your school's research databases that employs first person: "I"
    or "we." In what section is first person used, and how? Does its
    usage reflect one of the values this essay points out?

Works Cited

Clark, Susan G. "An Informational Approach to Sustainability: "Intel-
    ligence" in Conservation and Natural Resource Management Policy."
    Journal of Sustainable Forestry 28.6/7 (2009): 636–62. *Academic Search
    Premier*. Web. 22 Mar. 2010.
Kraemer, Jennifer M., and David X. Marquez. "Psychosocial Correlates and
    Outcomes of Yoga or Walking Among Older Adults." *Journal of Psycholo-
    gy* 143.4 (2009): 390–404. *Academic Search Premier*. Web. 22 Mar. 2010.
Terrill, Robert E. "Put on a Happy Face: *Batman* as Schizophrenic Savior."
    The Quarterly Journal of Speech 79.3 (1993): 319–35. *MLA International
    Bibliography*. Web. 22 Mar. 2010.

Reflective Writing and the Revision Process: What Were You Thinking?

Sandra L. Giles

"Reflection" and "reflective writing" are umbrella terms that refer to any activity that asks you to think about your own thinking.[*] As composition scholars Kathleen Blake Yancey and Jane Bowman Smith explain, reflection records a "student's process of thinking about what she or he is doing while in the process of that doing" (170). In a writing class, you may be asked to think about your writing processes in general or in relation to a particular essay, to think about your intentions regarding rhetorical elements such as audience and purpose, or to think about your choices regarding development strategies such as comparison-contrast, exemplification, or definition. You may be asked to describe your decisions regarding language features such as word choice, sentence rhythm, and so on. You may be asked to evaluate or assess your piece of writing or your development as a writer in general. Your instructor may also ask you to perform these kinds of activities at various points in your process of working on a project, or at the end of the semester.

A Writer's Experience

The first time I had to perform reflective writing myself was in the summer of 2002. And it did feel like a performance, at first. I was a doctoral student in Wendy Bishop's Life Writing class at Florida State University, and it was the first class I had ever taken where we English majors actually practiced what we preached; which is to say, we actually put ourselves through the various elements of process writing. Bishop led us through invention exercises, revision exercises, language activities, and yes, reflective writings. For each essay, we had to write what she called a "process note" in which we explained our processes of working on the essay, as well as our thought processes in developing the ideas. We also discussed what we might want to do with (or to) the essay in the future, beyond the class. At the end of the semester, we composed a self-evaluative cover letter for our portfolio in which we discussed each of our essays from the semester and recorded our learning and insights about writing and about the genre of nonfiction.

My first process note for the class was a misguided attempt at good-student-gives-the-teacher-what-she-wants. Our assignment had been to attend an event in town and write about it. I had seen an email announcement about a medium visiting from England who would perform a "reading" at the Unity Church in town. So I went and took notes. And wrote two consecutive drafts. After peer workshop, a third. And then I had to write the process note, the likes of which I had never done before. It felt awkward, senseless. Worse than writing a scholarship application or some other mundane writing task. Like a waste of time, and like it wasn't real writing at all. But it was required.

So, hoop-jumper that I was, I wrote the following: "This will eventually be part of a longer piece that will explore the Foundation for Spiritual Knowledge in Tallahassee, Florida, which is a group of local people in training to be mediums and spirituals healers. These two goals are intertwined." Yeah, right. Nice and fancy. Did I really intend to write a book-length study on those folks? I thought my professor would like the idea, though, so I put it in my note. Plus, my peer reviewers had asked for a longer, deeper piece. That statement would show I was being responsive to their feedback, even though I didn't agree with it. The peer reviewers had also wanted me to put myself into the essay more, to do more with first-person point of view rather than just writing a reporter-style observation piece. I still disagree with them, but what I should have done in the original process note was go into why: my own search for spirituality and belief could not be handled in a brief essay. I wanted the piece to be about the medium herself, and mediumship in general, and the public's reaction, and why a group of snarky teenagers thought they could be disruptive the whole time and come off as superior. I did a better job later—more honest and thoughtful and revealing about my intentions for the piece—in the self-evaluation for the portfolio. That's because, as the semester progressed and I continued to have to write those darned process notes, I dropped the attitude. In a conference about my writing, Bishop responded to my note by asking questions focused entirely on helping me refine my intentions for the piece, and I realized my task wasn't to please or try to dazzle her. I stopped worrying about how awkward the reflection was, stopped worrying about how to please the teacher, and started actually reflecting and thinking. New habits and ways of thinking formed. And unexpectedly, all the hard decisions about revising for the next draft began to come more easily.

And something else clicked, too. Two and a half years previously, I had been teaching composition at a small two-year college. Composition scholar Peggy O'Neill taught a workshop for us English teachers on an assignment she called the "Letter to the Reader." That was my introduction to reflective writing as a teacher, though I hadn't done any of it myself at that point. I thought, "Okay, the composition scholars say we should get our students to do this." So I did, but it did not work very well with my students at the time. Here's why: I didn't come to understand what it could do for a writer, or how it would do it, until I had been through it myself.

After Bishop's class, I became a convert. I began studying reflection, officially called metacognition, and began developing ways of using it in writing classes of all kinds, from composition to creative nonfiction to fiction writing. It works. Reflection helps you to develop your intentions (purpose), figure out your relation to your audience, uncover possible problems with your individual writing processes, set goals for revision, make decisions about language and style, and the list goes on. In a nutshell, it helps you develop more insight into and control over composing and revising processes. And according to scholars such as Chris M. Anson, developing this control is a feature that distinguishes stronger from weaker writers and active from passive learners (69–73).

My Letter to the Reader Assignment

Over recent years, I've developed my own version of the Letter to the Reader, based on O'Neill's workshop and Bishop's class assignments.

For each essay, during a revising workshop, my students first draft
their letters to the reader and then later, polish them to be turned
in with the final draft. Letters are composed based on the following
instructions:

> This will be a sort of cover letter for your essay. It should
> be on a separate sheet of paper, typed, stapled to the top
> of the final draft. Date the letter and address it to "Dear
> Reader." Then do the following in nicely developed, fat
> paragraphs:
>
> 1. Tell the reader what you intend for the essay to do for its
>   readers. Describe its purpose(s) and the effect(s) you want
>   it to have on the readers. Say who you think the readers
>   are.
>   - Describe your process of working on the essay. How did
>   you narrow the assigned topic? What kind of planning did
>   you do? What steps did you go through, what changes did
>   you make along the way, what decisions did you face, and
>   how did you make the decisions?
>   - How did comments from your peers, in peer workshop,
>   help you? How did any class activities on style, editing,
>   etc., help you?
> 2. Remember to sign the letter. After you've drafted it, think
>   about whether your letter and essay match up. Does the
>   essay really do what your letter promises? If not, then use
>   the draft of your letter as a revising tool to make a few
>   more adjustments to your essay. Then, when the essay is
>   polished and ready to hand in, polish the letter as well
>   and hand them in together.

Following is a sample letter that shows how the act of answering
these prompts can help you uncover issues in your essays that need
to be addressed in further revision. This letter is a mock-up based on
problems I've seen over the years. We discuss it thoroughly in my writing classes:

Dear Reader,

This essay is about how I feel about the changes in the financial aid rules. I talk about how they say you're not eligible even if your parents aren't supporting you anymore. I also talk a little bit about the HOPE scholarship. But my real purpose is to show how the high cost of books makes it impossible to afford college if you can't get on financial aid. My readers will be all college students. As a result, it should make students want to make a change. My main strategy in this essay is to describe how the rules have affected me personally.

I chose this topic because this whole situation has really bugged me. I did freewriting to get my feelings out on paper, but I don't think that was effective because it seemed jumbled and didn't flow. So I started over with an outline and went on from there. I'm still not sure how to start the introduction off because I want to hook the reader's interest but I don't know how to do that. I try to include many different arguments to appeal to different types of students to make the whole argument seem worthwhile on many levels.

I did not include comments from students because I want everyone to think for themselves and form their own opinion. That's my main strategy. I don't want the paper to be too long and bore the reader. I was told in peer workshop to include information from other students at other colleges with these same financial aid problems. But I didn't do that because I don't know anybody at another school. I didn't want to include any false information.

Thanks,

(signature)

Notice how the letter shows us, as readers of the letter, some problems in the essay without actually having to read the essay. From this (imaginary) student's point of view, the act of drafting this letter should show her the problems, too. In her first sentence, she announces her overall topic. Next she identifies a particular problem: the way "they" define whether an applicant is dependent on or independent of parents. So far, pretty good, except her use of the vague pronoun "they" makes me hope she hasn't been that vague in the essay itself. Part of taking on a topic is learning enough about it to be specific. Specific is effective; vague is not. Her next comment about the HOPE scholarship makes me wonder if she's narrowed her topic enough. When she said "financial aid," I assumed federal, but HOPE is particular to the state of Georgia and has its own set of very particular rules, set by its own committee in Atlanta. Can she effectively cover both federal financial aid, such as the Pell Grant for example, as well as HOPE, in the same essay, when the rules governing them are different? Maybe. We'll see. I wish the letter would address more specifically how she sorts that out in the essay. Then she says that her "real purpose" is to talk about the cost of books. Is that really her main purpose? Either she doesn't have a good handle on what she wants her essay to do or she's just throwing language around to sound good in the letter. Not good, either way.

When she says she wants the readers to be all college students, she has identified her target audience, which is good. Then this: "As a result, it should make students want to make a change." Now, doesn't that sound more in line with a statement of purpose? Here the writer makes clear, for the first time, that she wants to write a persuasive piece on the topic. But then she says that her "main strategy" is to discuss only her own personal experience. That's not a strong enough strategy, by itself, to be persuasive.

In the second section, where she discusses process, she seems to have gotten discouraged when she thought that freewriting hadn't worked because it resulted in something "jumbled." But she missed the point that freewriting works to generate ideas, which often won't come out nicely organized. It's completely fine, and normal, to use freewriting to generate ideas and then organize them with perhaps an outline as a second step. As a teacher, when I read comments like this in a letter, I write a note to the student explaining that "jumbled" is normal, perfectly fine, and nothing to worry about. I'm glad when I read that sort of comment so I can reassure the student. If not for the letter, I probably wouldn't have known of her unfounded concern. It creates a teaching moment.

Our imaginary student then says, "I'm still not sure how to start the introduction off because I want to hook the reader's interest but don't know how to do that." This statement shows that she's thinking along the right lines—of capturing the reader's interest. But she hasn't quite figured out how to do that in this essay, probably because she doesn't have a clear handle on her purpose. I'd advise her to address that problem and to better develop her overall strategy, and then she would be in a better position to make a plan for the introduction. Again, a teaching moment. When she concludes the second paragraph of the letter saying that she wants to include "many different arguments" for "different types of students," it seems even more evident that she's not clear on purpose or strategy; therefore, she's just written a vague sentence she probably thought sounded good for the letter.

She begins her third paragraph with further proof of the problems. If her piece is to be persuasive, then she should not want readers to "think for themselves and form their own opinion." She most certainly should have included comments from other students, as her peer responders advised. It wouldn't be difficult to interview some fellow students at her own school. And as for finding out what students at other schools think about the issue, a quick search on the Internet would turn up newspaper or newsletter articles, as well as blogs and other relevant sources. Just because the official assignment may not have been to write a "research" paper doesn't mean you can't research. Some of your best material will come that way. And in this particular type of paper, your personal experience by itself, without support, will not likely persuade the reader. Now, I do appreciate when she says she doesn't want to include any "false information." A lot of students come to college with the idea that in English class, if you don't know any information to use, then you can just make it up so it sounds good. But that's not ethical, and it's not persuasive, and just a few minutes on the Internet will solve the problem.

This student, having drafted the above letter, should go back and analyze. Do the essay and letter match up? Does the essay do what the letter promises? And here, does the letter uncover lack of clear thinking about purpose and strategy? Yes, it does, so she should now go back and address these issues in her essay. Without having done this type of reflective exercise, she likely would have thought her essay was just fine, and she would have been unpleasantly surprised to get the grade back with my (the teacher's) extensive commentary and critique. She never would have predicted what I would say because she wouldn't have had a process for thinking through these issues—and might not have known how to begin thinking this way. Drafting the letter should help her develop more insight into and control over the revising process so she can make more effective decisions as she revises.

How It Works

Intentions—a sense of audience and purpose and of what the writer wants the essay to do—are essential to a good piece of communicative writing. Anson makes the point that when an instructor asks a student to verbalize his or her intentions, it is much more likely that the student will have intentions (qtd. in Yancey and Smith 174). We saw this process in mid-struggle with our imaginary student's work (above), and we'll see it handled more effectively in real student examples (below). As many composition scholars explain, reflective and self-assessing activities help writers set goals for their writing. For instance, Rebecca Moore Howard states that "writers who can assess their own prose can successfully revise that prose" (36). This position is further illustrated by Xiaoguang Cheng and Margaret S. Steffenson, who conducted and then reported a study clearly demonstrating a direct positive effect of reflection on student revising processes in "Metadiscourse: A Technique for Improving Student Writing." Yancey and Smith argue that self-assessment and reflection are essential to the learning process because they are a "method for assigning both responsibility and authority to a learner" (170). Students then become independent learners who can take what they learn about writing into the future beyond a particular class rather than remaining dependent on teachers or peer evaluators (171). Anson echoes this idea, saying that reflection helps a writer grow beyond simply succeeding in a particular writing project: "Once they begin thinking about writing productively, they stand a much better chance of developing expertise and working more successfully in future writing situations" (73).

Examples from Real Students

Let's see some examples from actual students now, although for the sake of space we'll look at excerpts. The first few illustrate how reflective writing helps you develop your intentions. For an assignment to write a profile essay, Joshua Dawson described his purpose and audience: "This essay is about my grandmother and how she overcame the hardships of life. [. . .] The purpose of this essay is to show how a woman can be tough and can take anything life throws at her. I hope the essay reaches students who have a single parent and those who don't know what a single parent goes through." Joshua showed a clear idea of what he wanted his essay to do. For a cultural differences paper, Haley Moore wrote about her mission trip to Peru: "I tried to show how, in America, we have everything from clean water to freedom of religion and other parts of the world do not. Also, I would like for my essay to inspire people to give donations or help in any way they can for the countries that live in poverty." Haley's final draft actually did not address the issue of donations and focused instead on the importance of mission work, a good revision decision that kept the essay more focused.

In a Composition II class, Chelsie Mathis wrote an argumentative essay on a set of controversial photos published in newspapers in the 1970s which showed a woman falling to her death during a fire escape collapse. Chelsie said,

> The main purpose of this essay is to argue whether the [newspaper] editors used correct judgment when deciding to publish such photos. The effect that I want my paper to have on the readers is to really make people think about others' feelings and to make people realize that poor judgment can have a big effect. [. . .] I intend for my readers to possibly be high school students going into the field of journalism or photojournalism.

Chelsie demonstrated clear thinking about purpose and about who she wanted her essay to influence. Another Comp II student, Daniel White, wrote, "This essay is a cognitive approach of how I feel YouTube is helping our society achieve its dreams and desires of becoming stars." I had no idea what he meant by "cognitive approach," but I knew he was taking a psychology class at the same time. I appreciated that he was trying to integrate his learning from that class into ours, trying to learn to use that vocabulary. I was sure that with more practice, he would get the hang of it. I didn't know whether he was getting much writing practice at all in psychology, so I was happy to let him practice it in my class. His reflection showed learning in process.

My students often resist writing about their composing processes, but it's good for them to see and analyze how they did what they did, and it also helps me know what they were thinking when they made composing decisions. Josh Autry, in regards to his essay on scuba diving in the Florida Keys at the wreck of the Spiegel Grove, said, "Mapping was my preferred method of outlining. It helped me organize my thoughts, go into detail, and pick the topics that I thought would be the most interesting to the readers." He also noted, "I choose [sic] to write a paragraph about everything that can happen to a diver that is not prepared but after reviewing it I was afraid that it would scare an interested diver away. I chose to take that paragraph out and put a few warnings in the conclusion so the aspiring diver would not be clueless." This was a good decision that did improve the final draft. His earlier draft had gotten derailed by a long discussion of the dangers of scuba diving in general. But he came to this realization and decided to correct it without my help—except that I had led the class through reflective revising activities. D'Amber Walker wrote, "At first my organization was off because I didn't know if I should start off with a personal experience which included telling a story or start with a statistic." Apparently, a former teacher had told her not to include personal experiences in her essays. I reminded her that in our workshop on introductions, we had discussed how a personal story can be a very effective hook to grab the reader's attention. So once again, a teaching moment. When Jonathan Kelly said, "I probably could have given more depth to this paper by interviewing a peer or something but I really felt unsure of how to go about doing so," I was able to scold him gently. If he really didn't know how to ask fellow students their opinions, all he had to do was ask me. But his statement shows an accurate assessment of how the paper could have been better. When Nigel Ellington titled his essay "If Everything Was Easy, Nothing Would Be Worth Anything," he explained, "I like this [title] because it's catchy and doesn't give too much away and it hooks you." He integrated what he learned in a workshop on titles. Doing this one little bit of reflective thinking cemented that learning and gave him a chance to use it in his actual paper.

How It Helps Me (the Instructor) Help You

Writing teachers often play two roles in relation to their students. I am my students' instructor, but I am also a fellow writer. As a writer, I have learned that revision can be overwhelming. It's tempting just to fiddle with words and commas if I don't know what else to do. Reflection is a mechanism, a set of procedures, to help me step back from a draft to gain enough distance to ask myself, "Is this really what I want the essay (or story or poem or article) to do? Is this really what I want it to say? Is this the best way to get it to say that?" To revise is to re-vision or re-see, to re-think these issues, but you have to create a critical distance to be able to imagine your piece done another way. Reflection helps you create that distance. It also helps your instructor better guide your work and respond to it.

The semester after my experience in Bishop's Life Writing Class, I took a Fiction Writing Workshop taught by Mark Winegardner, author of *The Godfather Returns* and *The Godfather's Revenge*, as well as numerous other novels and short stories. Winegardner had us create what he called the "process memo." As he indicated in an interview, he uses the memo mainly as a tool to help the workshop instructor know how to respond to the writer's story. If a writer indicates in the memo that he knows something is still a problem with the story, then the instructor can curtail lengthy discussion of that issue's existence during the workshop and instead prompt peers to provide suggestions. The instructor can give some pointed advice, or possibly reassurance, based on the writer's concerns that, without being psychic, the instructor would not otherwise have known about. Composition scholar Jeffrey Sommers notes that reflective pieces show teachers what your intentions for your writing actually are, which lets us respond to your writing accurately, rather than responding to what we think your intentions might be ("Enlisting" 101–2). He also points out that we can know how to reduce your anxiety about your writing appropriately ("Behind" 77). Thus, without a reflective memo, your teacher might pass right over the very issue you have been worried about.

The Habit of Self-Reflective Writing

One of the most important functions of reflective writing in the long run is to establish in you, the writer, a habit of self-reflective thinking. The first few reflective pieces you write may feel awkward and silly and possibly painful. You might play the teacher-pleasing game. But that's really not what we want (see Smith 129). Teachers don't want you to say certain things, we want you to think in certain ways. Once you get the hang of it and start to see the benefits in your writing, you'll notice that you've formed a habit of thinking reflectively almost invisibly. And not only will it help you in writing classes, but in any future writing projects for biology class, say, or even further in the future, in writing that you may do on the job, such as incident reports or annual reports for a business. You'll become a better writer. You'll become a better thinker. You'll become a better learner. And learning is what you'll be doing for the rest of your life. I recently painted my kitchen. It was a painful experience. I had a four-day weekend and thought I could clean, prep, and paint the kitchen, breakfast nook, and hallway to the garage in just four days, not to mention painting the trim and doors white. I pushed myself to the limit of endurance. And when I finished the wall color (not even touching the trim), I didn't like it. The experience was devastating. A very similar thing had happened three years before when I painted my home office a color I now call "baby poop." My home office is still "baby poop" because I got so frustrated I just gave up. Now, the kitchen was even worse. It was such a light green it looked like liver failure and didn't go with the tile on the floor. Plus, it showed brush marks and other flaws. What the heck?

But unlike three years ago, when I had given up, I decided to apply reflective practices to the situation. I decided to see it as time for revision-type thinking. Why had I wanted green to begin with? (Because I didn't want blue in a kitchen. I've really been craving that hot dark lime color that's popular now. So yes, I still want it to be green.) Why hadn't I chosen a darker green? (Because I have the darker, hotter color into the room with accessories. The lighter green has a more neutral effect that I shouldn't get sick of after six months. Perhaps I'll get used to it, especially when I get around to painting the trim white.) What caused the brush strokes? (I asked an expert. Two factors: using satin finish rather than eggshell, and using a cheap paintbrush for cut-in-areas.) How can they be fixed? (Most of the brush strokes are just in the cut-in areas and so they can be redone quickly with a better quality brush. That is, if I decide to keep this light green color.) Is the fact that the trim is still cream-colored rather than white part of the problem? (Oh, yes. Fix that first and the other problems might diminish.) What can I learn about timing for my next paint project? (That the cleaning and prep work take much longer than you think, and that you will need two coats, plus drying time. And so what if you didn't finish it in four days? Relax! Allow more time next time.) Am I really worried about what my mother will say? (No, because I'm the one who has to look at it every day.) So the solution? Step one is to paint the trim first and then re-evaluate. Using a method of reflection to think back over my "draft" gives me a method for proceeding with "revision." At the risk of sounding like a pop song, when you stop to think it through, you'll know what to do.

Revision isn't just in writing. These methods can be applied any time you are working on a project—of any kind—or have to make decisions about something. Establishing the habit of reflective thinking will have far-reaching benefits in your education, your career, and your life. It's an essential key to success for the life-long learner.

Discussion

1. Define what metacognitive or reflective writing is. What are some of the prompts or "topics" for reflective writing?

2. Have you ever been asked to do this type of writing? If so, briefly discuss your experience.

3. Why does reflective writing help a student learn and develop as a better writer? How does it work?

4. Draft a Letter to the Reader for an essay you are working on right now. Analyze the letter to see what strengths or problems it uncovers regarding your essay.

Works Cited

Anson, Chris M. "Talking About Writing: A Classroom-Based Study of Students' Reflections on Their Drafts." Smith and Yancey 59–74.

Bishop, Wendy. "Life Writing." English Department. Florida State University, Tallahassee, FL. Summer 2002. Lecture.

Cheng, Xiaoguang, and Margaret S. Steffenson. "Metadiscourse: A Technique for Improving Student Writing." *Research in the Teaching of English* 30.2 (1996): 149–81. Print.

Howard, Rebecca Moore. "Applications and Assumptions of Student Self-Assessment." Smith and Yancey 35–58.

O'Neill, Peggy. "Reflection and Portfolio Workshop." Humanities Division. Abraham Baldwin Agricultural College, Tifton, GA. 25 January 2000. Lecture, workshop.

Smith, Jane Bowman. "'Know Your Knowledge': Journals and Self-Assessment." Smith and Yancey 125–38.

Smith, Jane Bowman, and Kathleen Blake Yancey, eds. *Self-Assessment and Development in Writing: A Collaborative Inquiry.* Cresskill, NJ: Hampton, 2000. Print.

Sommers, Jeffrey. "Behind the Paper: Using the Student-Teacher Memo." *College Composition and Communication* 39.1 (1988): 77–80. Print.

—. "Enlisting the Writer's Participation in The Evaluation Process." *Journal of Teaching Writing* 4.1 (1985): 95–103. Print.

Winegardner, Mark. Personal interview. 3 February 2003.

Yancey, Kathleen Blake, and Jane Bowman Smith. "Reflections on Self-Assessment." Smith and Yancey 169–76.

Wikipedia Is Good for You!?

James P. Purdy

"I actually do think Wikipedia is an amazing thing. It is the first place I go when I'm looking for knowledge. Or when I want to create some."

—*Stephen Colbert*

You may not realize it, but creating knowledge is one reason you are asked to do research-based writing[1] in college.[*] And a popular resource you may already use can help you with this task—though perhaps not in the way you might initially think. Wikipedia, the free wiki "encyclopedia,"[2] can provide information to assist you with and model some of the activities frequently characteristic of college-level research-based writing. As with any resource you use, your success with Wikipedia depends on how and why you use it. The goal of this chapter is to show you how and why you might use Wikipedia to help you complete research-based writing tasks for your first year composition class. It offers suggestions for two ways to use—and not to use—Wikipedia. The first is as a source. The second is as a process guide.

My premise for the first is that you are going to use Wikipedia as a source for writing assignments regardless of cautions against it, so it is more helpful to address ways to use it effectively than to ignore it (and ignoring it precludes some potentially beneficial uses of Wikipedia anyway). My premise for the second is that, as I argue else-

---

[*] This work is licensed under the Creative Commons Attribution-Noncommercial-Share Alike 3.0 United States License and is subject to the Writing Spaces Terms of Use. To view a copy of this license, visit http://creativecommons.org/licenses/by-nc-sa/3.0/us/ or send a letter to Creative Commons, 171 Second Street, Suite 300, San Francisco, California, 94105, USA. To view the Writing Spaces Terms of Use, visit http://writingspaces.org/terms-of-use.

where, Wikipedia can reinforce approaches to research-based writing that many composition teachers support. Wikipedia, that is, can help to illustrate (1) recursive revision based on idea development, (2) textual production based on participation in a conversation rather than isolated thinking, and (3) research based on production rather than only critique (Purdy). The process of successfully contributing to a Wikipedia article, in other words, parallels the process of successfully creating a piece of research-based writing. Both involve putting forth ideas in writing and developing them in response to feedback based on audience members' perceptions of the usefulness, accuracy, and value of those ideas.

I offer two caveats before I proceed. All first year writing instructors teach research-based writing differently and ask you to produce different kinds of texts for assignments, so you will need to adapt the suggestions offered in this essay for your particular course and assignment. My goal is not to mandate one correct, universally applicable process of research-based writing. There is none. Nor is it to claim that products of research-based writing should look like a Wikipedia article. They should not. Wikipedia articles are a different genre than academic research-based writing. Wikipedia seeks to emulate an encyclopedia (that's where the "pedia" part of the name comes from) and, thereby, requires that articles be written in what it calls "NPOV," or neutral point of view; articles are intended to represent all significant sides of a topic rather than to persuade readers to believe one is correct (Bruns 113–114, "Wikipedia:Neutral"). Research-based writing assignments in first year composition commonly ask you to advance and develop your own argument on a topic by drawing on and responding to relevant outside sources. While you may be asked to represent multiple views on a topic for such an assignment, you will frequently be asked to argue for one, so your writing will likely be more overtly persuasive than a Wikipedia article.

Despite these important differences, I believe that some of the practices often involved in successfully writing a Wikipedia article are also often involved in successfully writing a research-based text for college classes: reviewing, conversing, revising, and sharing. As Australian scholar Axel Bruns asserts, "Wikipedia . . . is closely aligned with the live processes of academic exchanges of knowledge" (208, italics in original). Thus, this chapter proceeds with the assumption that it is useful to consider Wikipedia as both a product (i.e., a source) and a representation of process (i.e., a guide to practices).

USING WIKIPEDIA AS A SOURCE

The first way you may think to use Wikipedia is as a source—that is, as a text you can quote or paraphrase in a paper. After all, Wikipedia is easy to access and usually pretty easy to understand. Its articles are often current and frequently provide interesting facts and information that can support your ideas. What's not to like?

Usually teachers do not like two primary aspects of Wikipedia. The first is its open participation: anyone, regardless of background, qualifications, or expertise, can write Wikipedia articles. As a result, articles can display incorrect information. There are many examples of such incorrect information on Wikipedia. Perhaps the most infamous involves the Wikipedia article on John Seigenthaler (former journalist, political advisor, and father of the reporter of the same name on NBC news). Brian Chase changed the article to indicate that Seigenthaler played a role in the assassination of President John F. Kennedy and his brother Robert. This untrue contribution lasted for 132 days (Page, "Wikipedia Biography"). Seigenthaler was understandably upset, which he reported vociferously in an article in *USA Today* (Seigenthaler). Were someone to take Wikipedia's John Seigenthaler[3] article at face value during this time, she or he would come to the wrong conclusion about Seigenthaler. If you quote or paraphrase a Wikipedia article as an authoritative source, then, you are potentially making a claim based on wrong information, and using incorrect information is not a good way to make a convincing argument. Of course, misinformation isn't limited to Wikipedia. As Jim Giles reports in *Nature*, Encyclopaedia Britannica has errors in some of its articles, too; he claims that Wikipedia is almost as accurate as Britannica for a series of articles on science topics (900–901; see also Bruns 127–133, Levinson 93). You should, therefore, read critically all sources, not just Wikipedia articles. It's always a good idea to verify information in multiple sources. To ensure a better chance of accuracy, though, college-level research-based writing assignments generally ask you to use sources written by academic professionals and recognized experts.

The second aspect of Wikipedia that many teachers do not like is its changeability: Wikipedia articles do not remain the same over time. The *Michael Jackson* article makes this explicit. Its 19:35, 27 June 2009 version begins with a header: "This article is **about a person who has recently died**. Some information, such as that pertaining to the circumstances of the person's death and surrounding events, may change rapidly as more facts become known" (emphasis in original). As this notice implies, the article didn't stay the same for long given the unfolding details of Jackson's death. As a result of such changeability, Wikipedia articles are unreliable; the article you cite today may not exist in that form tomorrow. This variability challenges prevailing understanding of how published texts work so causes some anxiety. Because print texts are (relatively) stable, we expect texts we read (and cite) to be the same when we go back to them later. Even Wikipedia contributors express worry about the implications of article changeability for citation:

> Among other problems . . . if several authors cite the same Wikipedia article, they may all cite different versions, leading to complete confusion. That just linking to the article sans version information is not enough can be seen by those Wikipedia articles themselves which refer to others, where it is clear from following the link that a different version was referred to (and there is no clue which of the many versions in the history was actually read by the person who cited it). ("Why Wikipedia Is Not So Great")

As Wikipedians explain, article variability makes citing hard because it is difficult for readers to know which version of a Wikipedia article an author cited. And academic audiences like to be able to return to the texts you cite to verify the conclusions you draw from them. If the texts you cite don't exist anymore, they cannot do that.

Teachers have concerns about you using Wikipedia as a source for another reason—one that has less to do with Wikipedia itself and more to do with the kinds of texts you are expected to use in research-based writing. Most college-level writing asks you to engage more deeply with a subject than does an encyclopedia, and doing so entails reading more than the general overview of a topic that encyclopedia articles provide.[4] So articles from any encyclopedia are not usually good sources to quote, paraphrase, or summarize in your writing. Indeed, in response to Middlebury College's history department officially banning students from using Wikipedia as a source in their papers, Sandra Ordonez, a spokesperson for Wikipedia, and Roy Rosenzweig, Director of the Center for History and New Media at George Mason University, agreed "the real problem is one of college students using encyclopedias when they should be using more advanced sources" (Jaschik n. pag.). If you wouldn't cite an encyclopedia article in a project, then citing a Wikipedia article likely isn't a good idea either.

Because of their open participation, unreliability, and (potentially) shallow topic coverage, you generally should not cite Wikipedia articles as authoritative sources in college-level writing. This does not mean that Wikipedia is not useful, or that you cannot read it, or that you should not cite it if you do use it. It does mean that Wikipedia is better used in other ways.

Using Wikipedia as a Starting Place

There are productive ways to use Wikipedia. In fact, Wikipedia can be a good source in three different ways. Rather than a source to cite, it can be a source of (1) ideas, (2) links to other texts, and (3) search terms.

To use Wikipedia as a source of ideas, read the Wikipedia article on your topic when you begin a research-based writing project to get a sense of the multiple aspects or angles you might write about. Many Wikipedia articles include a table of contents and headings that provide multiple lenses through which you might frame an argument (e.g., origins, history, economics, impact, production). Looking at the table of contents and headings can help you view your topic from vantage points you might not otherwise consider and can give you directions to pursue and develop in your writing.

You can also use Wikipedia as a gateway to other texts to consult for your research. Wikipedia's Verifiability Policy requires that material posted to articles be verifiable—that is, be cited (Bruns 114, "Wikipedia:Verifiability")—so articles include bibliographies, as shown in figure 1. They also frequently include "further reading," "external link," or "see also" lists, as shown in figure 2. These lists provide the names of—and often direct links to—other sources. Take advantage of these leads. When you have decided on a topic and are searching for sources to develop and support your thinking, look at these references, external links, and further reading lists. Wikipedia's Verifiability Policy, however, does not stipulate what kinds of sources contributors must cite to verify the information they post, so these reference and further reading lists do not necessarily provide connections to trustworthy, valid texts appropriate for citing in an academic paper (but, then again, neither do other sources). You still need to evaluate a source to determine if it is suitable for use.

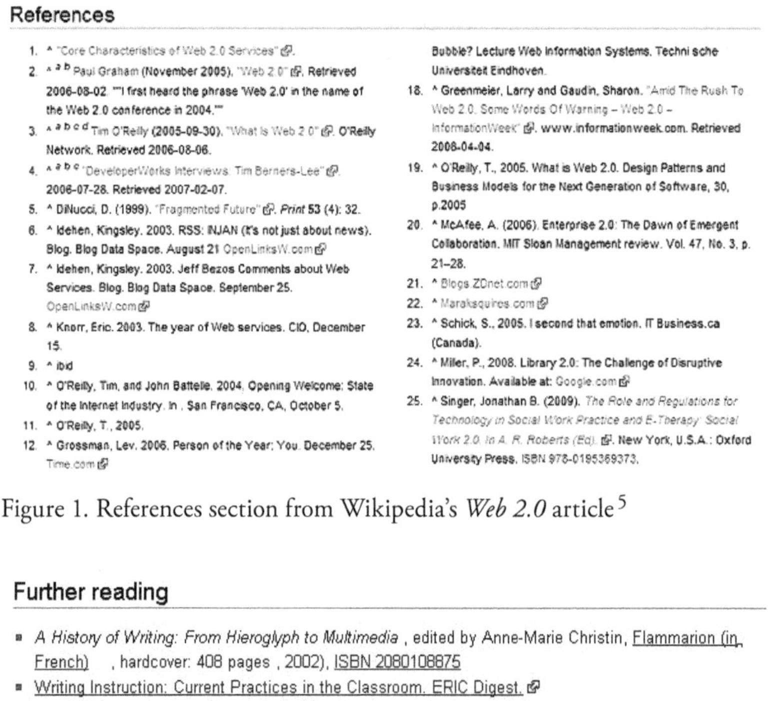

References

1. ^ "Core Characteristics of Web 2.0 Services" 🔗.
2. ^ a b Paul Graham (November 2005). "Web 2.0" 🔗. Retrieved 2006-08-02. "'I first heard the phrase 'Web 2.0' in the name of the Web 2.0 conference in 2004.'"
3. ^ a b c d Tim O'Reilly (2005-09-30). "What Is Web 2.0" 🔗. O'Reilly Network. Retrieved 2006-08-06.
4. ^ a b c 'DeveloperWorks Interviews: Tim Berners-Lee" 🔗. 2006-07-28. Retrieved 2007-02-07.
5. ^ DiNucci, D. (1999). "Fragmented Future" 🔗. Print 53 (4): 32.
6. ^ Idehen, Kingsley. 2003. RSS: INJAN (it's not just about news). Blog. Blog Data Space. August 21 OpenLinksW.com 🔗
7. ^ Idehen, Kingsley. 2003. Jeff Bezos Comments about Web Services. Blog. Blog Data Space. September 25. OpenLinksW.com 🔗
8. ^ Knorr, Eric. 2003. The year of Web services. CIO, December 15.
9. ^ ibid
10. ^ O'Reilly, Tim, and John Battelle. 2004. Opening Welcome: State of the Internet Industry. In . San Francisco, CA, October 5.
11. ^ O'Reilly, T., 2005.
12. ^ Grossman, Lev. 2006. Person of the Year; You. December 25. Time.com 🔗

Bubble? Lecture Web Information Systems. Techni sche Universiteit Eindhoven.
18. ^ Greenmeier, Larry and Gaudin, Sharon. "Amid The Rush To Web 2.0, Some Words Of Warning – Web 2.0 – InformationWeek" 🔗. www.informationweek.com. Retrieved 2008-04-04.
19. ^ O'Reilly, T., 2005. What is Web 2.0. Design Patterns and Business Models for the Next Generation of Software, 30, p.2005
20. ^ McAfee, A. (2006). Enterprise 2.0: The Dawn of Emergent Collaboration. MIT Sloan Management review. Vol. 47, No. 3, p. 21–28.
21. ^ Blogs.ZDnet.com 🔗
22. ^ Maraksquiros.com 🔗
23. ^ Schick, S., 2005. I second that emotion. IT Business.ca (Canada).
24. ^ Miller, P., 2008. Library 2.0: The Challenge of Disruptive Innovation. Available at: Google.com 🔗
25. ^ Singer, Jonathan B. (2009). The Role and Regulations for Technology in Social Work Practice and E-Therapy. Social Work 2.0 In A. R. Roberts (Ed). 🔗. New York, U.S.A.: Oxford University Press. ISBN 978-0195369373.

Figure 1. References section from Wikipedia's *Web 2.0* article [5]

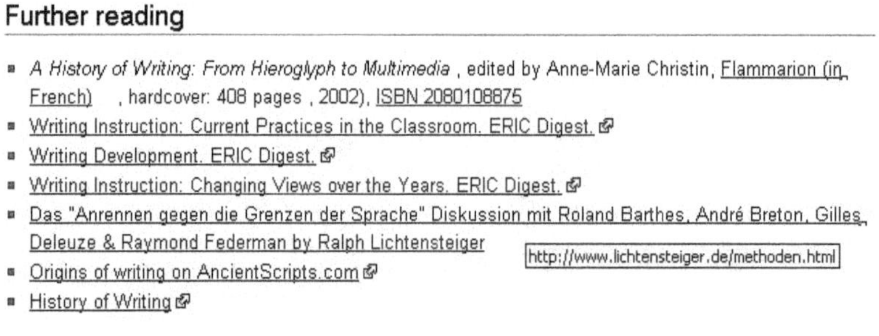

Further reading

- *A History of Writing: From Hieroglyph to Multimedia* , edited by Anne-Marie Christin, Flammarion (in French)   , hardcover: 408 pages , 2002), ISBN 2080108875
- Writing Instruction: Current Practices in the Classroom. ERIC Digest. 🔗
- Writing Development. ERIC Digest. 🔗
- Writing Instruction: Changing Views over the Years. ERIC Digest. 🔗
- Das "Anrennen gegen die Grenzen der Sprache" Diskussion mit Roland Barthes, André Breton, Gilles Deleuze & Raymond Federman by Ralph Lichtensteiger   http://www.lichtensteiger.de/methoden.html
- Origins of writing on AncientScripts.com 🔗
- History of Writing 🔗

Figure 2. Further reading section from Wikipedia's *Writing* article

Utilizing Wikipedia as a gateway to other sources should not replace going to the library or using your library's online databases. In fact, reviewing the Wikipedia article on your topic can help you better discover sources in your school's library. You might read Wikipedia articles to help you generate search terms to use for finding sources in your school library's catalog and online databases. Ashley Gill (who, like all students quoted in this essay, consented to the use of her real name) explains how she used Wikipedia in this way for an award-winning research project for her school's first year composition class:

> For this project, I began on Wikipedia, knowing that results were not accurate, but also knowing I could find useful search terms there. I was only slightly familiar with the psychology angle I was using for my paper, and so Wikipedia gave me a rough sketch of the general background. From here, I used the information I gained from Wikipedia to search for books form [*sic*] the . . . Library. ("Research" 2–3)

Gill acknowledges Wikipedia's problem with accuracy but outlines ways in which Wikipedia was still really useful in helping her get some general background information to determine search terms to use to find sources through the library. You might find Wikipedia similarly useful.

USING WIKIPEDIA AS A PROCESS GUIDE

Not only is Wikipedia potentially useful for generating ideas, finding sources, and determining search terms, but it is also potentially useful for remembering and understanding some of the tasks that are frequently part of good research-based writing: reviewing, conversing, revising, and sharing. To be clear, I am not suggesting that all types of research-based writing ask you to do these tasks in exactly the same way or that your writing should emulate a Wikipedia article. However, some of what happens in making successful contributions to Wikipedia parallels some of what happens in producing effective research-based writing. Looking at Wikipedia can help to demystify these practices. These practices happen recursively—that is, they repeat—so the order in which I present them here is not necessarily the best or correct one. While you do not need to move through these practices in a specific order, you will want to engage in these activities for many research-based writing assignments.

The Wikipedia Interface

Before proceeding, let me offer an overview of the Wikipedia interface so that the following discussion, which points to specific aspects of the interface, makes sense. A Wikipedia article's interface has four tabs, as shown in figure 3. These tabs are labeled "article," "discussion," "edit this page," and "history." The "article" tab contains the content of the article. This content is what displays automatically when you open an article in Wikipedia. The "discussion" tab provides access to the conversation surrounding the article, how it is being written, and the topic being written about. On this page users can, among other things, suggest changes to an article, justify changes they made to an article, and ask why other users made changes to an article. You can participate in this conversation. The "edit this page" tab provides a space for users to add, delete, or revise content of an article. This page is where people write the content that is displayed on the "article" page. You can make these changes. Finally, the "history" tab lists all the versions of the article, when they were written, who updated them, and what changes each user made (each author can provide a summary of his or her changes). On the "history" tab users can also compare and contrast selected article versions.

| article | discussion | edit this page | history |

Web 2.0

From Wikipedia, the free encyclopedia

Web 2.0 is a term describing the trend in the use of World Wide Web technology and web design that aims to enhance creativity, information sharing, and, most notably, collaboration among users. These concepts have led to the development and evolution of web-based communities and

Figure 3. A Wikipedia article interface's four tabs as shown for the Web 2.0 article

Each of the sections below is devoted to a practice common to both successful Wikipedia contributions and research-based writing. In each, I explain how Wikipedia authors engage in that practice, outline how you can learn from what Wikipedians do to engage in that practice for your research-based writing, and finally provide a specific way you can use Wikipedia for help with that practice.

REVIEWING

Examining the role of reviewing in contributing to a Wikipedia article can help you understand the role of reviewing in research-based writing. To make a successful contribution to Wikipedia, authors must review what other contributors have already written about the topic. They don't want to include information that the community of people interested in and knowledgeable about the topic has determined to be inappropriate, off topic, or unimportant, or to simply repeat information already published. Such contributions will be deleted—usually quickly—because they do not offer anything new to people's understanding of the topic.

To do this review, successful Wikipedia contributors read texts in and outside of Wikipedia. They look at previous versions of an article on the history page, including the change summaries provided by authors, and read the discussion surrounding an article on the discussion page. To show that they have reviewed other texts published on the topic of the article they are contributing to, Wikipedians also provide citations for material they post. As I indicate above, Wikipedia requires that material posted to articles be verifiable (Bruns 114, "Wikipedia:Verifiability"), so contributors need to demonstrate that they can verify material they post by citing its source. As shown in figure 4, an absence of citations often results in a warning that someone needs to cite a source to support what is written or the text will be removed.

 This article may contain original research. Please improve it by verifying the claims made and adding references. Statements consisting only of original research may be removed. More details may be available on the talk page. *(February 2010)*

Figure 4. Wikipedia's warning to provide citations to verify claims from the research article

This process parallels what you can do for research-based writing assignments. Review what other contributors have already published about your topic so you avoid writing something that is inappropriate, off topic, or repetitive. Doing this review in formal course writing is somewhat different than doing it in Wikipedia, though. You need to acknowledge in the texts you write that you have reviewed what others have previously published by doing what is called a literature review. A literature review entails summarizing main points from your sources, identifying their insights and/or limitations, and situating these texts in relation to one another and your writing.

Let's look at an example. Gill provides a literature review in her essay "The Analogical Effects of Neural Hemispheres in 'The Purloined Letter'":

> There are approaches to cognitive, and consequently behavioral, functioning that stem from ideas that each side of the brain thinks differently. Michael Grady asserts that a person who thinks with one side of his brain will differ greatly than a person who thinks with the opposite side (20–21). According to Thomas Regelski, the left side is said to think in the following ways: "linear, sequential, logical, analytical, verbal, fragmenting, differentiating, convergence (seeks closure) . . . conventional symbols, facts (objective, impersonal, confirmable), precision, explicit, Scientific Empiricism/Logical Positivism/certitude/surety" (30). Conversely, Regelski establishes that the right side is responsible for thinking in the subsequent ways, which seemingly oppose the first set of thinking methods: "circular, simultaneous, paradoxical, combinative, holistic, divergence (content with open-endedness) . . . expressive, vague, implicit . . . Immanence/Introspectionism/Intuitionism/Intuitive Cognition/indwelling/insight/intuition" (30). Sally Springer and Georg Deutsch assert in their book *Left Brain, Right Brain* that the human brain is divided in this model, and an easier way to interpret this model is "the left hemisphere is something like a digital computer, the right like an analog computer"

> (185), and that depending on which hemisphere the individual uses most primarily, the individual will think and therefore act in accord with said attributed qualities (186). Poe incorporates many of these characteristics into his characters['] methods during the investigation. The Prefect exemplifies the left side thinking with his systematic and complex approach to finding the purloined letter, while the Minister and Dupin utilize both right and left side attributes, thinking about the cognitions of the other and acting accordingly. (12–13)

Here Gill shows that she has reviewed the work of Grady, Regelski, and Springer and Deutsch by over-viewing their claims about brain function and then connecting those claims to her argument about "The Purloined Letter." Like a successful Wikipedia contributor, she also offers citations, though the form of these citations is different than in Wikipedia. Wikipedia generally uses hyperlinked endnotes, while the most popular academic citation styles from the American Psychological Association (APA) and Modern Language Association (MLA), which Gill uses here, require in-text parenthetical citations and reference and works cited lists, respectively. Despite these differences, the larger idea is the same: in your research-based writing you need to show you have reviewed other relevant texts to demonstrate conversance with appropriate source material and to allow readers to verify your conclusions.

I end this section suggesting a way you can use Wikipedia to help you with this reviewing process. My intention here is to not to prepare you to contribute to a Wikipedia article itself, but rather to use Wikipedia to prepare you to do the reviewing that is part of successful research-based writing. When you are beginning a research-based writing assignment, read the discussion page for the Wikipedia article on the topic you are writing about and identify the debates, questions, and absences that you find. In other words, list what contributors (1) argue about (i.e., what ideas are contentious), (2) have questions about, and (3) think is missing from and should be included in coverage of that topic. Then identify these debates, questions, and absences for the published literature (i.e., books, articles) on your topic. Review what other authors have written about them. Looking at the discussion page first allows you to enact on a smaller scale what you need to do with a wider range of sources for a literature review in a research-based writing project.

Let's consider an example. If you read the discussion page for the Wikipedia article *History of the board game Monopoly*, a section of which is shown in figure 5, you will find that contributors argue about when the game originated and the role Elizabeth Magie played in its creation; they ask questions about the rules for players selling property to one another; and they think information on the volume of game sales, McDonald's Monopoly games/promotions, and the World Monopoly Championships is missing and should be addressed more fully. Were you to write about the history of the board game Monopoly, you now have several avenues (no pun intended!) to read about and know what you might need to review in making an argument on the topic.

The First Paragraph   [edit]

Why does the first paragraph not say what country it is talking about? It could be talking about Indonesia for all i know. Shouldn't this have been read before putting it on the front page? *sigh* Cokehabit 01:43, 13 December 2006 (UTC)

> It's a board game, originally developed in the USA, which IS mentioned in the first paragraph. The introduction is no more specific than that because of the game's international history. Adding geography to a non-geographic subject would seem to make no sense. -- JohnDBuell 01:54, 13 December 2006 (UTC)

>> It is a terrible start to an article: *The history of the board game Monopoly can be traced back to the early 1900s.* Where? How? References?

>>> Yes we do give references. But you have to read them yourself to get the information you're asking for... -- Derek Ross | Talk 07:49, 13 December 2006 (UTC)

Based on original designs by Elizabeth Magie - If it can be traced back to Elizabeth Magie how come there were *several designs* over 30 years? Why is her name in there if the origin, date and original designer isn't known? When were her designs made? Which of the several designs were hers?

> That's because Monopoly was like a wikipedia article. Magie made the first few versions, then other people tweaked it over 30 years. So the name and the design both changed as time went by. It's still basically the same game though. Very much like a Wikipedia article really. -- Derek Ross | Talk 07:49, 13 December 2006 (UTC)

Figure 5. Section of the discussion page from Wikipedia's *History of the board game Monopoly* article

CONVERSING

A second practice successful Wikipedia contributors engage in that reflects a successful practice of research-based writing is conversing. Productive Wikipedia authors situate their contributions to an article in relation to those of past authors, recognizing that making a contribution to an article is like stepping into an ongoing conversation. Wikipedia authors engage in this practice by posting to the discussion page—for example, by asking questions of and responding to other contributors and by arguing for why they made certain changes—and by providing change summaries for their contributions when they edit an article, particularly change summaries that identify briefly why they made a certain change—for example, "corrected factual errors in introduction," "deleted irrelevant information to maintain article focus."

As with reviewing, conversing is another practice frequently characteristic of successful research-based writing. You should respond to the sources you use rather than just report on or parrot them. While Wikipedia contributors can literally insert themselves into a conversation on a Wikipedia article discussion page, you can engage in conversation with sources in research-based writing by quoting, paraphrasing, and summarizing them; by indicating agreements, disagreements, and connections among them and you; and by showing their insights, limitations, and applications.

Consider the following example. In a paragraph from "Literacy," an award-winning first year composition essay on the need to "broaden the range of serious reading material for youth to include comic books and the [I]nternet" (16), Lindsey Chesmar acknowledges what two other sources, Bob Hoover (italicized below) and Janell D. Wilson and Linda H. Casey (bolded below), have written about youth reading behaviors and inserts what she wishes to say in response to them (unformatted text below):

> *The NEA report, "To Read or Not to Read," [sic] shows "the startling declines, in how much and how well Americans read" (Hoover 1).* Although many people could have already guessed, this NEA report officially states what has been on the decline since the early 1990s. However, it seems as though the NEA left out some important data when conducting their study. **According to Wilson and Casey, "comic books have been at the top of the student preference list for sometime, yet it seems that they may not count as 'serious' reading material" (47). Children and young adults have been reading comics and comic books since their beginning. Some educators also use comics in class as a way to interest students who would be otherwise unwilling to read (Wilson and Casey 47).** However, literary studies rarely include

comic books in their questions and surveys of youth. If a young adult spends 3 hours a week reading comic books, the study will not include that in their overall findings. It is as if that time the young adult spends reading means nothing. *The NEA itself did not include the "double-digit growth in recent years" in sales of books aimed at teens (Hoover 1).* This statistic leads me to believe that teens are actually reading more than what the recent studies suggest. Leaving out some young adults' reading time and the growing popularity of young adult books could lead to misrepresentations in the results of the overall literacy studies. This also may lead the young adult to believe that what they are reading is not worthy enough, or "serious" enough, to count towards anything. They may feel discouraged and give up reading all together after finding out the things they like to read are not valid in the literary and educational worlds. (17, italics and boldface added)

In this paragraph, Chesmar makes clear that she knows important components of the ongoing conversation about literacy and reading: the National Endowment for the Arts (NEA) released a study that reports reading (amount and proficiency) has declined in the United States and, though popular among young adults, comic books did not count as reading material for the study. She puts sources discussing these ideas into conversation; note the back and forth between the bold, italics, and unformatted text. She then responds to these sources, writing, "This statistic leads me to believe that teens are actually reading more than what the recent studies suggest" (17). Chesmar thereby establishes her role in the conversation: she thinks the NEA report provides misleading results because it ignores certain types of reading material, which, for her, can have some troubling consequences.

Again, I end this section offering a suggestion for how you can use Wikipedia to help you with the research-based writing process—in this case, by putting your sources into conversation with one another and with you. One way to engage in a conversation like Chesmar does is to construct a dialogue between your sources like the dialogue on a Wikipedia article discussion page. Identify topics your sources address and create headings for them (e.g., concerns, benefits, history). Then quote and paraphrase relevant material from your sources and group it under the appropriate heading. Finally, situate these quotes and paraphrases in relation to one another and add yourself to the discussion. Literally construct a dialogue between them and you. The idea is to see yourself as a participant with a voice in the conversation.

Revising

Another practice that is part of successful Wikipedia and research-based writing is revising. Effective Wikipedia contributors revise articles frequently. They take advantage of the wiki capability to edit the articles they read. To be successful, they do not give up when other people delete or change their contributions but instead revise in response to the feedback they receive (be that from posts to the discussion page, change summaries on the history page, or administrator explanations for why something was removed). The history page for nearly any Wikipedia article provides evidence of how frequently Wikipedians revise. Figure 6, for instance, shows that authors made eleven revisions to the *Michael Jackson* article in one hour on 28 June 2009. As this page illustrates, making an enduring contribution to a Wikipedia article is an ongoing process of negotiation with the reading audience. Moreover, those contributors who revise the most and have their article contributions last for a long time can gain in status

Figure 6. Section of the history page from Wikipedia's *Michael Jackson* article.

among the Wikipedia community and be promoted to administrators. It is, in other words, through revising that Wikipedia contributors earn respect.

To succeed at research-based writing, you, like a successful Wikipedian, should also revise your texts multiple times in response to feedback you receive. You might receive such feedback from teachers, peers, writing center consultants, roommates, and friends who offer advice and suggestions rather than from strangers who change the text itself, as is the case for Wikipedia contributors. But the larger idea remains: creating an effective text involves multiple iterations of recursive revision. You need to write a draft, get some feedback, respond to that feedback in your next draft, and repeat the process. Good writing entails thinking through your ideas on the page or screen. Rarely do people record perfectly what they think the first time they write it down. Indeed, you often don't know what you think until you write it down. It is not uncommon, therefore, to find at the end of your first draft the thesis to develop in your second. That's okay! Knowledge production through writing is an ongoing process.

One way to use Wikipedia to help with revising a course assignment is to post a change to a Wikipedia article based on a draft you are writing, see how others respond and analyze those responses. In other words, give your idea a test drive with a public audience. If you aren't comfortable posting directly to an article or are afraid your contribution might get taken down, suggest a change on the discussion page and likewise chronicle the responses. Then revise your draft based on the feedback and responses you receive. The point of this activity isn't just to revise the Wikipedia article itself (though you might chose to do that later), but to use responses and what you learn by posting to Wikipedia to help you revise your research-based writing for class.

SHARING

A final practice successful Wikipedians engage in that reflects a successful practice of research-based writing is sharing. To get feedback, Wikipedia contributors share their writing; they post it for public viewing by editing an article and/or contributing to the discussion page for that article. Otherwise, they do not get feedback, their writing cannot have an impact on others' understanding of a topic, and they cannot gain in status among the Wikipedia community. To more fully participate in this sharing, they might even register and create a profile so other contributors and readers know who they are and can contact them. Professor Mark A. Wilson, for example, identifies contact with other people as a beneficial outcome of sharing his writing and photographs on the *Great Inagua Island* Wikipedia article. He was even invited to speak at the school of someone who saw what he shared.

You also need to share your writing to be successful. While this may seem obvious on some level, sharing involves more than turning in a final draft to a teacher. You have to be willing and prepared to share your writing earlier in your writing process. You can share by taking your writing to the writing center,[6] giving it to a classmate for a peer workshop, or reviewing it in a conference with an instructor. This sharing is clearly less public than posting to a widely accessible website like Wikipedia, but it still entails making written work available to a reading audience and is a critical part of the learning process. Key is that in order to get the most benefit from sharing—that is, to get feedback to which you can respond—you need to be prepared to share your writing prior to its due date. In other words, you cannot procrastinate.

Using Wikipedia as I suggest above in the revising section is also a good way to share your writing. After all, a goal of sharing is to get feedback to revise. You can, however, use wiki technology in another way to share your writing. You can record in a course wiki (or another wiki you create) your writing of a text, provide change summaries for all of the different versions along the way, and ask others to review your progress. Using a wiki in this way allows you to reflect on what you are doing and provides an accessible venue for you to share your work—one where your peers and your teacher can respond.

Conclusion

Understanding how to use (and not to use) Wikipedia as a source can help you avoid relying on Wikipedia in unproductive ways and can help you see sources as more than static products to plunk into your writing. In other words, looking at Wikipedia as a starting place (for ideas, sources, search terms, etc.) shows the importance of engaging with rather than ventriloquizing sources—of viewing sources as means to spur and develop your thinking rather than as means to get someone else to do your thinking for you.

Doing research-based writing can also be less daunting—and more fulfilling and fun—when you understand the practices involved and realize that these activities are an important part of knowledge creation. No one assigned Wikipedia contributors to proceed as they do. Since their goal, however, is to add to our understanding of a topic—the very same goal you have for the research-based writing you do in first year composition—they engage in certain activities: reviewing, conversing, revising, and sharing. Not all Wikipedians perform these practices in the same order in the same way, but successful Wikipedians do them. And the most dedicated contributors stay involved even after their text is shared: they read, respond, and revise, over and over again. The process doesn't stop when their writing is made public. That's just the beginning. If you approach your research-based writing in a similar fashion, it'll likely be the beginning of a journey of knowledge creation for you, too.

Notes

1. You may be familiar with the term *research paper* and may have been asked to write one for some of your classes. I don't use that term here, however. There are two primary reasons: (1) Research "papers" need not be papers anymore. That is, what you write need not be in the form of a print document. It might be a web site or a video or a poster or some other multimedia form. The term *research paper* doesn't encapsulate all these possibilities. (2) Research papers are often associated with presentations of what other people have written about a topic. When people hear *research paper*, in other words, they often think of compiling what other authoritative, smart people have to say about a topic and calling it a day. The kind of writing you are asked to do in college, however, requires more than that. It asks for your response to and application of what others have written. You need to do something with the sources you read (other than just string together quotes from them in your paper). So instead of *research paper*, I use *research-based writing*. This term emphasizes the activity (writing) rather than the medium (paper). This term also presents research as the basis (research-based), a beginning rather than an end.

2. I put the word "encyclopedia" in quotation marks because I argue that calling Wikipedia an encyclopedia and evaluating it based on the stan-

dards of print-based encyclopedias misrepresents the way it works (see Purdy W352, W357, W365).

3. For clarity, I italicize the names of Wikipedia articles in this chapter.

4. That Wikipedia provides the same shallow coverage as other encyclopedias, or even that it should be considered an encyclopedia, is debatable (Bruns 101–133, Levinson 95–98). Nonetheless, its prevailing classification as an encyclopedia raises concern.

5. This image, like all the images in this chapter, comes from the English version of Wikipedia (http://en.wikipedia.org/) and, like all Wikipedia content (except the logo, which Wikipedia does not allow to be reproduced), is licensed under the Creative Commons Attribution-Share Alike (http://creativecommons.org/licenses/by-sa/3.0) and GNU Free Documentation License (http://www.gnu.org/copyleft/fdl.html), which permit reproduction of content with attribution for non-commercial purposes, as explained by Wikipedia's official policy on reusing Wikipedia content ("Wikipedia:Reusing Wikipedia Content").

6. See Ben Rafoth's "Why Visit Your Campus Writing Center?" chapter in this *Writing Spaces* volume.

Works Cited

Bruns, Axel. *Blogs, Wikipedia, Second Life, and Beyond: From Production to Produsage*. New York: Peter Lang, 2009. Print.

Chesmar, Lindsey. "Literacy." *First Class: A Journal of First-Year Composition*. Pittsburgh, PA: Duquesne University, 2009. 16–19. Print.

Colbert, Stephen. Interview with Jimmy Wales. *The Colbert Report*. Comedy Central TV Network, 24 May 2007. Web. 28 June 2009.

Giles, Jim. "Internet Encyclopedias Go Head to Head." *Nature* 438.15. (15 Dec. 2005): 900–901. Web. 28 April 2006.

Gill, Ashley. "The Analogical Effects of Neural Hemispheres in 'The Purloined Letter.'" *First Class: A Journal of First-Year Composition*. Pittsburgh, PA: Duquesne University, 2009. 12–15. Print.

Gill, Ashley. "Research Log Reflection." Course Paper. Duquesne University, 2009. Print.

Jaschik, Scott. "A Stand against Wikipedia." *Inside Higher Ed*. Inside Higher Ed, 26 Jan. 2007. Web. 4 March 2008.

Levinson, Paul. *New New Media*. Boston: Allyn and Bacon, 2009. Print.

"Michael Jackson." *Wikipedia*. Wikimedia Foundation, 19:35, 27 June 2009. Web. 27 June 2009.

Page, Susan. "Author Apologizes for False Wikipedia Biography." *USA Today*. Gannett Co., 11 Dec. 2005. Web. 30 June 2009.

Purdy, James P. "When the Tenets of Composition Go Public: A Study of Writing in Wikipedia." *College Composition and Communication* 61.2 (2009): W351-W373. Print/Web. < http://www.ncte.org/library/NCTE-Files/Resources/Journals/CCC/0612-dec09/CCC0612When.pdf>.

"Revision History of Michael Jackson." *Wikipedia*. Wikimedia Foundation, 28 June 2009. Web. 28 June 2009.

Seigenthaler, John. "A False Wikipedia Biography." *USA Today*. Gannett Co., 29 Nov. 2005. Web. 25 June 2006.

"Talk:History of the Board Game Monopoly." *Wikipedia*. Wikimedia Foundation, 13 December 2006. Web. 13 Dec. 2006.

"Web 2.0." *Wikipedia*. Wikimedia Foundation, 15:13, 30 June 2008. Web. 30 June 2008.

"Why Wikipedia Is Not So Great." *Wikipedia*. Wikimedia Foundation, 14 Nov. 2004. Web. 22 Nov. 2004.

"Wikipedia Biography Controversy." *Wikipedia*. Wikimedia Foundation, 02:23, 30 June 2009. Web. 30 June 2009.

"Wikipedia in Research." *Wikipedia*. Wikimedia Foundation, 09:25, 16 Feb. 2010. Web. 20 Feb. 2010.

"Wikipedia:Neutral Point of View." *Wikipedia*. Wikimedia Foundation, 22:40, 6 Feb. 2010. Web. 8 Feb. 2010.

"Wikipedia:Reusing Wikipedia Content." *Wikipedia*. Wikimedia Foundation, 09:40, 13 July 2007. Web. 28 July 2007.

"Wikipedia:Verifiability." *Wikipedia*. Wikimedia Foundation, 17:42, 6 Feb. 2010. Web. 8 Feb. 2010.

Wilson, Mark A. "Professors Should Embrace Wikipedia." *Inside Higher Ed*. Inside Higher Ed, 1 April 2008. Web. 1 April 2008.

"Writing." *Wikipedia*. Wikimedia Foundation, 11:13, 9 June 2004. Web. 9 Nov. 2004.

Composing the Anthology: An Exercise in Patchwriting

Christopher Leary

Rebecca Moore Howard defines "patchwriting" as a method of composing in which writers take the words of other authors and patch them together with few or no changes (233).* Although associated with plagiarism, it is an extremely useful writing strategy with a very long and noble tradition, and I hope that, by the end of this essay, you will be convinced that the opportunities (great writing) far outweigh the risks (accusations of dishonesty). With that as my goal, I'll start by telling you the story of how I worked through my own fears and uncertainties about plagiarism and patchwriting.

Nowadays, I consider myself to be a frequent practitioner of patchwriting, especially early in my writing process. I also happen to really *enjoy* it—for one thing, it gets me past the stage of staring at a blank white page. Likewise, my students report that (in addition to being frustrating and time-consuming) patchwriting is "fun," "confidence-building," and "extremely interesting." I consider us to be the latest in a long-running line of writers [1] spanning centuries who view this type of work as crucial to their identities as writers.

Patchwriting was a mode I gravitated toward while studying for a degree in English at Long Island University in Brooklyn. Underemployed, single, without the kind of budget that would allow me to really partake in New York's "nightlife," without any cable TV or Internet access, I had, during much of this time, nothing to entertain myself in my bare apartment except for a bookshelf full of books.

During one notable phase of this period, I went one-by-one through each of my books, copying out short sentences until I had three or four pages worth of lines. Since the books were from different countries, times, genres, and personalities, I anticipated a sharp contrast in styles. "If I put tens of sentences from different times and eras and places all on the same page," my thinking went, "I'll be able to witness these eras bumping up against each other and rubbing elbows." In much the same way I find it interesting to view, say, automobiles from different times and places all in the same room.

After copying them into one Microsoft Word document, I started moving the sentences around, hoping to find sentences that *play weirdly* against each other. I was looking for that jarring effect, not expecting the exercise to go any further than that.

But once these lines were in the same document, I found that some were attracted to each other and others repelled. I dragged some over here, and some over there, deleting a lot, pruning a lot. The lines grouped themselves into stanzas, puzzlingly falling into place. For the most part, intuition told me where to move them, how to group them together, and which ones to delete. Much to my surprise, the lines that I had copied from the books in my bookshelf started to take a shape resembling the shape of a poem. And out of the original mess of lines, a scenario or situation—if not a story—started to emerge. (If you are getting visions of Ouija boards, I don't blame you.) I ended up spending a whole month on this project that was really meant to kill time one night.

Here is a small excerpt from the poem. I compiled it from work by Chinua Achebe, Milan Kundera, Gabriel Garcia Marquez, a lost source, and Henry James respectively.

> Then something had given way inside him.
> What about the hero who keeps his mouth shut?
> The intoxication of power began to break apart under the waves
>   of discomfort.
> "I can't help dreaming what I dream," he thought.
> Yet even as he afresh made this out, he felt how strange it all was.

This odd project got stickier when I decided I wanted to submit a few of the "poems" to my school's literary magazine, *Downtown Brooklyn*. I was held back by a concern and a strong feeling of guilt about authorship. I had to really wrestle with the question, "Am I the author of these texts?" When I got to the stage where I wanted to submit them as my own and put my name as the author, something felt very wrong and even dastardly. It didn't strike me as at all appropriate to put my own name as the author because I could not have written them "from scratch," by any means. The phrasings and language outstrip my capabilities.

I felt like a cheater. I worried I'd be accused of plagiarism or academic dishonesty. Ungenerous readers could fairly accuse me of trying to pass myself off as a better writer than I really am by stealing the language of established greats. Worse, my classmates and teachers could dismiss me as a parasite who, being completely unable to write his own poems, leeches off the work of others instead. The Dane Cook of poetry, so to speak.

At the same time, I recognized that, even if I didn't exactly write the things, I did sort of *make* them . . . and that ought to count for something.

My unshakeable moral dilemma propelled me to seek advice from a few knowledgeable poets whom I trust.

Conveniently, I shared a cubicle in the English Department during that time with someone I consider a "real" poet, a friend named Valerie. She's always blunt and I knew she'd give it to me straight. As the submission deadline approached, I found her in our graduate assistant cubicle. She was deep in thought, responding to a pile of work submitted by her undergraduate students. I plunked my shady texts on the top of her pile and peppered her with my doubts.

"Are these poems?" I asked Valerie. "Can I call them mine? Does it seem at all ethical to submit them to *Downtown Brooklyn*?"

She started off by saying that she did not particularly like what I'd shown her. ("That's not what I asked," I replied.) Yet she affirmed, technically speaking, they *are* poems and there was no reason not to submit them. She explained that what I was doing has a name—"found poetry"—and that it is a pretty conventional poetic strategy. She even found an old quote from her notebook and read it aloud: "The spider's web is no whit the better because it spins it from its own entrails; and my text no whit the worse because, as does the bee, I gather its components from other authors' flowers."

"Case closed," she said, slapping the quotebook shut and returning to her work.

Still, I wanted a second opinion, so I visited a faculty member and resident poet at LIU, Professor Moss, to ask him whether the work could legitimately be called mine and submitted to *Downtown Brooklyn* under my name. He agreed with Valerie that, yes, the poem is not very strong, and that, yes, it is in the tradition of "found poetry." He brought up another term, "the cento": it is a method of constructing poems (or even prose) out of quotations that are displaced and relocated. It's an ancient form that is still used today. One example my professor showed me was written by council members at the Academy of American Poets. They used lines from Charles Wright, Marie Ponsot, Emily Dickinson, Sylvia Plath, and Samuel Beckett, respectively, to compose the following:

> In the Kingdom of the Past, the Brown-Eyed Man is King
> Brute. Spy. I trusted you. Now you reel & brawl.
> After great pain, a formal feeling comes—
> A vulturous boredom pinned me in this tree
> Day after day, I become of less use to myself,
> The hours after you are gone are so leaden.

For a prose version, Professor Moss referred me to the essayist Walter Benjamin. Benjamin created a huge book, entitled *The Arcades Project*, consisting mostly of other people's writing about malls in Paris. Paradoxically, the book is "by" Benjamin, but there is not that much of his own writing in it. It's more like he just selects and arranges the writing of others. Below is a selection from *The Arcades Project*, with Benjamin's writing in bold, and other people's writing in italics:

> **In reference to Hausmann's success with the water supply and the drainage of Paris:** *"The poets would say that Hausmann was more inspired by the divinities below than by the gods above."* **Metro.** *"A great many of the stations have been given absurd names. The worst seems to belong to the one at the corner of the Rue Breguet and the Rue Saint-Sabin, which ultimately joined together, in the abbreviation 'Breguet-Sabin,' the name*

of a watchmaker and the name of a saint." **June Insur-
rection.** *"Most of the prisoners were transferred via the
quarries and subterranean passages which are located
under the forts of Paris and, which are so extensive that
most of half the population of the city could be contained
there. The cold in these underground corridors is so in-
tense that many had to run continually or move their
arms about to keep from freezing, and no one dared lie
down on the cold stones . . . The prisoners gave all the
passages names of Paris streets, and whenever they met
one another, they exchanged addresses."* (89)

Benjamin goes on like this—arranging the quotes of other writers—
for around a thousand extraordinary pages.

In the end, after we look at these examples together, and as we wrap
up our conversation, Professor Moss encouraged me in the exercises I
was doing but pointedly stated: "you must also mine your *own* writing,
not just other people's, for language that you like."

I point to my experience drafting and publishing those so-called
poems in *Downtown Brooklyn* because it played a pretty big role in my
own education in writing and language. One of the things you come
to realize as a patchwriter is that the shifting boundaries between writing, editing, and cheating are not problems you need to resolve, but
rather opportunities you can exploit.

ANTHOLOGIZING IN THE COMPOSITION CLASSROOM

One of the most obvious contemporary examples of patchwriting is
the anthology. This essay, for example, is part of an anthology called
Writing Spaces. The editors, Charles Lowe and Pavel Zemliansky,
didn't write the book, but they played a huge role in its construction.
In fact, if you have ever made a portfolio of your work, then you already pretty much understand anthologizing. The only difference is
that anthologies are collections mostly of *other* people's writing, instead of your own. And it turns out that many of the goals of portfolio
work equally apply to anthologizing in the classroom:

- Anthologizing and portfolio creation require you to move large
  chunks of texts around in relation to each other, almost as if
  you were rearranging a bookshelf.

- These practices help you to realize that texts, no matter the size, derive their meaning from the relationships of the parts that make it up.
- Each is an exercise in coherence. As Alan Schrift mentions, "For an anthology to work, the pieces must hang together, they must build on each other and if not articulate a thesis, at least give voice to several related theses" (192).
- In both portfolios and anthologies, you can inflect the pieces by placing them in different contexts, and you will begin to understand "how ideas fluctuate in specific types of spaces and contexts" (Rice 131).
- The anthologist and the portfolio manager have to manage what Ann Moss calls a "peculiar property": their "inherent capacity to balance unity and multiplicity" (430).

As convincing as this list might be to me, students don't always immediately warm to patchwriting as a brand of composition. For example, on the first day of class last year, during a break, Lorraina caught up with me in the hallway. "I am probably going to switch to a different section," she said. Drops are normal, I thought to myself, but not necessarily after the first hour of the first class.

"Are you concerned about the amount of work?" I said.

"Not the amount so much . . . more the type of work. I don't see how this so-called anthologizing is going to help me. We're going to be editing other people's work and writing introductory prefaces but none of that is what I need to do in my job."

"What is your job?"

"I work 9 to 5 all week for an insurance company, writing letters to customers," she said. "I want to get better at that, and I don't see how this type of work is going to help me."

Another student, Lisa, was on the brink of quitting as well. She was listening in on the hallway conversation, but, unlike Lorraina, decided to stick around. Months later, as the semester was finishing up, Lisa told me, "I thought I was going to drop this class after day one. I wanted to run when I heard about the anthologizing." She added, "But I'm glad I didn't."

Not to say there wouldn't be a lot more drops by other students throughout this particular semester. I can't say whether it was students fleeing from the odd Sunday morning hours, the pockets of swine flu that kept flaring up in our region of Queens, or the challenging coursework. Many students, I realized more and more as the semester progresses, plainly didn't have time to do all of the work that I asked them to do. They had full-time jobs, families to take care of, and a heavy course load of other classes. And, quite frankly, successful patchwriting requires a ton of reading.

WHAT IS READING LIKE FOR AN ANTHOLOGIST?

Creating an anthology with twenty-five texts in it doesn't mean you only have to read twenty-five texts. It's like photography—if a magazine photographer knows she is going to publish around ten photos in next month's issue, she won't take only ten photographs when she gets out in the field. A filmmaker creating a two-hour movie would be unwise to shoot only two hours of footage. As far as visual art goes, Winston Smith says, in an interview with SF Live, that for each collage that he composes, "I go through literally thousands of images looking for ones that are the right size and position for juxtaposing" (Stentz).

The same principle applies to patchwriters. In the midst of editing her anthology on family morality, Gail, a Queensborough Community College student, writes, "I am starting off working on the Internet reading different types of sources. This includes memoirs, court cases, newspaper articles, impact statements from those families affected. I am also working with poems and possibly works of art. After I gather a wide variety of work, I am going to narrow them down to the ones that have the greatest to do with my topic and help to tell my story." You might notice from Gail's writing that anthologists consider a slightly different set of questions than other readers. In other circumstances, when she doesn't have her editing cap on, Gail might read for plot, to see what happens, or to be able to say that she's read it. Or she might read for theme, main ideas, musicality, or pleasure.

However, during the anthologizing process, Gail reads for these reasons and a few others. It doesn't always matter so much what she learns from a piece, nor whether she agrees or disagrees with the author, nor whether she can identify the main points in it. It's more about what she can do with the text, how she can utilize it . . . how she can put it to work. It's a different kind of reading, and anthologists ask different kinds of questions as they make their way through a text, sometimes skimming, sometimes reading more closely. A student named Iga writes, "As I read, I am thinking about how one piece might fit with the others in the section. I am also thinking about how it is 'different' from the others (to create variety). Also, I look at the style of writing to make sure it is not just some sloppy work but something worthwhile." Iga's reading is very opportunistic. How, she asks, can I exploit this text that I am reading so that it increases the power and overall richness of my anthology?

While anthologists read, they think very strategically, trying to figure out where in the anthology a piece might go, if it will make it into the anthology at all, and what section or subsection it will go into. Gail puts the matter succinctly, saying that anthologists "view the texts not only on a personal level but also from the point of view of the audience it is intended for."

Unlike Lorraina, the insurance agent who dropped the class, I view the considerable time spent working on patchwriting to be well spent. It is a great experience in an underappreciated kind of composition, a kind that requires "working with information on higher levels of organization, pulling together the efforts of others into a multilayered multireferential whole which is much more than the sum of its parts" (Von Seggern).

However, for all of my confidence (and as much as I would like to convince you to try patchwriting), I'll end by admitting that some questions remain. For example, I think Lorraina was right to question how our anthological work would improve the letters she writes to customers. How would all of this have helped her at her job? The question of scale plays a big role here. Does improvement at one scale of writing (portfolio management) translate into improvement at other scales (letter writing)? Will your spelling improve as you arrange the books in a library? Will your experiments in patchwriting help you to improve your "grammar"?

DISCUSSION

1. What are some other situations where you organize the work of other people?

2. How might you reorganize the table of contents of the Writing Spaces collection that this article is a part of?

Note

[1] For example, the German-Hebrew writer Micha Berdyczewski wrote that compiling religious texts is a "poetic" (Kagan 223) practice that shines "new light" (Kagan 219) on them. This was puzzling to his friends, who viewed compiling the work of others to be a mundane, non-intellectual task. Also, the twenty-first century writer Jerome Rothenburg talks fondly of his textual assembly as "a pulling together of poems & people & ideas about poetry & much else in the words of others and in our own" (Golding). And the sixteenth century essayist and patchwriter Michel Montaigne says of his own work, "I have here only made a nosegay of culled flowers, and have brought nothing of my own but the thread that ties them together."

Works Cited

Achebe, Chinua. *Things Fall Apart*. Oxford: Oxford UP, 1996. Print.

Beckett, Samuel and Paul Auster. "Cascando." *Samuel Beckett*. New York: McGraw-Hill, 2006. 33. Print.

Benjamin, Walter. *The Arcades Project*. Oxford: Oxford UP, 1999. Print.

Dickinson, Emily, and R. Franklin. "After Great Pain a Formal Feeling Comes." *The Poems of Emily Dickinson*. New York: McGraw-Hill, 1999. 170. Print.

García Márquez, Gabriel. *One Hundred Years of Solitude*. Trans. Gregory Rabassa. New York: Perennial Classics, 1998. Print.

Golding, Alan. "Anthologizing the Innovative." n.d. Web. 13 May 2010. <http://epc.buffalo.edu/authors/bernstein/syllabi/readings/golding1.html>

Howard, Rebecca Moore. "A Plagiarism Pentimento." *Journal of Teaching Writing* 11.3 (Summer 1993): 233–46. Print.

James, Henry. *The Wings of the Dove*. Oxford: Oxford UP, 2008. Print.

Kagan, Zipora. "Homo Anthologicus: Micha Berdyczewski and the Anthological Genre." *The Anthology in Jewish Literature*. Ed. David Stern. Oxford: Oxford UP, 2004. 211-223. Print.

Kundera, Milan. *The Joke*. Oxford: Oxford UP, 2001. Print.

Montaigne, Michel. "Essays." n.d. Web. 21 July 2009 <http://philosophy.eserver.org/montaigne-essays.txt>.

Moss, Ann. "The Politica of Justus Lipsius and the Commonplace-Book." *Journal of the History of Ideas* 59.3 (1998). 421–36. Print.

Plath, Sylvia. "The Hanging Man." *The Oxford Book of American Poetry*. Ed. David Lehman and John Brehm. Oxford: Oxford UP, 2006. 886. Print.

"Poetic Form: Cento." *Poets.org: From the Academy of American Poets*. n.d. Web. 9 Mar. 2010.

Ponsot, Marie. "One is One." *The Bird Catcher*. New York: Knopf, 1998. Print.

Rice, Jeff. "Networks and New Media." *College English* 69.2 (2006): 127–33. Print.

Schrift, Alan. "Confessions of an Anthology Editor." Ed. Jeffrey DiLeo. On Anthologies. Lincoln: U of Nebraska P, 2004. 186–205. Print.

Stentz, Zack. "Class Cut-Ups: Collagists and Assemblagists Gain New Respect." *SF Live*, Dec. 1996. Web. 8 Mar. 2010.

Von Seggern, John. *Postdigital Remix Culture and Online Performance*. n.d. Web. 11 Jan. 2007.

Wright, Charles. "In the Kingdom of the Past, the Brown-Eyed Man is King." *Appalachia*. New York: Farrar, Straus, and Giroux, 1999. Print.

Collaborating Online: Digital Strategies for Group Work

Anthony T. Atkins

INTRODUCTION

Much of what you do in school, on the job, and in your everyday life involves the ability to work well with others.* Here, in college, your teachers will ask you to collaborate or work together in a number of ways. For example, you may be paired with one person to complete an in-class assignment, or you may be required to work with a group of three or four of your classmates to complete a semester-long project. Collaborative activities and assignments may occur in a number of your classes (English, Business, History, and Political Science to name a few). You may work with non-profit organizations, for instance, where you and your classmates develop a newsletter or brochure, or you may compose a grant to help a local organization build a park near your neighborhood. Group assignments like these require you and your group members to work efficiently, and require everyone to contribute to the project equally. Your teachers are looking for how well you can manage tasks, orchestrate togetherness, and demonstrate that everyone can work together productively to complete a project as a team or a group. Even though working in groups can be challenging, the truth is that much of what you will do both here in college and on the job occurs as a group effort. Indeed, collaboration with others can be difficult. What follows are some productive technological alternatives to face-to-face collaboration. In this chapter of *Writing Spaces* you will learn more about:

- Assessing the project or task;
- Using technology to organize the project;
- Using technology to present the project.

Assessing the Project or Task

In this section we will consider the following questions:

- What does the project entail? What is its purpose?
- How long should the project take?
- How many group members are needed or required, and what should each one do?
- What will be each group member's role?

Teachers or employers request a number of tasks or projects that require collaborating with others. Sometimes group tasks can last for one hour, and sometimes group tasks can last for several months (and sometimes even years, depending on the nature of the project and its purpose). For example, in a classroom, you might be asked to complete a quick group project within the fifty minute class period, or you may be asked to complete a month-long group project. Projects in a classroom are usually completed for a grade, whereby projects completed for an employer or businesses are evaluated as part of your job performance. Once you and your group members have been assigned a specific project, it is important to have a meeting to assess the project and all of its facets or components, and so you can get to know your group members.

Consider, for example, a group project (we'll call this Project A) that requires four people to work together as a team to create a newsletter for a non-profit organization. You and your group members should begin by reviewing the components of the assignment and the project. Producing a newsletter can require designing a layout, conducting research, creating copy, gathering visuals, and collating, collecting, editing, and proofing the final product. In this type of scenario, the team will need to determine how best to delegate responsibilities to each member. For example, one person could design the layout and look of the newsletter, one or two people might be responsible for the research and content development, and another person on the team might manage the final production of the newsletter—including collating pieces and editing.

Once tasks are assigned and each group member knows her/his responsibilities, determine what technologies you and your group will need to facilitate the project collaboratively, and set deadlines for tasks. Deadlines and managing time is extremely important when working with groups. Make certain that everyone in the group is aware of deadlines and is confident that they can be met. It is not uncommon to fall behind schedule, but how you and your team members react to added challenges determines the success or failure of the project. Adjusting group duties and pitching in to help each other can reassert the team's to complete the task.

In addition to working with a team of other students, sometimes students work with teachers or professors on individual projects—like an honor's thesis or professor-driven independent projects. This example (we'll call it Project B) references three separate honors projects directed/guided by the same teacher. Three students selected a range of general topics for their honors projects. Over the course of one semester, the honors projects required that each student write a traditional research paper on their topic, and provide a "poster" presentation as well as a formal presentation to an audience in a classroom setting.[1]

Part of the challenge of Project B is that the three students needed to read and respond to each other's projects, and the teacher needed to read and respond to each student's specific project as well. Because of the collaborative nature of Project B, the teacher and three students held an initial face-to-face meeting to determine tasks, roles, and collaboration spaces so that all members of the group could adjust their calendars and set deadlines. When individuals have a number of tasks or assignments that demand their attention, frequently meeting face-to-face is not conducive or productive. However, in the beginning of a collaborative task, such as Project B, it is extremely necessary to have a meeting so that a thorough assessment of the project and its requirements can be determined, which then provides useful information to the group for how to proceed.

Both Project A and B provide examples of ways that group work may be assigned in your classes. To be sure, there are a number of projects and ways that collaborative work is assigned and required by your teachers and your classes. Importantly, you should remember to assess the task, delegate responsibilities, and determine a timeframe (deadlines).

USING TECHNOLOGY TO ORGANIZE THE PROJECT

In this section, we will consider the following questions:

- Which technology will work best for a specific project?
- Should you use or do you need multimedia files and documents?
- What kind of editing and revising is required or needed?

Many free technologies are available to help organize collaborative projects. Because Web 2.0 technologies like wikis and Google Docs are so common, they lend themselves to easy use when collaborating with others. Using technologies to organize group work and projects can make group work more productive, alleviate problems with group members who are absent (or who do not participate), and cost nothing to use. They are also easily accessible. A collaborative technology like a wiki can help group members organize their contributions, respond to others' ideas, communicate with members of the group (easily forwarding links or electronic documents, for example), and facilitate a way to present the final group project to an audience. While there are a number of these technologies out there, wikis (like Wetpaint, PBWorks, or Wikispaces) and project management tools (like Google Docs) will serve as examples here of how to orchestrate a productive group work experience for you and your group members.

The most well-known wiki is Wikipedia. What makes Wikipedia intriguing is that all Wikipedia readers can edit most entries on the Wikipedia website.[2] This same concept is a shared characteristic among wikis. In short, it is what makes a wiki a wiki. Wikis, like many online free tools, often require a username and password. Everyone

registered on the site can create and share pages or add to already existing pages (just like editing an entry in Wikipedia) by writing text, uploading images, or linking to videos, images, text/articles, or to other
websites. The beauty in this tool is that it is free and all you need is
an Internet connection. Moreover, your group can use a wiki to make
contributions to your group project without having to meet face-to-
face.

Mashing in other collaborative technologies can further help you
to create, organize, and present your group project. To enhance the
productivity of your group work, you might also consider employing
another digital tool: Google Docs. Google Docs, like wikis, allows
users to create and share documents electronically removing the neces-
sity for face-to-face meetings. Once you create an account via Google,
you will have access to other features that Google has, like Google
Docs, Google Talk, and Gmail to name a few[3]. The attractive feature
of Google Docs, is that it allows you to create many of the same types
of documents as Microsoft Office (Word, Excel, and PowerPoint). So,
a team member could write the first draft of a proposal using Google
Docs and share the document with the team for easy editing online.
Or you could all revise and edit the document simultaneously. A link
to the document can also be included on your group wiki page for easy
access. In fact, because Google Docs is so valuable and easy to use,
even teachers and researchers are using it to collaborate on their own
research projects.

In Projects A and B, the wiki serves as a "house," meaning this is
where all information for the projects will be stored. The pages in the
wiki are created as separate "rooms" in the house. Each room (or page)
will represent a task in the project. Once the wiki is created and all
members create an account and join, each group member can create
their own page within the wiki so that information concerning that
task can be available and edited by all group members. To keep with
the house metaphor, each member can create their own "space" or
room and put in their room only the things they need. For example, in
Project A, the wiki might have a page for the contents of the newsletter whereby a group member can keep the other members up-to-date
on currently drafted articles or information, and provide a timeframe
for when other information will be available. For project A, you might
set-up a wiki this way:

1. Create three pages that correspond to the individual tasks. The three pages might be named: Newsletter Design, Newsletter Content, and Newsletter Production.

2. Each member of the group is responsible for a section and should post information pertaining to his or her task. This might include drafts of articles for the newsletter—as mentioned previously—sample or mock-up drafts of the design of the newsletter, or ideas pertaining to how the newsletter should be created.

3. Significantly, each member should contribute to the wiki in their specified area, or in their own room, but should also be visiting the other members' areas—or rooms—to provide helpful feedback and ideas as needed.

Figure 1. The wiki for Project A.

Similarly, Project B integrates wikis and Google Docs by following similar principles. For example, in Project B, each of the three students created their own page (room) within the wiki (house) that the teacher created for them. Each of their projects was located within the wiki, making it easy for the members of Project B to read and respond to each other's work (visit each other's rooms).

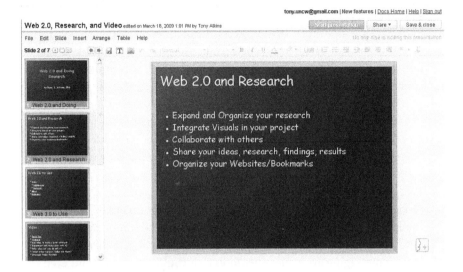

Figure 2. The wiki for Project B.

In Project B, all three students were expected to create their own projects, but were encouraged to collaborate with the other students working on individual projects for help with revising, brainstorming research questions, and finding articles or other multimedia files that could help another student. Working together was the best course of action because each group member had a detailed project that required a high quality product. The wiki allowed group members to post and share information with each other. Together, Project B group members felt that using a wiki would be the best technology to use for collaborating and sharing each others' work and progress.

How is using a wiki better or more helpful than simply meeting face-to-face? Aside from getting around schedule constraints trying to get all group members in the same room at the same time to work face-to-face, it also allows you and your group to always work in an electronic medium where all text, images, and links are saved at all times in one space, without having to trade files by email. All members have access to the same material from any location, and any group member can edit any of the documents at any time. Online collaboration also facilitates participation because group members who are often quiet in face-to-face meetings may feel less inhibited to participate or contrib-

ute to the project. You can also share the wiki with your teacher so she/
he can see your progress as your group completes the project.

There are a number of ways to share documents on a wiki, but an
easy option is to create your documents using Google Docs. For example, while some drafting can be done in a wiki, it is even easier to
create a Google Doc, draft an article for the project, then simply link
to it from the wiki, allowing all group members to see the link and edit
if they choose to do so. Regardless of whether you use wikis or Google
Docs, both also provide the added benefit of revision tracking, which
keeps a record of all changes made to the document and by whom.

With each group project, you will want to determine the best technological tool to complete the task. In Projects A and B, a wiki and
Google Docs seem to be the best tools for the purpose, but it should be
noted that there are a number of many Internet communication and
productivity tools available (blogs, Facebook, drop.io file sharing, and
instant messaging are some other tools that could assist you), and each
group should determine what works best for that particular group and
that particular project. Questions you might think about when determining which tool to use are:

- Will documents need to be edited, revised, or otherwise
  changed?
- Will group members need to be able to upload multimedia files
  and documents, and if so, what kinds and how large are they?
- Will documents need to be shared with more than assigned
  group members?

Answering these questions can help you determine the best technological tool for the task.

Assessing your project and determining the technological tools that
will help complete it are not the only challenges when it comes to group
work. Simply working with your group members can be difficult.
Some group members do not participate, lack motivation or desire,
or simply leave the bulk of the work to other group members, making excuses along the way. "Is this a group grade?" you might ask after
learning about a group project assigned in one of your classes. Why is
this a common question? By far, the biggest complaint of group work
from students is that some members do not contribute fairly, and then
the students who do the work must share the grade with the person

who did very little. Certainly, teachers have come up with numerous ways to track work among students within a collaborative project like progress reports, end-of-project reflections, and asking group members to "grade" each other. These attempts at making sure all members of a group participate equally come with mixed results. However, using wikis or Google Docs, and inviting the teacher to review your group's progress, gives your group and your instructor a permanent and visible record of the contributions each group member made.

Beyond using Web 2.0 technologies to help police non-contributing group members, using Web 2.0 tools can increase participation in your group by changing attitudes about group work. One of the reasons group projects can be successful is because group members can get excited by using a Web 2.0 technology to organize the project, and this has the potential to eliminate virtually all face-to-face meetings. Group members should decide on an exciting way to conduct and complete group work. Using a technology like a wiki, Google Docs, or a blog (or even a social networking site), can do more than excite group members about the project; it can also alleviate the problems associated with face-to-face discussion-based meetings and facilitate participation by all group members.

Once the project is complete, often you are asked to present the project to the class or to the group of people for whom you were working. As you will see in the next section, online digital tools can also help your group develop the presentation.

USING TECHNOLOGY FOR PRESENTATION

In this section we will consider the following questions:

- What type of presentation (or end product) is required?
- What tools will best help the group deliver a coherent presentation of the project?
- What technologies can help create the presentation?

Often, group work requires the presentation of the project to the class, teacher and/or people invested in the project. Presentations can take various forms. What kind of presentation you create is determined largely by the nature of the project itself. For example, if the group project you completed involved many numbers or statistics, you might consider creating graphs and charts to display the statistics in an honest and visually appealing format. Web 2.0 technologies can aid in this part of the project, too. Let's look at the two projects described earlier.

Projects A and B required two types of presentations. Project A required the development of a newsletter. Certainly, the audience will want to see the completed newsletter, but your teacher, the non-profit organization, and/or your classmates will also want to see how you collected the information to write the content of the newsletter and the process your group went through to design the newsletter. For example, how did your group decide on the design and layout of the newsletter? To illustrate the work your group completed, consider the technologies you used to organize the project and your group. When you and your group members use Google Docs and a wiki to house and create a project, your information is readily available in electronic format. An easy way to illustrate what you have done is by showing the audience your group wiki pages (your house and the rooms) to help explain the decision-making process. Likewise, you and your group could also use Google Docs' presentation tool, which resembles Microsoft PowerPoint, to show and share more concretely the major points and ideas of the newsletter. Once you create a Google Doc presentation, you could link to it from your wiki (house), and email a link to the presentation to all audience members for easy reference. Additionally, your presentation is available from almost any location that has an Internet connection. You do not even have to carry a USB flash drive containing the presentation.

Project B, on the other hand, required a slightly different dynamic for group members because each group member had to present the project orally, as well as put together a poster that summarized the project as a whole. Like Project A, students could use Google Docs' presentation tool to develop the oral presentation because they had maintained their work in the wiki.

The posters were created by another software program that was also shared electronically among group members. While group members shared the posters via email, they also reviewed and edited each other's presentations by using Google Docs. Eventually, links to the posters were added to the wiki.

As you will discover in your own projects, creating presentations in Google Docs functions like a review system that allows you and your classmates to access the presentations from home, encourages group

Figure 3. An example Google Doc presentation in edit mode.

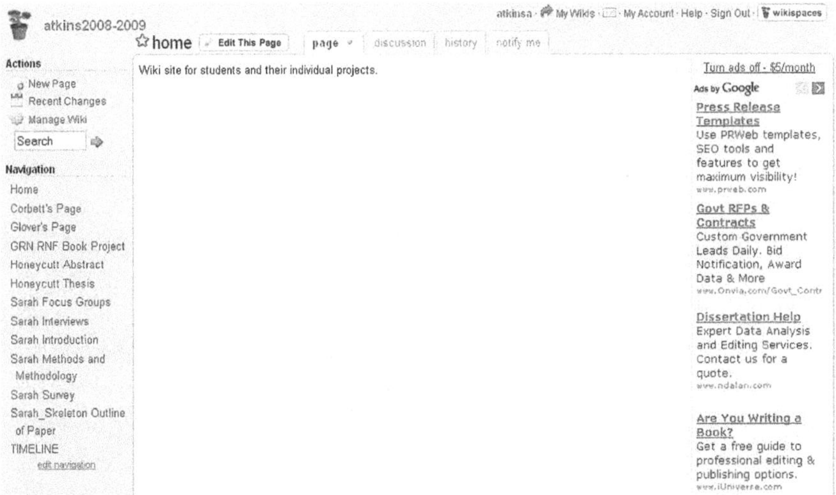

Figure 4. Project B's Google Doc presentation in edit mode.

members to participate, and increases the quality of work produced by the group. When presentations are meant to be interactive, having the project and presentation in an electronic format will allow others to participate in your project and further illustrate the time, work, and effort put into a specific project.

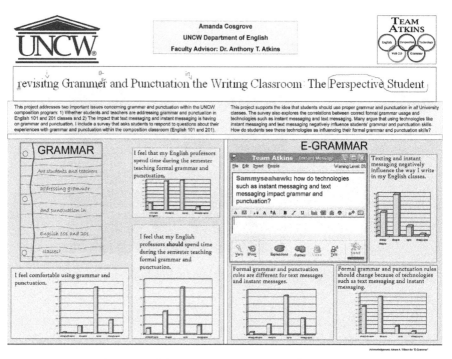

Figure 5. Final version of the poster. (© 2008 Amanda Cosgrove.)

Review

Working in a collaborative environment can be tricky and certainly if group members decide not to contribute, it can become more challenging than it should be. There are a number of ways to improve the quality of group work. Assessing your project or what you have been asked to do is the first step in determining how best to proceed. Once groups have been formulated, having an initial group meeting is imperative. If your teacher does not provide time during class, you could meet face-to-face in the library, a coffee shop, or if you are taking the course as a distance or online course, hold a phone conference using a free service such as FreeConferenceCall.com, Skype, or talk online in a chat room. During this meeting, it is important to determine group member roles. What should each group member do to help facilitate the completion of a project? Remember to consider the following when getting ready for group work:

- What does the project entail? What is its purpose?
- How long should the project take?
- How many group members are needed or required and what should each one do?
- What technologies can help the group complete the project collaboratively?
- What is the best way to present the project?

The newsletter project (Project A), ended successfully. Using a wiki called Wikispaces, the group was able to post all content concerning the newsletter to the wiki for everyone to view and evaluate. Because all group members could follow the progress of the newsletter on the wiki, all group members were able to communicate and share information, manage their deadlines, and complete their tasks in a timely manner. The group could also share the wiki and other project information with the non-profit organization's stakeholders. Keeping the client organization up-to-date with the progress of the project is an important positive attribute to using Web 2.0 tools to develop collaborative projects. The presentation of the project included a Google Doc with links to pertinent material associated with how group member contributed directly to the project, which included research gathered about the organization and the adaptation of a logo/image. The group maintained a large house filled with rooms of information that was easy to mange, access, and use. Indeed, the work and contributions of group members, the full development of the project, and the end-product delivered are a direct result of employing Web 2.0 tools like wikis and Google Docs. When assigned a group task or group project, you should consider what free digital tools are available that can most help you and your group members organize the project.

DISCUSSION

1. Consider some of your previous experiences doing collaborative work. What important concepts in this essay would have been useful for your group to know? Why?

2. Think about what online tools (websites) you have used to communicate or share content. Would any of them be useful for doing collaborative work with a group? Why?

3. Create a Google Docs account (if you don't have one already). Experiment with it. Think about the individual work you do as a college student. How might Google Docs be useful to you for your non-group work?

Notes

1. The students were required to create a poster for a presentation to faculty, and in this situation the students simply stood next to their poster and explained the project to those who chose to stop by and review them. The students were also required to provide a more formal presentation of their work in a classroom setting (where a computer and LCD projector could also be used).

2. Wikipedia controls the edits of some entries more than others; they also allow anonymous edits for some entries. Users should read the restrictions and limitations surrounding some Wikipedia entries.

3. For those who simply want access to Google Docs, they can create an account using a school email address. In other words, a full Google account is not necessary for access to Google Docs.

Navigating Genres

Kerry Dirk

There's a joke that's been floating around some time now that you've likely already heard.* It goes something like the following:

Q: What do you get when you rewind a country song?
A: You get your wife back, your job back, your dog back . . .

Maybe this joke makes you laugh. Or groan. Or tilt your head to the side in confusion. Because it just so happens that in order to get this joke, you must know a little something about country music in general and in particular country music lyrics. You must, in other words, be familiar with the country music genre.

Let's look into country music lyrics a bit more. Bear with me on this is if you're not a fan. Assuming I want to write lyrics to a country song, how would I figure out what lyrics are acceptable in terms of country songs? Listening to any country station for a short period of time might leave one with the following conclusions about country songs:

- Country songs tend to tell stories. They often have characters who are developed throughout the song.
- Country songs often have choruses that are broad enough to apply to a variety of verses.

- Country songs are often depressing; people lose jobs, lovers, and friends.
- Country songs express pride for the country style and way of life.
- Country songs are often political, responding to wars and economic crises, for example.

Given these characteristics, I would feel prepared to write some new country lyrics. But what would happen if I wanted to write a country song that didn't do any of the above things? Would it still be a country song?

You are probably already familiar with many genres, although you may not know them as such; perhaps your knowledge of genres is limited to types of books, whether mystery, horror, action, etc. Now I'm going to ask you to stick with me while I show you how knowledge of genres goes far beyond a simple discussion of types. My purposes are to expand your definition of genre (or to introduce you to a definition for the first time) and to help you start thinking about how genres might apply to your own writing endeavors. But above all, I hope to give you an awareness of how genres function by taking what is often quite theoretical in the field of rhetoric and composition and making it a bit more tangible. So why was I talking about country songs? I think that using such references can help you to see, in a quite concrete way, how genres function.

When I started writing this essay, I had some ideas of what I wanted to say. But first, I had to determine what this essay might look like. I've written a lot—letters, nonfiction pieces, scholarly articles, rants—but this was my first time writing an essay to you, a composition student. What features, I asked myself, should go into this essay? How personal could I get? What rhetorical moves might I use, effectively or ineffectively? I hoped that a similar type of essay already existed so that I would have something to guide my own writing. I knew I was looking for other essays written directly to students, and after finding many examples, I looked for common features. In particular, I noted the warm, personal style that was prevalent through every essay; the tone was primarily conversational. And more importantly, I noticed that the writer did not talk as an authoritative figure but as a coach. Some writers admitted that they did not know everything (we don't), and others even went so far as to admit ignorance. I found myself doing what Mary Jo Reiff, a professor who studies rhetoric and composition, did when she was asked to write about her experience of writing an essay about teaching for those new to the field of composition. She writes, "I immediately called on my genre knowledge—my past experience with reading and writing similar texts in similar situations—to orient me to the expectations of this genre" (157).

I further acknowledged that it is quite rare that teachers of writing get to write so directly to students in such an informal manner. Although textbooks are directed at students, they are often more formal affairs meant to serve a different purpose than this essay. And because the genre of this essay is still developing, there are no formal expectations for what this paper might look like. In my excitement, I realized that perhaps I had been granted more freedom in writing this essay than is typical of an already established, although never static, genre. As a result, I decided to make this essay a mix of personal anecdotes, examples, and voices from teachers of writing. Such an essay seems to be the most fitting response to this situation, as I hope to come across as someone both informative and friendly. Why am I telling you this? Because it seems only appropriate that given the fact that I am talking about genre awareness, I should make you aware of my own struggles with writing in a new genre.

I will admit that the word genre used to have a bad reputation and may still make some people cringe. Genre used to refer primarily to form, which meant that writing in a particular genre was seen as simply a matter of filling in the blanks. Anne Freadman, a specialist in genre theory, points out that "it is this kind of genre theory with its failures that has caused the discredit of the very notion of genre, bringing about in turn its disuse and the disrepair many of us found it in" (46). But genre theory has come a long way since then. Perhaps the shift started when the rhetorician Lloyd Bitzer wrote the following:

> Due to either the nature of things or convention, or both, some situations recur. The courtroom is the locus for several kinds of situations generating the speech of accusation, the speech of defense, the charge to the jury. From day to day, year to year, comparable situations occur, prompting comparable responses; hence rhetorical forms are born and a special vocabulary, grammar, and style are established. (13)

In other words, Bitzer is saying that when something new happens that requires a response, someone must create that first response. Then when that situation happens again, another person uses the first response as a basis for the second, and eventually everyone who encounters this situation is basing his/her response on the previous ones, resulting in the creation of a new genre. Think about George Washington giving the first State of the Union Address. Because this genre was completely new, he had complete freedom to pick its form and content. All presidents following him now have these former addresses to help guide their response because the situation is now a reoccurring one. Amy Devitt, a professor who specializes in the study of genre theory, points out that "genres develop, then, because they respond appropriately to situations that writers encounter repeatedly" ("Generalizing" 576) and because "if each writing problem were to require a completely new assessment of how to respond, writing would be slowed considerably. But once we recognize a recurring situation, a situation that we or others have responded to in the past, our response to that situation can be guided by past responses" ("Generalizing" 576). As such, we can see how a genre like the State of the Union Address helps for more effective communication between the president and citizens because the president already has a genre with which to work; he/she doesn't have to create a new one, and citizens know what to expect from such an address.

The definition of genre has changed even more since Bitzer's article was written; genres are now viewed as even more than repeating rhetorical situations. Carolyn Miller, a leading professor in the field of technical communication, argues that "a rhetorically sound definition of genre must be centered . . . on the action it is used to accomplish" (151). How might this look? These actions don't have to be complex; many genres are a part of our daily lives. Think about genres as tools to help people to get things done. Devitt writes that:

> genres have the power to help or hurt human interaction, to ease communication or to deceive, to enable someone to speak or to discourage someone from saying something different. People learn how to do *small talk* to ease the social discomfort of large group gatherings and meeting new people, but advertisers learn

> how to disguise *sales letters* as *winning sweepstakes entries*. (*Writing* 1)

In other words, knowing what a genre is used for can help people to accomplish goals, whether that goal be getting a job by knowing how to write a stellar resume, winning a person's heart by writing a romantic love letter, or getting into college by writing an effective personal statement.

By this point you might realize that you have been participating in many different genres—whether you are telling a joke, writing an email, or uploading a witty status on Facebook. Because you know how these genres function as social actions, you can quite accurately predict how they function rhetorically; your joke should generate a laugh, your email should elicit a response, and your updated Facebook status should generate comments from your online friends. But you have done more than simply filled in the blanks. Possibly without even thinking about it, you were recognizing the rhetorical situation of your action and choosing to act in a manner that would result in the outcome you desired. I imagine that you would probably not share a risqué joke with your mom, send a "Hey Buddy" email to your professor, or update your Facebook status as "X has a huge wart on his foot." We can see that more than form matters here, as knowing what is appropriate in these situations obviously requires more rhetorical knowledge than does filling out a credit card form. Devitt argues that "people do not label a particular story as a joke solely because of formal features but rather because of their perception of the rhetorical action that is occurring" (*Writing* 11). True, genres often have formulaic features, but these features can change even as the nature of the genre remains (Devitt, *Writing*, 48). What is important to consider here is that if mastering a form were simply a matter of plugging in content, we would all be capable of successfully writing anything when we are given a formula. By now you likely know that writing is not that easy.

Fortunately, even if you have been taught to write in a formulaic way, you probably don't treat texts in such a manner. When approaching a genre for a the first time, you likely view it as more than a simple form: "Picking up a text, readers not only classify it and expect a certain form, but also make assumptions about the text's purposes, its subject matter, its writer, and its expected reader" (Devitt, *Writing* 12). We treat texts that we encounter as rhetorical objects; we choose be-

tween horror movies and chick flicks not only because we are familiar
with their forms but because we know what response they will elicit
from us (nail-biting fear and dreamy sighs, respectively). Why am I
picking popular genres to discuss? I think I agree with Miller when
she argues the following:

> To consider as potential genres such homely discourse
> as the letter of recommendation, the user manual, the
> progress report, the ransom note, the lecture, and the
> white paper, as well as the eulogy, the apologia, the
> inaugural, the public proceeding, and the sermon, is
> not to trivialize the study of genres; it is to take seri-
> ously the rhetoric in which we are immersed and the
> situations in which we find ourselves. (155)

In other words, Miller is saying that all genres matter because they
shape our everyday lives. And by studying the genres that we find familiar, we can start to see how specific choices that writers make result
in specific actions on the part of readers; it only follows that our own
writing must too be purposefully written.

I like examples, so here is one more. Many of you may be familiar
with *The Onion*, a fictitious newspaper that uses real world examples
to create humorous situations. Perhaps the most notable genre of *The
Onion* is its headlines. The purpose of these headlines is simple: to
make the reader respond by laughing. While many of the articles are
also entertaining, the majority of the humor is produced through the
headlines. In fact, the headlines are so important to the success of the
newspaper that they are tested on volunteers to see the readers' immediate responses. There are no formal features of these headlines besides
the fact that they are all quite brief; they share no specific style. But
they are a rhetorical action meant to bring about a specific response,
which is why I see them as being their own genre. A few examples for
those of you unfamiliar with this newspaper would help to explain
what I'm saying. Here are a few of my personal favorites (politically
charged or other possibly offensive headlines purposefully avoided):

- "Archaeological Dig Uncovers Ancient Race of Skeleton
  People"
- "Don't Run Away, I'm Not the Flesh-Eating Kind of Zombie"
- "Time Traveler: Everyone In The Future Eats Dippin' Dots"

- "'I Am Under 18' Button Clicked For First Time In History Of Internet"
- "Commas, Turning Up, Everywhere"
- "Myspace Outage Leaves Millions Friendless."
- "Amazon.com Recommendations Understand Area Woman Better Than Husband"
- "Study: Dolphins Not So Intelligent On Land"
- "Beaver Overthinking Dam"
- "Study: Alligators Dangerous No Matter How Drunk You Are"
- "Child In Corner To Exact Revenge As Soon As He Gets Out" (*The Onion*)

I would surmise with near certainty that at least one of these headlines made you laugh. Why? I think the success lies in the fact that the writers of these headlines are rhetorically aware of whom these headlines are directed toward—college students like you, and more specifically, educated college students who know enough about politics, culture, and U.S. and world events to "get" these headlines.

And now for some bad news: figuring out a genre is tricky already, but this process is further complicated by the fact that two texts that might fit into the same genre might also look extremely different. But let's think about why this might be the case. Devitt points out, "different grocery stores make for different grocery lists. Different law courts make for different legal briefs. And different college classes make for different research papers. Location may not be the first, second, and third most important qualities of writing, as it is for real estate, but location is surely among the situational elements that lead to expected genres and to adaptations of those genres in particular situations" ("Transferability" 218). Think about a time when you were asked to write a research paper. You probably had an idea of what that paper should look like, but you also needed to consider the location of the assignment. In other words, you needed to consider how your particular teacher's expectations would help to shape your assignment. This makes knowing a genre about much more than simply knowing its form. You also need to consider the context in which it is being used. As such, it's important to be aware that the research paper you might be required to write in freshman composition might be completely different than the research paper you might be asked to write for an introductory psychology class. Your goal is to recognize these shifts in location and to be aware of how such shifts might affect your writing.

Let's consider a genre with which you are surely familiar: the thesis statement. Stop for a moment and consider what this term means to you. Ask your classmates. It's likely that you each have your own definition of what a thesis statement should and should not look like. You may have heard never to start a thesis statement with a phrase like "In this essay." Or you might have been taught that a thesis statement should have three parts, each of which will be discussed in one paragraph of the essay. I learned that many good thesis statements follow the formula "X because Y," where "X" refers to a specific stance, and "Y" refers to a specific reason for taking that stance. For example, I could argue "School uniforms should be required because they will help students to focus more on academics and less on fashion." Now, whether or not this is a good thesis statement is irrelevant, but you can see how following the "X because Y" formula would produce a nicely structured statement. Take this a step further and research "thesis statements" on the Internet, and you'll find that there are endless suggestions. And despite their vast differences, they all fit under the genre of thesis statement. How is this possible? Because it comes back to the particular situation in which that thesis statement is being used. Again, location is everything.

I think it's time to try our hand at approaching a genre with which I hope all of you are only vaguely familiar and completely unpracticed: the ransom note.

A Scenario

I've decided to kidnap Bob's daughter Susie for ransom. I'm behind on the mortgage payments, my yacht payments are also overdue, and I desperately need money. It is well known that Bob is one of the wealthiest people in Cash City, so I've targeted him as my future source of money. I've never met Bob, although one time his Mercedes cut me off in traffic, causing me to hit the brakes and spill my drink; the stain still glares at me from the floor of the car. The kidnapping part has been completed; now I need to leave Bob a ransom note. Let's look at a few drafts I've completed to decide which one would be most appropriate.

Ransom Letter 1:

If you ever want to see your daughter alive again, leave 1 million dollars by the blue garbage can at 123 Ransom Rd. at Midnight. Come alone and do not call the police.

Ransom Letter 2:

Hav daughter. Million $. Blu grbg can 123 Ransom Rd. 12AM. No poliz.

Ransom Letter 3:

Dear Bob,

Thank you for taking the time to read this letter. You have a lovely house, and I very much enjoyed my recent visit while you were out of town. Unfortunately, I have kidnapped your daughter. As I am currently unable to meet several financial demands, I am graciously turning to you for help in this matter. I am sure that we will be able to come to some mutually beneficial agreement that results in the return of your daughter and the padding of my wallet. Please meet with me at the Grounds Coffee House on First Street so that we may discuss what price is most fitting. Your daughter, meanwhile, remains in safe and competent hands. She is presently playing pool with my son Matt (a possible love connection?), and she says to tell you "Hi."

Yours truly,

Jim

P.S. Please order me a skim vanilla latte, should you arrive before I do.

Immediately, you can probably determine that ransom letter one is the best choice. But have you considered why? What does the first letter have that the other two are lacking? Let's first eliminate the most obvious dud—letter number three. Not only does it mimic the friendly, familiar manner of two friends rather than the threatening note of a deranged kidnapper, but it also suggests both that there is no rush in the matter and that the price is negotiable. Letters one and two are closer; they both contain the same information, but letter two fails to be as rhetorically strong as number one. The spelling errors and choppy feel might suggest that the writer of the note is not intelligent enough to get away with the kidnapping. The first letter is the most rhetorically strong because it is well written and direct. All of these letters would qualify as fitting the genre of ransom letter, but the first one most obviously fits the rhetorical situation.

It may be worthwhile to note some particular challenges you might have to approaching your writing genres as rhetorical situations. Perhaps you have come from a writing background where you learned that certain rules apply to all writing. Just nod if these sound familiar:

- You must have a thesis statement at the end of the introduction.
- Every thesis statement should introduce three points of discussion.
- You cannot use "I" in writing.
- You cannot begin a sentence with a coordinating conjunction.
- Every paragraph should start with a topic sentence.

You get the point. These rules are appealing; they tell us exactly what to do and not to do with regard to writing. I remember happily creating introductions that moved from broad to specific (often starting with "In our world"), constructing three point thesis statements, and beginning paragraphs with "first," "second," and "third." I didn't have to think about audience, or purpose, or even much about content for that matter. All that really mattered was that essay followed a certain formula that was called good writing. But looking back, what resulted from such formulas was not very good; actually, it was quite bad.

That is, of course, not to say that there aren't rules that come with genres; the difference is that the rules change as the genre changes, that no rules apply to all genres, and that genres require more effort than simply following the rules. Because genres usually come with established conventions, it is risky to choose not to follow such conventions. These similarities within genres help us to communicate successfully; imagine the chaos that would ensue if news broadcasts were done in raps, if all legal briefs were written in couplets, or if your teacher handed you a syllabus and told you that it must first be decoded. In sum, "too much choice is as debilitating of meaning as is too little choice. In language, too much variation results eventually in lack of meaning: mutual unintelligibility" (Devitt, "Genre" 53).

But on a brighter note, genres also help us to make more efficient decisions when writing, as we can see how people have approached similar situations. Creating a new genre each time that writing was required would make the writing process much longer, as we would not have past responses to help us with present ones (Devitt, "Generalizing" 576). As a result, the more you are able to master particular genres, the better equipped you may be to master genres that you later encounter:

> When people write, they draw on the genres they
> know, their own context of genres, to help construct
> their rhetorical action. If they encounter a situation
> new to them, it is the genres they have acquired in
> the past that they can use to shape their new action.
> Every genre they acquire, then, expands their genre
> repertoire and simultaneously shapes how they might
> view new situations. (Devitt, *Writing* 203)

Taking what Devitt says into account, think back to the previous discussion of the research paper. If you already have some idea of what a research paper looks like, you do not have to learn an entirely new genre. Instead, you just have to figure out how to change that particular genre to fit with the situation, even if that change just comes from having a different teacher.

Learning about genres and how they function is more important than mastering one particular genre; it is this knowledge that helps us to recognize and to determine appropriate responses to different situations—that is, knowing what particular genre is called for in a particular situation. And learning every genre would be impossible anyway, as Devitt notes that "no writing class could possibly teach students all the genres they will need to succeed even in school, much less in the workplace or in their civic lives. Hence the value of teaching genre awareness rather than acquisition of particular genres" (Writing

205). This approach helps to make you a more effective writer as well, as knowing about genres will make you more prepared to use genres that you won't learn in college. For example, I recently needed to write a letter about removing a late fee on a credit card. I had never written this particular type of letter before, but I knew what action I was trying to accomplish. As a result, I did some research on writing letters and determined that I should make it as formal and polite as possible. The body of the letter ended up as follows:

> I have very much enjoyed being a card carrier with this bank for many years. However, I recently had a late fee charged to my account. As you will note from my previous statements, this is the first late fee I have ever acquired. I do remember making this payment on time, as I have all of my previous payments. I hope to remain a loyal customer of this bank for many years to come, so I would very much appreciate it if you would remove this charge from my account.

You can see that this letter does several things. First, I build credibility for myself by reminding them that I have used their card for many years. Second, I ask them to check my records to show further that I am typically a responsible card carrier. And third, I hint that if they do not remove the late fee, I might decide to change to a different bank. This letter is effective because it considers how the situation affects the genre. And yes, the late fee was removed.

Chances are that I have left you more confused than you were before you began this essay. Actually, I hope that I have left you frustrated; this means that the next time you write, you will have to consider not only form but also audience, purpose, and genre; you will, in other words, have to consider the rhetorical effectiveness of your writing. Luckily, I can leave you with a few suggestions:

- First, determine what action you are trying to accomplish. Are you trying to receive an A on a paper? Convince a credit card company to remove a late fee? Get into graduate school? If you don't know what your goal is for a particular writing situation, you'll have a difficult time figuring out what genre to use.
- Second, learn as much as you can about the situation for which you are writing. What is the purpose? Who is the audience?

How much freedom do you have? How does the location affect the genre?

- Third, research how others have responded to similar situations. Talk to people who have written what you are trying to write. If you are asked to write a biology research paper, ask your instructor for examples. If you need to write a cover letter for a summer internship, take the time to find out about the location of that internship.
- And finally, ask questions.

Discussion

1. What are some genres that you feel you know well? How did you learn them? What are their common rhetorical features?

2. What rules have you been told to follow in the past? How did they shape what you were writing?

3. How much freedom do you enjoy when writing? Does it help to have a form to follow, or do you find it to be limiting?

Works Cited

Bitzer, Lloyd F. "The Rhetorical Situation." *Philosophy and Rhetoric* 1.1 (1968): 1–14. Print.

Devitt, Amy J. "Generalizing About Genre: New Conceptions of an Old Concept." *College Composition and Communication* 44.4 (1993): 573–86. Print.

—. "Genre as Language Standard." *Genre and Writing: Issues, Arguments, Alternatives.* Ed. Wendy Bishop and Hans Ostrom. Portsmouth, NH: Boynton/Cook, 1997. 45–55. Print.

—. "Transferability and Genres." *The Locations of Composition.* Ed. Christopher J. Keller and Christian R. Weisser. Albany, NY: SUNY P, 2007. 215–27. Print.

—. *Writing Genres.* Carbondale: Southern Illinois UP, 2004. Print.

Freadman, Anne. "Anyone for Tennis." *Genre and the New Rhetoric.* Ed. Aviva Freedman and Peter Medway. Bristol: Taylor & Francis, 1994. 43–66. Print.

Miller, Carolyn R. "Genre as Social Action." *Quarterly Journal of Speech* 70.2 (1984): 151–67. Print.

The Onion: America's Finest News Source. 20 July 2009. Web. 20 July 2009. <http://www.theonion.com>.

Reiff, Mary Jo. "Moving Writers, Shaping Motives, Motivating Critique and Change: A Genre Approach to Teaching Writing." *Relations, Locations, Positions: Composition Theory for Writing Teachers*. Ed. Peter Vandenberg, Sue Hum, and Jennifer Clary-Lemon. Urbana, IL: National Council of Teachers of English, 2006. 157–64. Print.

Contributors

Sarah Allen is an Assistant Professor of English at the University of Northern Colorado, where she teaches courses in rhetoric, composition theory, and creative nonfiction. She is currently working on a book project on imitation practices in writing—how the practices of imitation can be re-conceptualized and rendered as practices in the care of the self.

Susan E. Antlitz completed her PhD in English Studies at Illinois State University in 2005. Her interests include digital writing environments, online communities, alternative textual structures, and the connections among technology, spirituality, and writing. Susan is currently an online writing instructor for Joliet Junior College and South University Online.

Anthony T. Atkins (Tony) is an assistant professor of English and the composition coordinator at UNC Wilmington. He teaches courses in professional writing, rhetorical theory, composition theory/pedagogy, and writing technologies. He has published in *Kairos* and *Composition Studies*. His recent article (co-authored with Colleen Reilly) is titled "Stifling Innovation: The Impact of Resource-poor Techno-ecologies on Student Technology Use" and published in *Technological Ecologies & Sustainability* by Computers and Composition Digital Press. His latest article is titled "It's Complicated [with] Student-Professor Relationships: Using Facebook to Create Emotional Connections" and is forthcoming in the 2010 winter edition of *The Journal of the Assembly for Expanded Perspectives on Learning*.

Laura Bolin Carroll holds a PhD in Discourse Studies from Texas A&M University and is an associate professor of English at Abilene Christian University. Her current research includes the use of religious metaphor in British and American political discourse.

Collin Craig has a PhD in Cultural Rhetoric and Composition and teaches writing at Michigan State University. He is interested in the intersections of literacy and rhetoric as well as masculinity and writing. He enjoys writing courses that focus on popular culture, rhetorical analysis, race, and new literacies. His most recent work includes a co-edited freshman reader, *A Reader for Writers,* that is used by Michigan State's first year writing program. He is currently working on a project exploring the literacy practices of young black college males from underrepresented communities. He will be teaching writing at Wake Forest University in the Fall of 2010.

Robert E. Cummings is Director of the Center for Writing and Rhetoric at the University of Mississippi. His most recent work includes *Wiki Writing: Collaborative Learning in the College Classroom* (co-edited with Matt Barton) (Michigan UP 2008) and *Lazy Virtues: Teaching Writing in the Age of Wikipedia* (Vanderbilt UP 2009).

Kerry Dirk is currently a PhD student in Rhetoric and Writing at Virginia Tech. Her research interests include genre theory, activity systems, computers and composition, and composition pedagogy. She has published short works in *TETYC* and *Harlot,* as well as an article on participation in *Composition Studies.*

Sandra L. Giles holds a Master's Degree in Literature from Valdosta State University and a PhD in Creative Writing and Composition/Rhetoric from Florida State University. She is an Associate Professor of English at Abraham Baldwin Agricultural College, a small state college in Tifton, Georgia. She has published a range of creative writing and articles in such places as *The Southeast Review, AWP Pedagogy Papers, On Writing: A Process Reader, Feeling Our Way: A Writing Teacher's Sourcebook,* and *Pegasus.* She is Faculty Co-Advisor to her school's literary magazine and serves as a Teacher-Consultant for the Blackwater Writing Project.

Beth Hewett holds a PhD from The Catholic University of America in English (Rhetoric and Composition). She is an adjunct Associate Professor at University of Maryland University College and an expert in online writing instruction. She is the author of *The Online Writing Conference: A Guide for Teachers and Tutors* and co-author of *Preparing Educators for Online Writing Instruction: Principles and Processes,* as well as numerous articles about teaching and tutoring in online and traditional settings. Dr. Hewett is the chair of the CCCC Committee for Best Practices of Online Writing Instruction and an NCTE Professional Development

Consultant. She is an academic writing and educational consultant with Defend & Publish, LLC.

Corrine E. Hinton is currently the Student Success Center Coordinator at University of the West (Rosemead, CA). She is completing her PhD at Saint Louis University in English with an emphasis in Rhetoric & Composition. Her research interests include Renaissance rhetoric, first year composition, writing centers, student-veterans, and the first year student experience. For her dissertation, Corrine is investigating the effects of military service and education on the experiences of student-veterans in the first year composition classroom.

L. Lennie Irvin teaches first year writing at San Antonio College, and has been a community college writing teacher since 1989. He is the Co-Director of the San Antonio Writing Project, and a PhD Candidate in Technical Communication and Rhetoric at Texas Tech University (projected to finish 2010).

Megan Lynn Isaac is an Associate Professor of English at Elon University and teaches writing, Shakespeare, and assorted other courses. Her most recent book is titled *Suzanne Staples: The Setting is the Story* (2010), and her newest project explores surveillance and observation in children's and young adult literature.

Rebecca Jones is an Assistant Professor of Rhetoric and Composition at the University of Tennessee, Chattanooga. She feels lucky to be able to teach courses in argument theory, rhetorical analysis, rhetorical theory, writing, and women's studies. Her published work includes articles on argument theory, activism, protest rhetoric, and pedagogies for HSI's. She is currently working on a project about the intersection of belief and public discourse.

Christopher Leary worked as a consultant in writing centers at New York City College of Technology, Long Island University in Brooklyn, and Skidmore College before joining the St. John's University Writing Center as an Associate Director in 2007. He is pursuing a doctorate in Composition Studies at CUNY's Graduate Center and serves on the steering committee for the Northeast Writing Centers Association (NEWCA).

Steven T. Lessner is Research Assistant to the Director of Tier I Writing at Michigan State University and teaches a first year writing course that explores intersections between masculinities and writing. He also consults with student athletes in the MSU Student Athlete Support Services Writing Center and serves as an Assistant Editor on *CCC Online*. He is currently pursuing a PhD at MSU in Rhetoric and Writing. His current research focuses on examining the activist practices of Writing Program Administration work as well as promoting writing pedagogies inclusive of first generation college students and their transitions into higher education.

Kate McKinney Maddalena is an instructor in North Carolina State University's First Year Writing Program. She is currently pursuing a PhD at NCSU in Communication, Rhetoric, and Digital Media. Kate is interested in the intersections of sociolinguistics and rhetoric. Her most recent research describes the negotiation of social capital and the evocation of expertise in academic, political and popular writing about science.

James P. Purdy is an assistant professor of English/writing studies at Duquesne University, where he teaches composition and digital writing and directs the University Writing Center. He has published his research in *College Composition and Communication, Computers and Composition, Computers and Composition Online, Kairos,* and *Pedagogy* and has chapters forthcoming in *Reading (and Writing) New Media* and *The New Work of Composing*. He (along with Joyce R. Walker) received the 2008 *Kairos* Best Webtext Award for "Digital Breadcrumbs: Case Studies of Online Research."

Ben Rafoth directs the Writing Center and is University Professor at Indiana University of Pennsylvania. He teaches courses in writing, research methods, and composition theory and pedagogy. His essays and articles have appeared in *Research in the Teaching of English, Written Communication, Assessing Writing,* and the *Writing Lab Newsletter*. He is the author of *A Tutor's Guide,* 2nd ed., and, with Shanti Bruce, *ESL Writers,* both published by Heinemann Boynton/Cook. He is a recipient of the Ron Maxwell Award from the National Conference on Peer Tutoring in Writing.

Michelle D. Trim holds a PhD in Rhetoric and Technical Communication and teaches writing and writing intensive seminars in gender and technology studies as a Lecturer at Elon University. Her most recent article argues for a reconsideration of compositionists' motives in the use of service learning. Her current project investigates the transformative effects of an ethnographic-based assignment designed to increase students' critical awareness of technology.

Index